Laughter in the Air

An Informal History of British Radio Comedy

BRITISH BROADCASTING CORPORATION

THIS REVISED AND ENLARGED PAPERBACK EDITION FIRST PUBLISHED IN GREAT BRITAIN IN 1981 BY ROBSON BOOKS LTD., 28 POLAND STREET, LONDON W1V 3DB. ORIGINALLY PUBLISHED IN HARDBACK BY ROBSON BOOKS IN 1976

ISBN 0 86051 149 9

AND BY THE BRITISH BROADCASTING CORPORATION, 35, MARYLEBONE HIGH STREET, LONDON W1M 4AA.

ISBN 0 563 17197 9

Printed in Hungary

Contents

For Lyn—with love

Acknowledgements

Since this book was first published in hardback in 1976 many people whose advice I sought and who gave their time and knowledge of radio unstintingly, have died or moved on to other areas of broadcasting.

I'd like to remember particularly those who are no longer with us but who, to a greater or lesser extent, influenced the course of radio history. They include, and the list is sadly a long one: Peter Sellers, Peter Eton, Sir Charles Curran, Ronnie Waldman, Bob Oliver Rogers, Ben Lyon, Ted Ray, Mrs Phyllis Cranston (Robb Wilton's niece and executor of his estate), Kenneth Tynan, Ronnie Taylor, Hattie Jacques, Peter Butterworth and Jack Benny. Happily many of those who helped in the preparation of this book are still active and their contribution to radio, and thus this slim history, has been immeasurably valuable.

I'd like particularly to thank Pat Daniels, Barbara Varley, Peter James and Adrian Preston of the BBC Script Library; Anthony Jennings who as BBC's Head of Copyright in 1975 gave me much help both legal and general, Tessa Le Bars for her help with the chronology of 'Hancock's Half Hour', Elizabeth Rose and Anna Selby of Robson Books for their advice, patience and help, and finally the BBC—just for *being* there.

B.T.

Introduction

As a race, the British have one peculiarity that sets them apart from the rest of mankind: their extraordinary sense of humour; their ability to laugh at themselves, to laugh at others, to laugh at the sublime *and* the ridiculous, to laugh at disaster and at triumph, to be indifferent to the subject of the joke but to seek and find humour in everything. As a comedy script-writer, I am frequently told that 'If you spent a day here [in this shop, this factory, this hospital or wherever] you'd have enough humour to last you a lifetime.' The British see themselves as unbelievably comic and cannot conceive of a situation that hasn't got a funny side, whether it's spoiled holidays, the IRA, or economic collapse. I have a hunch that laughter is a symbol of freedom. It's anti-totalitarian. A free man can laugh, a slave cannot; and it's possible to assess the amount of freedom in a society by the quantity of laughter it generates.

Not that all laughter is about freedom. A lot of it records the survival of the person who's laughing. It says: 'There's always someone worse off than yourself.' It says, in short: 'He died, I didn't.' Then there's the laughter of recognition—the 'He's just like our Winnie's Arthur' type of laughter, the cosy chuckle that comes from sharing someone else's observation and knowing it to be true. There's also the laughter that comes from someone saying what you've always felt but never dared to say—the laughter of instinct, the laughter of ideas. The great radio comedies—the ones that stay fresh in the memory—embodied these various sorts of laughter, often unconsciously, and put such weighty abstracts as freedom, fear, guilt, surprise, into situations in which they effortlessly revealed their potential for humour.

In radio's great years the variations on the theme of laughter were infinite. No idea was ignored, no concept was passed over, and just as the needs of people change as time goes on, so radio comedy itself changed to echo the prevailing tastes of its audience. The history of its development is not a cut-and-dried, compartmentalized affair. The men who made BBC comedy—Eric Maschwitz, John Watt, Harry S. Pepper, Michael Standing, Ronnie Waldman, Pat Hillyard, Jim Davidson, Roy Rich, Con Mahoney, and the rest—were not cast in one mould. The thoughtful and the instinctive, the practical and the theorist, the saints and the crooks, jostled each other in the corridors of Aeolian Hall and Broadcasting House, learned from each other, and put what they learned into practice.

In the fifty-plus years of radio there have been thousands of comedy shows and tens of thousands of comedians, and it's just not possible to describe accurately and in detail everything that went on the air from 1922 to the present day. In fact, trying to write a history of radio comedy is rather like attempting to draw a detailed map of the Mekong Delta on a grain of rice. There just isn't room for it all.

What I have tried to do is chart what seem to me the important shows, comedians, character actors, producers and writers. Many people and programmes have had to be left out, and let me apologise now for these omissions. I have compiled this informal history from many interviews; from the BBC archives; from observations; and from my own personal experience: I've worked with, learned from, been friends with, made enemies of many of the people who made radio great. I shared a little in the Indian summer of wireless comedy through my association with 'Round The Horne', and for that I am grateful. I have sat in BBC studios and been deafened by the laughter of the studio audience as they howled their approval of 'I'm Sorry, I'll Read That Again' or 'Take It From Here', Frankie Howerd or Kenneth Williams. I've writhed with embarrassment at lesser men and awful shows. On the air myself, I have been funny and I've been frightful, but in my radio life I've lived among giants, and for that, too, I shall be eternally grateful.

I have quoted from as many scripts as space and the generosity of the authors permit, because I believe that describing comedy isn't as useful as demonstrating it. I have tried to put these shows in context, and above all, wherever possible I have quoted eye-witness accounts of how they came to be made.

The biographies of the leading broadcasters of the day from Arthur Askey to Lord Reith all tell much the same story—small beginnings, minor triumphs, major triumphs, and a more or less serene old age. Mind you, it's difficult for people writing about themselves to be objective because, mercifully, we tend to forget unpleasant or embarrassing incidents and only have clear memories of the good days. It takes quite an effort of will to recall bad times, and this is as true of broad-

(Marconi Company)

Loudspeaker reception with the Marconiphone V2 wireless receiver in 1922

Tommy Handley and Heather Thatcher with the 'meatsafe' microphone, 1928

(BBC)

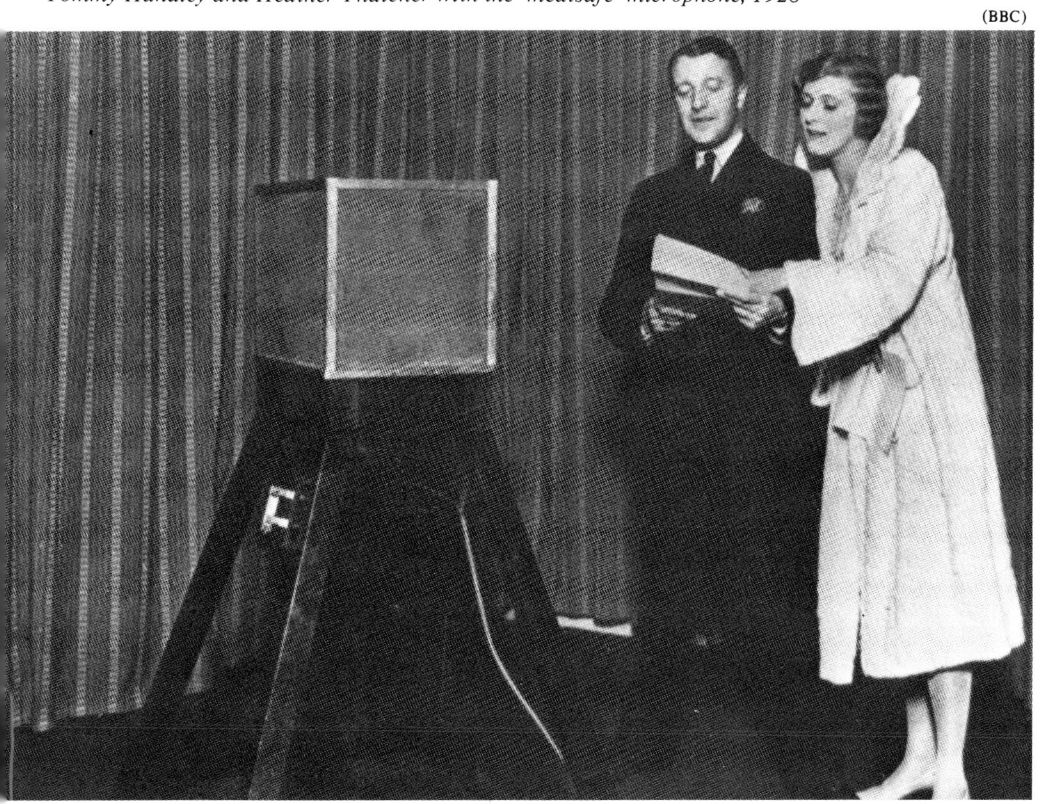

Lord Reith, 1967 (BBC)

Sir Hugh Greene (BBC)

Sir Charles Curran 
(BBC)

"THE VALVE SET" CONCERT PARTY.

8.0.—We Tune in.
8.5.—High and Low Tension will function.
8.10.—The set oscillates.
8.20.—The Mirth Condenser will function.
8.30.—High Tension again in evidence.
8.40.—A little more reaction is used.
8.50.—Whereby further howling is caused.
9.0.—Finer tuning is necessitated.
9.5.—Surely we've got America!
9.10.—The set again oscillates.
9.15.—The Authorities take action.
9.15.—Performance of Winning Items in "5WA" Competition for New Tunes suited to Country Dancing.

Wireless programme item from Radio Times, July 25, 1924

(Radio Times Hulton Picture Library)

Gillie Potter, 1930

Harry S. Pepper, 1942 (BBC)

Robb Wilton, 1954 (Popperfoto)

(BBC)

The original 'Band Waggon' team, Richard Murdoch and Arthur Askey in 1971

Ronald Waldman (with headphones) in action (Popperfoto)

casting as anything else. In 1975 I had a long conversation with Michael Standing, who was BBC Radio's Director of Variety from 1945 to 1953, and whose influence made the so-called Golden Years of post-war radio comedy possible. I complimented him on his bravery and foresight in promoting such programmes as 'Take It From Here' and 'The Goon Show', and backing them in their early days before they were established and, indeed, when they were nearly taken off the air. 'Ah,' he said, 'but I also showed the same "foresight" backing other shows that never made it, and in fact wasted a lot of people's time and a lot of the Corporation's money.' But fortunately successes are remembered and failures are quickly forgotten.

Let me give you a personal example. In the early 1950s I was a stand-up comedian (that is, I used to stand up and tell jokes) and served a brief and inglorious apprenticeship on 'Workers' Playtime', a lunchtime variety show which broadcast twice-weekly from factories and workshops all over the British Isles. It had started during the war as a morale booster and lingered on well into the 'sixties, when I suppose it eventually occurred to someone that the war was over. On one occasion I appeared at a smallish electronics laboratory in Cambridge where my jokes were received with delight and my finishing song was greeted with rapturous applause by the assembled boffins. I can remember every detail of *that* broadcast vividly, even the faces of the audience and details of the cold buffet we were served afterwards.

The next 'Workers' Playtime' I did (incidentally my last) was transmitted from a bicycle factory in Nottingham and took place in a canteen roughly the size of Wembley Stadium. All I remember of *that* occasion as I stood there in my dove grey lounge suit and salmon pink tie, making what I supposed were telling and apt comments on the state of Britain, was that no one looked up from their food during my act, except one man in the front row who was wearing grimy overalls and a trilby hat, and eating roast beef and Yorkshire pudding with a spoon. He smiled a lot (between mouthfuls), but the effect was marred by the fact that he had no teeth. Actually, that broadcast did make history of a sort. It was the only occasion on record when a comedian on a 'Workers' Playtime' didn't get one single laugh.

History, then, is a matter not so much of what happened as of what people care to remember happening, and people tend to remember events differently. I have tried to sort out the often widely-differing accounts of an incident and have used the version that seems to me to be most likely to be true. But, to quote the opening line of Dylan Thomas's *Under Milk Wood*, 'To begin at the beginning'.

1

Early Days

A. J. ALAN.

When radio began in Britain in 1922 it was greeted with enthusiasm by the handful of amateur wireless buffs then in existence, but with deep suspicion and even outright hostility by people whose livelihood depended upon other forms of communication and entertainment. Newspaper proprietors suspected that if news were broadcast regularly, people would no longer buy papers; and music-hall and theatre owners felt that if their stars were available, as it were, *free* to the listeners, then box office receipts would drop. Neither group dreamed that radio might, in fact, enhance both newspaper sales (since a good radio critic could add thousands to the circulation), and the size of theatre audiences, who would flock to see a star they had previously only heard.

The uneasiness of Fleet Street and Shaftesbury Avenue was understandable. By 1922 the victory of 1918 had turned sour; depression was in the wind, and the survivors of the Somme and Passchendaele, Jutland and the Dardanelles, were becoming aware that Britain, far from becoming a land 'fit for heroes to live in', was a hard place in which to live at all. Everyone, ex-serviceman and civilian alike, was sick of the tensions of wartime Britain, the never-ending casualty lists, the food shortages, the short leaves and the long separations, the constant and bloody death. They had become heartily sick of the exhortations to join up, to save for victory, to work harder and eat less, and by 1922 the grim fraud of the 'war to end war' had been revealed. The dole queues stretched across the land and the war leaders and their acolytes were no longer seen as heroes but as helpless, often foolish, and occasionally corrupt men who, having helped to win the war, were now clearly losing the peace. Hortatory propaganda lost its power, and all that people wanted was to be left alone.

Radio was cheap and it was cosy, and above all it was something that the whole family could share. Moreover, it was reassuring. The friendly voices of the broadcasters could and did reach the remotest parts of the country, and even more than the newspapers or the music hall, or even the infant cinema industry, it united the kingdom. Radio was a universally shared experience. Furthermore, radio was new and modern and untainted by war. It hadn't existed in 1914, and people looking for a new and better world seemed to hear it crackling through the earphones of their primitive crystal sets.

At first, the BBC was unable to provide much in the way of laughter. One reason was that music-hall proprietors forbade their big name performers to broadcast. Another was that John Reith, who ran the British Broadcasting Company (as it was called until 1927, when it became the British Broadcasting Corporation), didn't care that much for jokes—or at least, not for the rough vulgarities of common comedians—and so radio's early laughter-makers tended to be refined, middle-class, and eminently respectable. Nothing was broadcast that might bring a blush to a maiden's cheek, and if it didn't bring a laugh to her lips either—well, that was hard luck.

It took another World War to change the nature of broadcasting, when the BBC, having revolutionized public taste in the 'twenties and 'thirties, in turn had its own tastes radically altered. In 1922, amid the brass bands, the string quintets, and the 'sketches by humourists'—Reith's description of what he wanted in the way of comedy—such programmes as 'The Goon Show' or 'Take It From Here', or the many other tremendous successes by which we measure radio's greatness today, would have been inconceivable. And 'Round The Horne'? God, or rather, Reith, forbid.

At the *very* beginning, what comedy there was on the air was in the hands of the various 'uncles and aunties' who presented 'Children's Hour', in those days a very important programme. That, I suppose, gave the BBC the 'Auntie' tag that persisted well into the 'sixties—much to the disgust of Sir Hugh Greene, Director General from 1960 to 1969, who hated that particular image and had a fierce anger for any of his staff who used the expression. In the 'twenties, the 'package' shows were chiefly concert parties—semi-professional groups of entertainers, often drawn from local BBC staff and their friends—which rejoiced in such names as The Elite Concert Party, The Crotchets Concert Party, The Impossibles, The Moonstones, and The Valve Set Concert Party.

There'd be a soprano ('Maidens of Cadiz'), a baritone ('Drake's Drum'), a pianist ('Nola'), a light comedian ('Lily of Laguna'), a low comedian ('Two Lovely Black Eyes'), and a 'novelty' musical ensemble—the novelty probably being that they could actually play in tune. On Boxing Day, 1923 came the first-ever radio pantomime/revue, called 'Singbad the Wailer', of which no details, apart from its title, remain.

The early years of radio *did* produce stars, of course. Tommy Handley first broadcast in 1924, and Charles Penrose, who specialised in laughing songs, 'The Laughing Policeman' being perhaps the most famous, quickly became nationally-known names. There were others, too—John Henry and Blossom; Norman Long with his sophisticated songs at the piano; and Gillie Potter, whose anecdotes of the fictitious village of Hogsnorton and its local squire, Lord Marshmallow, were delivered in a deadpan voice and with a wealth of bizarre detail, such as his description of 'the temperance band who got so very drunk last year'. His invariable opening line, 'Good evening, England. This is Gillie Potter speaking to you in English', made him a national celebrity.

The first really big star that radio actually *created* was A. J. Alan, who first broadcast in 1924. A. J. Alan was the pseudonym of a civil servant named Leslie Harrison Lambert, and over the years the BBC had a lot of fun tempting listeners to guess Alan's real identity—almost to a point where the mystery assumed the same cause célèbre quality as the 'Who is Jack the Ripper?' outcry of the 1870s, the guesses including leading politicians and royalty. Alan was a perfectionist who invariably broadcast wearing a dinner jacket, even though he was alone in the studio. His style would, I suppose, today be called 'up-market'. It was certainly unashamedly middle-class, as witness this extract from one of his pieces, 'Wottie':

> 'The preparatory school I went to was near Haywards Heath, about sixteen miles from Brighton—in Sussex, you know. The headmaster was a man called Mercer, and he knew his job.
>
> He taught us cricket and rugger and how to behave and (I believe) one or two other things.'

Ronnie Waldman, who has had a long and distinguished career in both radio and television—who is, indeed, to radio what Machiavelli was to the Renaissance—was a young radio producer in the 'thirties and often produced the A. J. Alan short stories. He vividly remembers Alan as a perfectionist who, 'quite apart from being a man of impeccable craftsmanship in the writing of his stories and in the telling of them, was also an impeccable craftsman in the way he went about it. Let us assume that his story was due to last fifteen minutes—well, he'd send me the script with a letter saying, "I'm afraid this only runs for fourteen minutes and fifteen seconds, is this acceptable?" And I would write back and say yes, I thought it would be all right, and in due course he would turn up for rehearsal at Broadcasting House. He invariably brought a little attaché case. He'd be taken to the studio and he would sit down, open the attaché case and take out a flask of brandy which he put on one side of the mike in case he felt he needed it. Hard liquor was taboo in Broadcasting House in those days, but even Reith couldn't stop A. J. Then he'd produce his script, which was gummed to cardboard so it didn't rustle when he was turning over the pages, and then out came the rest of his equipment, which included an indiarubber and a pencil in case he wanted to make any amendments or alterations, a stopwatch so that he could time himself, a steel tape measure so that he could measure the distance from his mouth to the microphone (he'd been told once that eighteen inches was the right distance), and then, incredibly, a candle and a box of matches, because once the lights had failed during a broadcast. He would set it all up, light the candle and then say, "Engineers, if you can hear me, burn a blue light please." Then he'd rehearse.'

According to Waldman, A. J. Alan's timing never varied by as much as one second throughout rehearsals or transmission. In those days the Empire Service repeated programmes at all hours of the day and night to tie in with local time at the receiving end. But even when recording on disc became a practical possibility, Alan always insisted on reading his stories live, whether at midnight, two o'clock in the afternoon or at 6 in the morning, and they always ran exactly the same length of time and presumably he always wore his dinner jacket. 'He was a staggering man,' Waldman said. 'As a senior civil servant and an ex-Navy type, I suppose he had that sort of perfectionism built into him.' As someone has so aptly remarked, 'Broadcasting attracts the oddballs.' But it's the work, not the man, that should command our attention. The following extract is from another typical A. J. Alan radio story, called 'My Adventure on Dartmoor':

> 'Good evening, everyone. I always seem to bring my troubles here. I'm going to grouse tonight about a piece of ingratitude that someone's . . . treated me to . . . and it may make me feel a little less bitter to get it off my chest.
>
> Last November I was spending a few days in Devonshire with two very good friends of mine, a Mr and Mrs Harris. Charming people they are—I'm sure you'd like them. He writes books, and she illustrates 'em—or else it's the other way round—anyhow, there the matter seems to end. . . . That is, I've never heard of anything of theirs getting published. But it doesn't matter, as

they've enough to live on without that. They've a little cottage on Dartmoor, and they live in it all the year round. Quite a nice cottage, whitewashed; there's a little wooden porch in front and a sort of barn place at one end. They keep a cow and a car, which both live in the barn. The cow's called Constance, and the car's a runabout—you know the kind. They run about a mile and then, owing to a slight technical hitch, they stop.

Of course, they have to have something to get about in, because they are three miles from a village and twelve miles from a station. I tell you, it's pretty wild there—the last half mile of road leading to their place is little more than a sheeptrack. If you want a cocktail on Sunday morning you have to walk three miles across the moor to the nearest inn, and when you get there you have to show the man how to mix it. . . . He hasn't got half the things, and it tastes like death; and then you walk all the way home again. . . . Oh, it's *great* fun.'

Now, off-hand, who does that remind you of? That style, that turn of phrase . . .? Right first time. Frank Muir in 'My Word'. But although Muir doesn't admit to influences (I think he feels he sprang fully-formed into a radio studio), I wouldn't mind betting that the infant Muir unconsciously absorbed A. J. Alan if not at his mother's breast, than at least at her wireless set.

Frederick Laws wrote of A. J. Alan in the *News Chronicle* in 1928: 'He is the most complete personality yet projected by the microphone.' They still don't come much completer. Even Frank Muir doesn't take a candle and a tape measure to the studio!

Whereas in the USA in the 'twenties, radio was local and commercial—a free-for-all dogfight with hundreds of small companies competing for the audience and the sponsors—the BBC was a unified monopoly of eight regional stations working as an integrated federation, and was thus able to develop faster and more efficiently despite opposition from music-hall and newspaper interests. At least, *technically* it developed. By the 'thirties, Lord Reith, as he had then become, had created a set-up and a system that was to last unthreatened for nearly forty years, its programmes reflecting primarily the taste of the programme-makers and then—and only then—the taste of the listeners. During the 'thirties the development of Radio Luxembourg and Radio Normandie, both commercial stations complete with advertisements and a style that was unashamedly lowbrow, drove the BBC to compete on a more popular level, but right up to the arrival of commercial television in 1955, the BBC regarded its competitors rather in the way that Queen Victoria must have viewed the behaviour of the fuzzy-wuzzies in the Sudan in the 'nineties: irritating, even puzzling, but in reality not sufficiently important to lose any sleep over. After all, the BBC reasoned, it could always win when it chose to, and this simple faith has been the Corporation's guiding philosophy throughout its long and distinguished life, OBE's and knighthoods being the most common—and often the only—rewards for winning.

It's easy to forget, incidentally, how closely television followed upon radio's heels. However, though John Logie Baird first demonstrated television in January 1926 (a year before the BBC became a Corporation), in the late 'twenties and 'thirties television was still in the province of speculation—when it wasn't merely a joke. Radio was *the* thing.

1928 caption.—WHAT OUR TELEVISIONISTS MAY HAVE TO PUT UP WITH. Voice of Broadcasting Lecturer. "*Now I vill run through the Lithuanian vowel-sounds once again, and this time I want you all to watch my lips closely.*"

Reproduced by permission of Punch

By 1927 the number of wireless licences had risen from the 1922 figure of 35,000, to an astonishing 2,178, 259, and it can be assumed that there were many listeners who had not bothered to acquire a licence.

What made those millions laugh? Well, there was 'Charlot's Hour', a sort of genteel Variety programme which broadcast regularly from 1927 on, and vaudeville and topical revues replaced the more primitive Elite and Valve Set Concert Parties. Comedy was still very much 'sketches by humourists', the novelty of the settings in which these were placed being the only real artistic development. By 1933 'Non-Stop Variety' was being added to the vaudeville concept, the main difference being that in vaudeville the artistes appeared once, and in Variety, twice. It all sounds pretty deadly now, and even then not everybody was amused, as letters to the editor of the *Radio Times*, and indeed newspaper articles of the time, show. The author, critic and observer of the wireless scene, St John Ervine, wrote in 1932 in the *Radio Times:*

> 'I do not complain because many of the jokes are old. All jokes are old, and all jokes are fresh. The most depressing bore in the world is the gloomy fellow who says: "I've heard that one before!" He ought to be bumped off. Are nine persons to be deprived of a jest because the tenth has heard it? The most familiar joke in the world is new to millions of people, for millions of people are born every year, and there must be a period in their lives when any joke, however blue-mouldy with age it may be, must be fresh and sparkling. I will not grumble, therefore, when I hear a chestnut. Even the *Punch* joke about the curate's egg must be unknown to many persons. But I am entitled to grumble when a man delivers a joke to me with an apology for joking at all. That, too often, is what the BBC comedians seem to be doing. I could hit them when they mumble, and I would if I could get to them. They "fur" their voices and speak too quickly and make no allowance for the hollow laughter of the morgue-keepers who are listening in the studio. They do not time their stuff well. They have no sense of the unseen audience. If, that is to say, they are smart, up-to-date, bright young comedians. But if they are old stagers, like Sir Harry Lauder or Wilkie Bard or Bransby Williams, they can time their stuff with absolute precision. These old boys know how to catch the laughter of the unseen and can plant their jokes effectively every time. I cannot recall a single instance of failure by an old music-hall comedian to obtain an effect on me. But I can remember many melancholy nights when death would have been the portion of certain modern comedians if the ether could kill.'

A typical vaudeville bill from October 10, 1932 included Jeanne de Casalis, who did an act as a confused housewife aptly named 'Mrs Feather', generally on the phone to a tradesman ('I haven't had my brown, Mr. Brawn . . .'), plus Tommy Handley, a singer or two, and a lady violinist rejoicing in the name of Mrs Pullpleasure. I've searched but can find no other reference to her—could it really have been her name? Perhaps she'd been so called at the whim of an immigration officer with a distorted sense of humour, in the way that Sam Goldwyn was named Goldfish on his arrival in the USA. Or perhaps she changed it herself, as did our own Lord Delfont, who started life as Bernie Winogradsky in Tokmak in Russia. After all, it was 1932, and it's possible that the poor woman was an Italian expatriate on the run from Mussolini's fascists with their rubber truncheons and caster oil—a graduate of the Venice School of Music, perhaps, who was born Tirare-

Picere and made the literal translation to Pullpleasure. . . .

December 1, 1932 gave the world 'The All Male Novelty Variety Show'. No prizes for guessing that Tommy Handley was on the bill. Tommy Handley also appeared on December 10, 1932 with Max Miller. Or rather, as Asa Briggs points out in his *History of Broadcasting*, *was* to have appeared with the legendary Max, for although billed in *Radio Times*, George Black withheld permission for Miller to appear. Having Miller under contract, Black was able to enforce the 'no broadcasting' clause, even though he had a gentleman's agreement with the BBC to allow his contract artists to appear on radio. The suspicion that the impresarios nursed about the BBC was pathological, and even in later years when the boot was on the other foot, and the only big box office draws were radio 'names', the theatre magnates still held the whip hand, making offers they couldn't refuse to Arthur Askey and Jack Warner for stage versions of their hit radio shows, 'Band Waggon' and 'Garrison Theatre'. There were two main reasons for this. One is that pre-war radio paid its stars incredibly badly and the lesser known artists hardly at all, a guinea being the not unusual fee for a supporting player. The other is that the top men of radio regarded Variety as undignified, vulgar and at best a necessary evil. Their attitude was rather like that of a priest seeing a street-walker accosting a client—knowing that the flesh is weak but pitying or despising both parties involved in the sordid transaction. The sombre Reith has much to answer for.

On December 28, 1932, in a show that included Hermione Gingold (then Mrs Eric Maschwitz), there was a sketch by the *Daily Express* columnist 'Beachcomber'. On the face of it, not a particularly relevant piece of information—until you consider that hitherto radio had been anathema to Lord Beaverbrook, for whom 'Beachcomber' worked, and that Eric Maschwitz was about to take over as Director of Variety with instructions to shake things up a bit.

Maschwitz joined the BBC in 1926 and spent some time in the Outside Broadcasts department before being made editor of the staggeringly popular *Radio Times* in 1927. In 1933 he moved from that position to take charge of the newly-created Variety department, where his energy and enterprise soon pushed Variety (once described by Val Gielgud, the Head of Drama, as 'ukelele players and comedians') out of its parochial and often tediously homespun rut, into exciting, adventurous and above all romantic broadcasting. He did all he could to develop and groom young and untried performers. Among his finds were impressionist/comedienne Beryl Orde, and the female impersonator, Arthur Marshall. Marshall, a housemaster at Oundle public school, was spotted by a producer, C. Denis Freeman, doing an extremely funny act at a party at

Cambridge, and was soon dragged before the microphone in 'Charlot's Hour' where he performed one of his set pieces, a school-mistress addressing her girls. Maschwitz was impressed by Marshall's humour and inventiveness, and saw to it that he broadcast regularly. One of Marshall's funniest creations was Nurse Dugdale. The following extract is from a script broadcast in 1944, but it is typical of Arthur Marshall's radio style. Here, Nurse Dugdale tells a gripping tale of life in a girl's school, called 'Rivals Of The Platform':

> 'Ding-dong-ding. Ding-dong-ding. High noon boomed out its festive message over the crenelated pile that was Tudway Towers as the girls came trooping cheerily out of the stinks lab. "I say, by Jove," cried Elspeth Durrant, wiping her specs and dabbing the last drops of hydrochloric from her sensitive fingers, "don't forget, girls, it's the music comp. this afternoon for the coveted Butterworth Chalice. I'm off to polish up my double-stopping. What about it? Care to come along too?" she queried sportingly of Maud Bagshawe, her dreaded rival. But Maud frowned petulantly and with a muttered "No thanks" she slouched moodily off in the direction of the senior's cubies.
>
> Music had, alas, caused a life-long feud between the two girls, for each had, on occasion, scooped the handsome bronze Chalice from the other, Elspeth with a forceful 'cello solo in the spring of '42, and Maud a year later, with a breath-taking rendition of a completely unknown Patagonian chansonette.'

Elspeth is nobbled. As she settles her 'sturdy mahogany instrument between her knees' she finds to her horror that her reading glasses have been smashed. She realises that it's the work of her rival, Maud, but goes on to win the contest playing her 'cello from memory. After supper, Elspeth seeks Maud out—

> ' "Look here, old girl," she cried, "I vote we bury the hatchet, eh?" Maud bit her lip and forced herself to speak steadily. "Thanks, Elspeth, ever so," she said. "Tell you what," she added, "we're both pretty A1 at solos, but in Life you don't get far by playing a lone hand. What about turning our solos into a duet?" And, arm in arm, and humming a catchy stave from Eric Coates, the two girls strolled cheerily off to the grubber.'

Eric Maschwitz hoped to persuade the BBC to train 'Variety apprentices', but this idea came to nothing and so he turned to the young Canadian entrepreneur, Carroll Levis, to produce the required new talent. Carroll Levis, a former policeman, radio announcer and lumberjack from Vancouver, had tried the 'discovery' idea in Canada. It was really only an amateur talent contest in a skin but somehow Levis made it seem new and fresh.

I began my professional career with him in 1951, when I won a radio talent contest—the prize being congratulations from Hermione Baddeley! My own memory of Levis is of a man of hypnotic personality. Women adored him and he them, and often his dressing-room was like a busy doctor's surgery as woman after woman went in to 'pay her respects'—he may not have had talent but he certainly had stamina. On stage he specialized in the Hitleresque 'big lie', and a typical introduction to a discovery might go something like: 'Little Jimmy here is only thirteen, his mother's in hospital, his dad's out of work and he has to support his six kid sisters. He's going to whistle through his nose—and he's your own local boy, so give him a big hand.' After that, how could little Jimmy go wrong? The audience wasn't to know he was a thirty-five year old midget born three hundred miles away. Now, I'm six-foot-two, I come from a middle-class London suburban background and was, in those days, a teller of jokes, so clearly the 'poor kid from the sticks' approach wouldn't work. He described me variously as 'Lambeth's longest laugh', 'The lanky Londoner', and once 'That crazy character from Cricklewood'. However, I soon escaped the horrors of being 'a young man making his start in show business' when he made me the manager of a second-string touring company which travelled round the smaller and seedier theatres which littered Britain in the 'fifties. Apart from the regulars—harmonica players, xylophonists and the like, who were professionals—I used to hold auditions for amateurs in every town we visited, and recommend the better 'finds' to Carroll for his radio series. Comedians were hard to come by but some did make the grade, notably a boy called Jim Smith, who later changed his name to Jim Dale and became in turn a pop singer, a regular in the *Carry On* film series, and is today a considerable actor. Another find was a young impressionist named John Killick, better known today as the disc jockey, Tony Brandon.

But that was in 1951–52. In 1937, C. B. Rees interviewed Carroll Levis for *Radio Times:*

> 'I was ushered into the presence of a young man with a strong, round, clean-shaven face, an expectant blue eye, no trace of disillusionment or boredom, a grip like a vice, and an energy that was unmistakably a virtue. He had just been giving somebody a piece of his mind on the telephone. Happily for me, that had warmed him up, and in two minutes I was leaning back in a chair listening to the answers to questions I had not yet had time to ask. "I am 27 but I look more because my hair is grey and I'm over-

weight. I was a radio announcer in Canada—and I started a feature introducing new and unknown artists to the microphone. I conducted a search for talent from coast to coast in Canada, but I soon decided that there would be greater opportunities in the British Isles than in any other country in the world."

That was why he came over about eighteen months ago and began his quest for the stars of tomorrow here. His first broadcast on September 8, 1936, was one of the successes of the year. He presented thirteen new acts from all parts of the country.

"How do you find your discoveries?" I asked him. "I spend hours," he answered, "giving people auditions. I have heard more than a thousand people in one week."

Mr Levis told me that there are now twenty-four acts regularly employed by him at a salary of not less than £5 a week and expenses. One girl he discovered is in a West End show and doing well. Several have gone onto the Variety stage and are making good, and in one or two cases earning £25 a week. Those who are not found to be suitable return to their jobs none the worse and at least, as Mr Levis puts it, "they have had their hour of glory".'

Unfortunately, by 1937 Maschwitz's private interests and those of the BBC had become mutually incompatible and Maschwitz went to work for MGM in Hollywood. What he left was a tradition of operettas tailor-made for radio, *good* light music, internationally-known comedians (such as George Burns and Gracie Allen, Vic Oliver, and so on) to spice Variety shows, and a sense of lightness, a gaiety that was eagerly sought and cherished by the listening millions.

I first met and worked for Eric Maschwitz when he had returned to become the BBC's Head of Light Entertainment (Television) in April 1958. His sense of mischief hadn't deserted him, and he surrounded himself with good, clever people (Frank Muir and Denis Norden were his advisers), and drove both comedy—that's to say, scripted shows—and Variety—that is, song and dance shows—even further forward than his predecessor, Ronnie Waldman, had done. Incidentally, it's interesting to note in passing how many radio men subsequently became great influences on TV comedy. Maschwitz was a good example. When his restlessness caused him to leave the BBC yet again in 1961, he reappeared almost immediately at the commercial TV station, Associated Rediffusion, master-minding the comedy success, 'Our Man At St. Mark's'.

The year 1937 saw the teaming of two formidable radio talents—Robb Wilton and Max Kester—in 'Mr Muddlecombe J.P.', a series of fifteen-minute comedies. Kester was one of Maschwitz's young men, a young beanpole of an actor with a talent for writing and production. Robb Wilton was an established music-hall star who had already become well known both in radio and in films with his character studies of bumbling firemen, policemen, and the like. His rich Lancashire accent and his quirky, idiosyncratic turn of phrase were ideally suited to radio, and the character of Mr. Muddlecombe, the fumbling and disorganised Justice of the Peace, fitted him to perfection. Imagine him at the Bench, not at his best in the early morning, dealing with his first case of the day, a persistent offender named John Higgins who is on yet another charge of being drunk and disorderly. A BBC prohibition of the time actually forbade the phrase 'drunk and disorderly', and Kester substituted 'incapable'. Mention of public houses was also taboo, hence the curious reference in the script to a milk bar—but the actors' performance and the listeners' imagination filled in the gaps.

MUDDLECOMBE Call the first case.

WALLACE (*usher*) Yes, sir. Call John Higgins!

VOICE (*distant and calling*) John Higgins!

MUDDLECOMBE Where's my pen? What a court this is. Where the—?

HIGGINS (*cockney*) I'm here, sir.

MUDDLECOMBE Ah, morning, John. Well, what is it this time?

WALLACE (*reading*) Last night I found John Higgins in the Seven Cows Milk Bar. He was helpless. He *was* in a state.

MUDDLECOMBE Very nice, too—I mean, do you know this is your 217th conviction in this court—and always on the same charge?

HIGGINS 217 is it, sir? Just a minute while I check up on that. (*Mumbles to himself*) That's right.

MUDDLECOMBE It's getting a bit monotonous you know. I'd like to help you, John, but the charge always says incapable. Incapable! How do you do it? I like a drink myself and I'd like to know—I mean, what makes you do it?

HIGGINS Well, you see, sir, eleven years ago yesterday I met the wife and ever since then—well, you know how it is—you need a little something to help you over the hard times.

MUDDLECOME But you were here three weeks ago.

HIGGINS Yes, sir. That was the anniversary of our wedding.

MUDDLECOMBE And five weeks before that? November 9th?

HIGGINS That was the day I got work, sir

MUDDLECOMBE And you came in again on the 12th.

HIGGINS That was the day I got the sack.

MUDDLECOMBE You must pull yourself together, John.

HIGGINS I'll try, sir, but I haven't been well lately.

MUDDLECOMBE What's been the matter?

HIGGINS I've got a nasty pain in the lower part of my back.

MUDDLECOMBE I'm sorry to hear that, is it a kind of slow, stabbing pain?

HIGGINS Yes.

MUDDLECOMBE Catches your breath when you breathe?

HIGGINS That's it.

MUDDLECOMBE *I* get that. Are you doing anything for it?

HIGGINS I've been trying some ointment.

MUDDLECOMBE Oh, that's no good. Now when you go home tonight, if you *do* go home, try some of that stuff that cured me.

HIGGINS What was that, sir?

MUDDLECOMBE Oh, now you've got me, can't think of it for the life of me, but try it, and if you *don't* go home, get the warder to slip out and get you a double scotch. Get him to make it hot with a slice of lemon, boil you some onions, put a hot water bottle in your bed and then get him to sit and read to you till you fall off to sleep and you'll be as right as can be in the morning.

During the war, Robb Wilton was to coin one of the best-remembered phrases ever to have been created for the radio: 'The day war broke out'. Here's how his routine continued:

'The day war broke out, my Missus looked at me and she said, "What good are you?" I said, "Who?" She said, "You." I said, "How do you mean, what good am I?" She said, "Well, you're too old for the army, you couldn't get into the navy, and they wouldn't have you in the air force, so what good are you?" I said, "How do I know, I'll have to think."

So I joined the Home Guards. The first day I got my uniform I went home and put it on—and the Missus looked at me and said, "What are you supposed to be?" I said, "Supposed to be? I'm one of the Home Guards." She said, "One of the Home Guards, what are the others like?" She said, "What are you supposed to do?" I said, "I'm supposed to stop Hitler's army landing." She said, "What, YOU?" I said, "No, not *me*, there's Bob Edwards, Charlie Evans, Billy Brightside—there's seven or eight of us, we're in a group, we're on guard in a little hut behind 'The Dog and Pullet'." '

Besides Eric Maschwitz, the other big men of 'thirties Variety were

John Watt, Maschwitz's successor as Director of Variety; John Sharman, who looked after vaudeville and music-hall shows; Michael North; and Harry S. Pepper, whose main responsibility was for revue and concert party entertainment. They gathered around them a group of bright and dedicated young men, including Brian Michie, who started as a sound effects boy and soon ran that side of things for the department before becoming an interviewer; Gordon Crier, who became an outstanding producer; Vernon Harris, the writer; Max Kester; and Ronnie Waldman. In their new headquarters in St. George's Hall, Langham Place, and free from the stuffier atmosphere of Broadcasting House, they set about creating a new and more exciting kind of light entertainment—more dance bands, better Variety, bigger names, more novelty. 'In Town Tonight', a news miscellany in which the famous and the interestingly obscure were interviewed live on subjects of interest; 'The Kentucky Minstrels', a revived and remodelled version of the old minstrel troupe and forerunner of 'The Black and White Minstrel Show' so beloved by television audiences in the 'fifties and 'sixties; 'Music Hall'; 'Songs From the Shows'—all these programmes were given long runs, and the Variety team came to feel itself an independent group able to escape from the establishment-minded bureaucrats of Broadcasting House.

Ronnie Waldman was typical of these young lions. He'd been a producer in the theatre, had written songs, been an actor and was producing at Brighton when one day in 1937 he received a letter from John Watt suggesting an interview. Knowing nothing of Variety, Waldman suspected that it was his songs they were after, and duly turned up at St. George's Hall with a sheaf of them in his briefcase. However, it was Waldman the producer they wanted: without knowing it, he had acquired a reputation as a bright and inventive stage producer and that was just what BBC Variety felt it needed. He duly joined the Corporation in 1938 and became Harry S. Pepper's assistant, a job in which Waldman feels he really learnt from a master; for 'there was nothing about show business that "Pep" [Harry S. Pepper's nickname] didn't know.' Waldman absorbed it like a sponge, and his drive and mental agility soon outstripped the older man, though he is becomingly modest about his own contribution, attributing most of the department's hit shows to the combined efforts of that early think-tank.

'Band Waggon' is a case in point. Waldman recalls that 'BBC audience research came up with the information that dance band shows weren't as popular as we thought they were. They were all right but no more. After a lot of thought John Watt said, "We can't cut out dance bands altogether, but let's have a compère and a comedian and put something more into the show." And Gordon Crier, the producer, said, "There's a young chap called Richard Murdoch who's an extremely polished actor. He'd be a good compère." John said, "O.K. but who's going to be the comedian?" Well, Harry Pepper and I had just done our annual tour of the seaside summer shows and in our opinion there were only two comedians worth looking at for the job. They both happened to be in Shanklin, Isle of Wight. One was called Tommy Trinder, and the other Arthur Askey. They were equally good, so we tossed a coin, heads for Trinder and tails for Askey, and it came down heads.'

Thus 'Band Waggon's' comedian should have been Tommy Trinder. But as he wasn't available, they asked Arthur Askey and fortunately *he* was. A writer was hired to write a script for Askey and Murdoch but the first three or four shows were a disaster. The scriptwriter was quietly removed and the think-tank took over. Arthur Askey, Richard Murdoch and all crammed themselves into a tiny office under the roof of St. George's Hall for what Harry S. Pepper called a 'sit round', and 'Band Waggon' took shape.

Many people have fond memories of the programme, but if you tell them that Askey and Murdoch appeared for only ten minutes out of the hour the programme ran, they find it hard to believe. However, it's true. Those ten minutes might be said to have revolutionized radio comedy in Britain.

The comedy centred round the idea of Arthur Askey and Dicky Murdoch living in a flat upstairs in Broadcasting House. The 'sit-round' came up with Mrs Bagwash and her daughter, Nausea (whom Arthur was supposed to be courting), Lewis the goat, and pigeons Lucy and Basil. Ronnie Waldman remembers one particular sound effect which was a feature of the programme, and which became known as the 'Band Waggon crash', a forerunner of the wonderful effects noises of 'ITMA' and 'The Goon Show': 'We always made it a point that somewhere or other Arthur would be putting up the curtains or something and he would fall, and there was this terrible crash. A corner of the St. George's Hall stage was fenced off like a boxing ring and inside it was a pile, ten or twelve feet high, of metal chairs, metal trays, wastepaper baskets, etc. At the given moment the sound effects man would solemnly push this mass of metal very gently until it fell with a gargantuan clatter—and, of course, the studio audience adored it.' The chap who did the pushing joined in the spirit of the thing and started dressing for the part and taking a bow when the crash was applauded. This caused Askey to remark on one occasion, 'Oi—*I'm* the comedian. *I* get the laughs.' The sound effects man dressed more soberly after that!

In summing up 'Band Waggon', Waldman seems to me to describe the essence of all radio comedy: 'It's great quality was that it created something you felt you could see—characters that you could picture, even if they were invisible, or indeed non-existent.' All the great comedy shows did that; indeed it could be argued that radio is the best of all forms of communication because it allows the listener to participate in the act of creation. Sitting in front of the loudspeaker in 1939 you could imagine what Mrs Bagwash and Nausea looked like. When Arthur Askey pressed the wrong button on the mighty BBC organ and went through the roof of Broadcasting House, you could picture the scene—as you can when you read this extract involving the antics of Askey and Murdoch when asked to open the new BBC Social Club. It is taken from the tenth programme in the first series of 'Band Waggon' and is typical of its humour:

ANNOUNCER	Over now to the opening of the BBC Social Club, where Arthur and Dicky have been persuaded to perform the opening ceremony.
FX	*Applause, cheers, etc.*
MURDOCH	Come on, Arthur, you'll have to make a speech.
ASKEY	But they'll never see me.
MURDOCH	Well, we'll stand on this table.
ASKEY	It doesn't look any too safe and you know what usually happens when I stand on a table.
MURDOCH	Never mind. Be a brave little boy. They've all got to see you make your speech. Have you got the notes of your impromptu speech?
ASKEY	Yes.
MURDOCH	Go on, then.
ASKEY	Ladies and gentlemen—life without you would be a dreary blank. I long to feel your arms around me . . .
MURDOCH	What are you saying?
ASKEY	Oh, I'm sorry—it's one of Nausea's letters. . . . Oh, I've lost my notes.
MURDOCH	Well, as I wrote them for you I expect I shall be able to remember them, so I'll prompt you.
ASKEY	Right. Ladies and gentlemen, it is with great . . . er . . .
MURDOCH	Diffidation.
ASKEY	It is with great diffidation—what does that mean?
MURDOCH	I don't know, but it sounds good.
ASKEY	That I—that is to say, I rise to . . . er . . . to . . .
MURDOCH	My feet.

ASKEY Dicky's feet.

MURDOCH No, you fool—*your* feet.

ASKEY No, you fool—*your* feet—to declare, honour and obey . . .

MURDOCH To declare this club—

ASKEY To declare this club well and truly launched.

MURDOCH Here's a bottle of champagne. (*As commentator, sotto voce*) Arthur is now holding above his head a bottle of champagne—well, when I say champagne, a monster lemonade. He's now pushing the glass alley in with his thumb, he's just said something that I couldn't catch. The edge of the bottle appears to be a little jagged. Oh, he's done it! Heavens! He's drinking it himself. (*Aloud*) Arthur, Arthur—you shouldn't have drunk that.

ASKEY Well, I didn't know you wanted to have a drink. T'aint 'alf gassy.

MURDOCH Don't you realise what you were meant to do with that bottle? You see that stone over there?

ASKEY Yes.

MURDOCH Well, when the Secretary nods his head you must hit it with the bottle.

ASKEY I see.

FX *Glass crash, thud and cry of pain*

MURDOCH Oh dear—Arthur's launched the Secretary.

Another popular feature of 'Band Waggon' was 'Chestnut Corner' where jokes grown old in the service of comedy were exhumed for one last airing.

ANNOUNCER Ladies and gentlemen!

BAND *Fanfare*

MURDOCH 'Band Waggon' presents 'Chestnut Corner'.

BAND '*Dear Old Pals*'

Or—

FX *Gong*

MURDOCH I wonder why the ankle comes between the calf and the foot?

ASKEY I think it's to keep the calf from getting at the corn.

MURDOCH You *are* bandy!

ASKEY Yes, that's from eating crooked bananas.

MURDOCH What's an optimist?

ASKEY	A man who doesn't care what happens so long as it doesn't happen to him.
MURDOCH	And a pessimist?
ASKEY	The man who's lived a long time with an optimist.

MURDOCH	Does your watch go?
ASKEY	Regularly—every Monday.
MURDOCH	If you smoke fifty cigars like this, you get a gramophone.
ASKEY	If I did, I'd get a harp.

For the accomplished and versatile Arthur Askey it was his big break. Although the first three shows were near-disastrous the think-tank, thanks principally to Vernon Harris, saved the day, and from the fourth programme the show started to look up. Eighteen episodes were broadcast before Askey had to leave to fulfil a summer season contract. With Askey and Murdoch occupying ten minutes, the balance of the programme was made up with such guest stars as Harry Richman (the Frank Sinatra of his day), Art Tatum, the jazz pianist, and Cary Grant. Another regular feature of the programme was 'Mr Walker wants to know', in which Syd Walker, playing the part of a rag and bone man, posed social questions of the day and asked the audience to supply the answers. His catchphrase, 'What would you do, chums?', became nationally quoted and his post bag grew to monumental proportions. But even with that additional support, 'Band Waggon' was Askey's and Murdoch's triumph and it is for their contribution that the show is remembered. When it came off the air in the spring of 1939, a listener wrote to *Radio Times:*

> 'In all the years I have been a listener I have never heard anything so moving and upsetting as the end of "Band Waggon". When Arthur Askey and Richard Murdoch packed up in the flat and went sadly off with the goat and the pigeons, the female portion of the family broke down and cried, while the male showed its feelings by becoming very cross and going out.'

'Band Waggon' returned to the air in the autumn of 1939 for another run, but by then Arthur's career was developing fast, and his time was filled with stage shows and films. Richard Murdoch joined the RAF, and 'Band Waggon' was never to return. It had been pre-war radio's biggest comedy success, for Arthur Askey caught the mood of the time perfectly with his mixture of clowning, irreverence and insight, and he carried the show to the top with his own bubbling, irrepressible sense of humour.

2

Tommy, Ted and Francis

Radio comedy during the war years was dominated by 'ITMA' ('It's That Man Again'). It was created by Ted Kavanagh, its writer; Francis Worsley, its producer; and Tommy Handley, its star. Handley started broadcasting in 1924 and Kavanagh had first written for him in 1925, but by 1939, both their careers were at the crossroads and they needed a new direction in which to move, and a new stimulus to drive them forward.

'ITMA' was designed to replace, or at least emulate, 'Band Waggon', and it was planned over pints of beer in a pub. Perhaps that's not exactly a fitting description of the Langham Hotel in Portland Place, at that time a noted haunt of visiting clergymen, but that's where Ted Kavanagh, Handley and Worsley met one June afternoon in 1939 to discuss the new project. At that time, Kavanagh was writing a weekly show called 'Lucky Dip', which featured an unknown character actor named Jack Train. Though Train was later to make such an impact in 'ITMA' as Colonel Chinstrap, Funf, and many other roles, he did not feature in the first series, which starred Cecilia Eddy, Sam Heppner and Lionel Gamlin. It was decided that the show would be set on an ocean liner, 'a sort of mad hatters' strength-through-joy cruise ship', in which Tommy Handley would be in charge of festivities and Cecilia Eddy would play his dumb secretary, nicknamed Silly. In addition there was a mad Russian inventor, Vladivostooge, played by Eric Egan. Sam Heppner ran a feature called 'Man Bites Dog,' in which mundane situations were reversed, and Lionel Gamlin looked after the obligatory quiz—quizzes then, as now, being extraordinarily popular with listeners. Music was provided by Jack Harris's band, and Pat Taylor was the singer. The show was called after the 1939 catchphrase that related to Hitler's sinister antics of the time: whenever the Führer made a new threatening speech or some new territorial demand, the papers would headline the report, 'It's That Man Again', and Francis Worsley seized on this as his title. It was touch and go. For a time the show looked like being called 'M.U.G.' (the 'Ministry of Universal Gratification'), but Worsley's idea prevailed and 'ITMA' it became.

Thus named and organised, the new show was launched on Wednesday July 12, 1939. Kavanagh said of the occasion, 'It can be well imagined that with the whole of Europe like the proverbial tinder box, the BBC had to be very careful not to give offence. . . . Any slight deviation from the script might have caused another crisis, but Tommy had never been known to extemporise.' So in an atmosphere of mutual trust, but with fingers crossed, 'ITMA' went on the air.

On the face of it, the first 'ITMA' series doesn't seem to have been a world-beating innovation and indeed wasn't terribly successful. In fact, the war stopped it dead before the case could be proved either way, but it's doubtful whether that particular format would have turned out to be the classic that the subsequent 'ITMA', with its riot of characters and plethora of catchphrases, became.

During the late 'thirties the BBC had made plans for the dispersal of personnel and equipment throughout the British Isles, and as part of that plan the Variety department shifted to Bristol. When the 'ITMA' team reassembled in Bristol in early September 1939, the format had to be rethought. For a start the original team of actors was no longer available and, considering the times, a show set on a cruise ship was clearly out of the question. Kavanagh, Handley and Worsley set about creating a new situation and came up with the Ministry of Twerps in which Handley, as the Minister, was surrounded by a gallery of oddities who either worked for the Ministry or sought to gain some advantage from it. The 1939/40 cast included Sam Costa, up till then a dance band vocalist; Maurice Denham, a character actor; Jack Train; Vera Lennox; the Cavendish Three; and the Billy Ternant Orchestra. Francis Worsley and Michael North wrote the signature tune and the show became an instant and blazing success—its self-assurance and cheerful optimism a welcome relief in that time of fear and uncertainty. Handley's comedic style could be described as cocky—and the crisp and cheeky barrage of jokes and puns delivered at machine gun speed took people's minds off their own troubles. 'ITMA' was never a reflective show—its trump card was its exuberance, and its many catchphrases were easy to remember and quote the next day at factory and barracks: 'Mine's a persico', 'I always do the best for all my gentlemen', 'Vous pouvez crachez', 'What a common boy', and many others were soon common currency among the listening millions.

The show came off the air again in February 1940 and stayed off for seventeen months. It went on tour, but curiously it never had the same impact on theatre audiences as it had had on radio. But then, Tommy Handley had never been much of a draw on the halls. His sketch, 'The Disorderly Room', was a compendium of old army jokes and worked at that level, but Handley himself was at his best in, as it were, verbal close up. On radio the timbre of his voice and his skill in delivering a line made him a master of broadcasting, but in the theatre the intimacy was lacking.

During the seventeen months' break in the 'ITMA' transmissions, the BBC had moved from heavily-blitzed Bristol to the comparative safety of Bangor in North Wales. In the calmer atmosphere, Kavanagh did not forget his much-loved programme. 'I thought a lot about "ITMA" while I was isolated in Bangor and had jotted down a lot of new ideas and characters which, when presented to Francis Worsley, were at once accepted. Thus Lefty and Sam, the gentle gangsters, the diver, the Colonel, Ally Oop the pedlar, the cheery commercial traveller, Claud and Cecil the polite brokers' men, and many others were born.' The new series of 'ITMA' started broadcasting in 1941 and was set in the Middle East. It was called 'It's That Sand Again', but the title quickly reverted to the tried and trusted 'ITMA', and it stayed that way to the end of its radio life.

Sybil Dickinson, who was then a BBC secretary, remembers Bangor well as a haven where 'ITMA' 'flourished gloriously and in comparative peace'. She was working for Tom Ronald at that time on an 'Old Mother Riley' series: 'We had an office in the annexe to Bron Castell, and Francis Worsley and his secretary had theirs immediately opposite. Thursdays—the day the "ITMA" scripts were written—were marvellously funny days, with laughter from beginning to end. Francis, Ted and Tommy used to sit *in a row* at the desk, each capping the other's absurd jokes—many, of course, much too awful for the sedate BBC and/or censor of the day. It was in *this* office that the famous Royal Variety Performance for Windsor was written and then shouted and laughed up and down the corridor with heaps of saucy jokes that some of the Royal Family might have adored but which were, of course, instantly blue-pencilled.' During the early days in Bangor, Francis Worsley conducted some interesting experiments to find the optimum size of audience for a show like 'ITMA'. He said there were three possibilities, remembers Ronnie Waldman: 'You could do it at the theatre in Bangor or at a cinema in Llandudno with an audience of two thousand; you could do it with an audience of two hundred in the studio at Bangor; or you could do it with no audience at all. He tried all three. The audience of two thousand had the effect of slowing the show down. No audience at all somehow gave a sense of emptiness. Two hundred people turned out to be just right.' Worsley's discovery proved to be an important lesson. Since the 'forties, two or three hundred has been the standard size of radio and television studio audiences.

By 1942, Mrs Mopp, the archetypal charlady (played by Dorothy Summers) had become a firm favourite. Maurice Denham had created a similar character, Mrs Tickle, in the earlier series of 'ITMA', but had had to leave the show to go into the forces. However, when he came on leave, Ted Kavanagh wrote the following scene between these two charwomen. It captures the authentic flavour of mid-wartime 'ITMA':

MRS MOPP And what may you be doin' of, may I ask?
MRS TICKLE I'm tidying up this filthy office for Mr Itma.
MRS MOPP Oh you are, are you? Let me tell you, I do for His Worship, and no one else.
MRS TICKLE I always do my best for all my gentlemen.
MRS MOPP Then you don't do it in here. I'm Mrs Mopp, the Corporation Cleaner.
MRS TICKLE And I'm Lola Tickle, Mr Itma's fancy.
MRS MOPP Tickle by name and Tickle by nature no doubt.
MRS TICKLE Don't you cast excursions at me, Mrs Mopp.
MRS MOPP And don't you dust my gentleman's doings, Mrs Tickle.
MRS TICKLE He's mine. I did for him first.
MRS MOPP He's used to ladies' attention and you're no lady.
MRS TICKLE You're a woman—that's what you are, Mrs Mopp, a woman.

The two hundredth edition of 'ITMA' was broadcast on February 21, 1946. By then it was claimed for it that it had helped to win the war—which, for all I know to the contrary, it may have done. To mark the double century, *Radio Times* collected the plaudits of celebrated people: ' "ITMA" has made a unique contribution to radio comedy . . . it is the outstanding comedy creation of British radio,' said impresario C. B. Cochran. 'It is . . . a living proof that British radio shows, properly handled, can easily compete with American or any other programmes,' enthused Vic Oliver. 'For me, "ITMA" is *Alice in Wonderland* all over again,' was A. G. Street's charming tribute. However, Professor C. E. M. Joad, a national figure through his appearance on 'The Brains Trust', said: 'Alas, superior person, haughty highbrow, despiser of the common joys of humanity that I am, I have never heard "ITMA".' Adding insult to injury, he also sent Tommy Handley a telegram which read: 'Congratulations. For the two hundredth time I have not heard you.' To which Tommy replied: 'Thanks for all your good wishes. I'm always delighted to hear from a brother comic.'

Not that 'ITMA' hadn't had hard criticism over the years. In 1939 a London listener complained to *Radio Times:* 'Why should the producers in the Variety department assume that the listeners are a body of half-wits? The puns served up last night in "ITMA" were an insult to anyone's intelligence.' In 1940 a listener in Welwyn Garden City begged: 'I implore you please to have "ITMA" and Funf painlessly removed from future programmes.' And in February 1944 a listener from Lytham St. Annes wrote: 'I am constantly amazed by the number of otherwise intelligent people who rave about this programme. I have tried to discover some sort of level of culture or intelligence from which "ITMA" fans are drawn—but in vain.' However, the antis were overwhelmingly outnumbered by the pros, and in 1944 a staggering forty per cent of the population was listening every week.

By 1946 the 'ITMA' location had changed again—this time to the imaginary South Sea Island of Tomtopia, which presented an opportunity to introduce some new characters, among them Chief Bigga Banga and his daughter, Naieve. But the regulars continued—as the following typical exchange between Tommy, Major Munday (Carleton Hobbs) and Colonel Chinstrap (Jack Train), shows:

TRAIN — This gold rush's dangerous, Munday. I hope you carry a gun. I always have one with me.
HANDLEY — Have one with you, Colonel? I'll have a large gin and Jumbo.
HOBBS & TRAIN — Silence, civilian!
HANDLEY — Quiet, conscript!
HOBBS — I say, Chinstrap, my nephew, Montgomery Munday, once drank a toast to his Colonel's daughter out of her slipper and passed out—
HANDLEY — What was her size in shoes? Fourteen and a half?
HOBBS — She was engaged to Figgy Fitzwallaby.
TRAIN — Poor old Figgy. I sat next to him the night he smeared the General's face with mayonnaise and tried to shave him with a fish knife. Definitely dirty, what?

HANDLEY	Oh, I don't know. I sat next to Jimmy Wilde at dinner the other night—he jumped into the serviette ring, went three rounds with a black pudding, gave the steak pie a kidney punch and feinted into the trifle. Any questions?
TRAIN	By the way, Munday, do you know that a submarine can now go to America and back without coming to the surface?
HOBBS	Tchah! You shouldn't believe everything you read in Jules Verne.

Deryck Guyler joined the cast in 1946, and stayed with the show until Handley died in 1949. He was doing Euripides on the Third Programme when he got a phone call from Francis Worsley. 'I didn't know any people in Light Entertainment at that time,' Guyler remembers. 'He asked me to go and have a little chat with Tommy and himself and Ted Kavanagh. I asked him why and he said, "Well, we'd just like to have a little chat. I can't tell you any more now." So I was introduced to Tommy and he said, "I wonder if you'd like to read a few of these bits for me." Francis and Ted went into the control room and Tommy and I read the "bits", then *he* went into the control room. I stood there wondering what it was all about. I couldn't see Tommy, Ted and Francis—in fact the only person I *could* see was the studio engineer, and for no reason at all I said in a Liverpool accent, "I wonder what that's all about. Standing me here like a Charlie." And suddenly Tommy's head flashed round the studio door and he said, "Do you come from Liverpool?" I said, "Yes, it's my home town"—and that was that. But about five months later—I'd forgotten all about it by then—the phone went—and I was in. Ted invented this new character and I did it with a Liverpool accent. It didn't have a name for about four weeks and then one day Tommy, to dry me up, said, "Here's my old friend, Frisby Dyke." The name stayed. It was the name of a large store in Liverpool, rather like Harrods in London. It had gone out of business in 1936 and was completely flattened in the bombing, but in its day it was a Liverpool landmark.

'The following season I had a dreadful skin infection on my face. I wasn't allowed to shave or touch it with water and, of course, I grew a tremendous beard and Tom went to town on it. Every week he had a go. One week he said, "You stand there and look like a brush hanging outside a little window." The next, "You stand there like the underside of New Brighton pier at low tide"—and so on, and the audience loved it.'

For a time when Francis Worsley was ill, Ronnie Waldman produced

'ITMA'. He attributes the show's sparkle to the amazing ad-lib ability of Tommy Handley: 'The great moment was always 6 p.m. on Thursdays (two hours before we went on the air). We'd rehearse during the day but we'd stop at ten minutes to six, go into a dressing-room and listen to the six o'clock news. As we listened, Tommy would make jokes about each news item while a secretary took down everything he said. When the news was over we'd go over his cracks, pick out the best ones, put them into the script and then do the final rehearsal. People used to wonder how it was that the show was so unbelievably topical. It was Tom. He had this extraordinary ability to make a crack about any news item. I didn't start it; I don't know whether it was a tradition that went right back to the beginnings of the show, but I found it happening and I was delighted by it because it seemed to me that this was the essence of comedy—to make it alive and instantly topical.'

'ITMA' was a series that produced so many characters—each with its own catchphrases—that it's impossible to put them into order of popularity. They were all successful. Everyone had their own favourite. 'ITMA' was brilliantly written, exceptionally well played and impeccably produced, but above all it echoed, more than any other show before it, the world in which the listeners themselves lived. It was a world with which they could identify, and if 'ITMA' offered nothing but superficial fun—well, during the war no one had time to stop and really think about things, and it was reassuring to hear Colonel Chinstrap say every week, 'I don't mind if I do'. By 1949, when Tommy Handley died, the world had changed and, in fact, the popularity of 'ITMA' was declining. It had been overtaken by other radio programmes with which the audience could identify more. But during the war and the years of austerity which followed it, Handley and his gang of cheery lunatics reigned supreme. Actually, they weren't *all* cheerful. One of the most successful 'ITMA' characters was Mona Lott, created by Joan Harben, whose lugubrious delivery of an unending tale of woe contrasted hilariously with her catchphrase, 'It's being so cheerful as keeps me going':

HARBEN Good morning, sir. What a shocking day. Got rheumatism that bad you wouldn't believe. What with that and my catarrh. . . . Here's your laundry.

HANDLEY What's this? 'Enclosed please find buttons; shirt follows next week. P.S. In future please take socks out of boots before sending.' They're getting fussy. So you suffer from catarrh, do you?

HARBEN	Yes, something chronic; makes me deaf. I can't hear myself cough.
HANDLEY	Oh, I'll give you something to fix that.
HARBEN	What—make me hear better?
HANDLEY	No, make you cough louder. Cheer up!
HARBEN	Ah, it's all very well for you to laugh. You don't have to spend your time washing like me.
HANDLEY	I do, but I must admit I skip the back of the neck on Thursday. I've got my hands full anyway.
HARBEN	Don't talk about hands—swelled up something enormous, they have. Look at this.
HANDLEY	It *is* huge. Take it along to Carroll Levis. He's always asking for a big hand for his discoveries. By the way, what's your name?
HARBEN	Mona Lott, sir.
HANDLEY	Mona Lott. Any relation to Gordon Crier? Off you go and keep your pecker up.
HARBEN	I always do, sir. It's being so cheerful as keeps me going.

The cast list of 'ITMA' over the years was a long one. Actors came and went as new characters were required and old ones faded. Here, as far as I can ascertain, is the complete list of the character actors and actresses who helped Tommy Handley to build 'ITMA' into a national institution: Maurice Denham, Horace Percival, Clarence Wright, Dino Galvani, Dorothy Summers, Fred Yule, Sydney Keith, Paula Green, Kay Cavendish, Deryck Guyler, Hattie Jacques, Mollie Weir, Hugh Morton, Joan Harben, Lind Joyce, Diana Morrison, Jean Capra, Carleton Hobbs, Mary O'Farrell, Sam Costa, Michele de Lys, and, of course, Jack Train.

The last show, number 310, was recorded on January 5, 1949. Tommy Handley died on January 9, 1949 from a cerebral haemorrhage. 'ITMA' was over.

'ITMA' was not the only show that Kavanagh wrote. In fact, during the first ten weeks of the war he wrote thirty-four shows, though admittedly none of them was particularly memorable. He had always been a fast and prolific writer. It is said that it took him only three hours to write the entire script for an episode of 'ITMA'. Sybil Dickinson describes Ted Kavanagh as 'the only person I've ever met who could write as quickly as I could type. When it was done he'd wander off again with some pleasantry and kind of half-exploding with his special sort of suppressed *non*-laugh. An intensely funny and humorous man.' He was born in Auckland, New Zealand, and after the 1914–18 war, studied medicine at Edinburgh University. He forsook medicine for journalism in the early 'twenties and contributed to all kinds of periodicals. His first attempt at comedy was a joke column in G. K. Chesterton's magazine, *G. K.'s Weekly*.

'ITMA' was far and away Kavanagh's most successful show, and after it he never had another hit, but by then he had started a literary agency which is still flourishing today. He had long cherished a dream of combining radio writers under one roof for their better comfort and protection, and in 1945 he founded Kavanagh Associates. Many writers lined up under the Kavanagh banner, including Denis Norden who joined the agency in 1947, followed only a few weeks later by Frank Muir. They became directors in the 'fifties, along with Sid Colin, himself one of the agency's earliest clients. The business side of the agency was handled by John Hayes and Kavanagh's son, Kevin, with Ted Kavanagh acting as a cross between a recruiting officer and a collector of stray dogs. His generosity was legendary and he was a soft touch for anyone with a joke to tell. John Hayes remembers being in a pub with him 'and someone would come up to him and say, "Here, Ted, here's one for 'ITMA'," and tell him a story. Ted would laugh his head off, pull a fiver out of his pocket and give it to the joke-teller. I'd say, "Ted, you *know* that joke, I told it to you myself last night. You didn't have to buy it.' He'd say, "Ah, but he needs the money. That poor fellow's got six kids." '

Frank Muir became involved with Kavanagh Associates while he was still in the RAF. Having seen an article in the London *Evening Standard* saying that Ted had formed an agency for writers, he sent him some stuff that he'd written: 'He asked me to write a piece for a clarinettist who wanted to become a comedian. I did, and Ted paid me £10 out of his own pocket, I found out later. He was the kindest of all kind men.'

It's interesting to note that the script fee for 'ITMA' at its peak was £50, and for that the BBC got one of the most creative minds of the day. In his book on Tommy Handley, Kavanagh writes, 'My own idea of radio writing was an obvious one—it was to use sound for all it was worth, the sound of different voices and accents, the use of catch-phrases, the impact of funny sounds in words, of grotesque effects to give atmosphere—every device to create the illusion of rather crazy or inverted reality. In Francis Worsley I found the ideal producer, unafraid of innovations, helpful, receptive and unfailingly understanding. Tommy, too, got on well with him, admired his breadth of judgement and knew instinctively that he could put perfect trust in him. What was more, he liked him.' Clearly the three men were in perfect accord, each stimulating the other.

Listening to recordings of 'ITMA' thirty-five or more years after the event, one might be forgiven for wondering why the audience found it so funny. The programme was only on rare occasions witty, it had the shallowest of plots—if in fact they could be called plots at all—and yet in its time its dominance cannot be denied. I think the secret of its success lay in its unselfconscious larkiness—its vitality and its good natured irreverence, and surely that's the stuff of all the best in British humour, from Chaucer to Monty Python. If today you wonder at it—well, it was about *then*, when it happened.

Tommy Handley enjoyed a parallel career with 'ITMA' as half of the quickfire patter act, Murgatroyd and Winterbottom (the other half was Ronald Frankau). Both men operated solo—Frankau in music hall, cabaret and radio, Handley mainly in radio—but came together before the microphone to rattle off some of the fastest cross-talk in the history of broadcasting. This is a snatch of a typical routine:

MURGATROYD How are you, Mr Winterbottom?
WINTERBOTTOM I feel a bit funny.
MURGATROYD Only a bit? Oh, I feel frightfully funny.
WINTERBOTTOM Well, it ought to be a good act tonight.
MURGATROYD It won't be appreciated by the audience in the studio.
WINTERBOTTOM Why not?
MURGATROYD Well, *look* at them—there's a fellow there eating a bit of cheese.
WINTERBOTTOM Yes. He got it on the strength of that. They certainly don't look a very intelligent lot.
MURGATROYD No. Obviously friends of the producer; but we must think of the listener.
WINTERBOTTOM I'm thinking of her. There won't half be a row when I get home.
MURGATROYD Why?
WINTERBOTTOM I threw a shoe at her.
MURGATROYD It isn't June yet.
WINTERBOTTOM What's that got to do with it?
MURGATROYD Ne'er cast a clout till May is out. Yes, Mr Winterbottom, we must always study the listener—the Mr and Mrs Everyman.
WINTERBOTTOM The Jones and Smiths.
MURGATROYD The Robinsons and Browns.
WINTERBOTTOM The Gilberts and Sullivans.
MURGATROYD The Tristans and Isoldes.
WINTERBOTTOM The Hengists and Horsas.

MURGATROYD	The Moodies and Sankeys.
WINTERBOTTOM	And the Derbys and Joans.
MURGATROYD	Cut out the Joans and let's think of the Derby. What have you backed?
WINTERBOTTOM	My car into a shop window. Joan a car?
MURGATROYD	Cut out the Joan and let's think of the Derby again.

In many ways, Handley might still be considered the best radio comedian ever. He was swift, accurate and disciplined, yet quick-witted and inventive at the crucial moment—that's to say, *before* the broadcast, when the contribution of the comedian can transform a good script into a brilliant one. Others had these qualities too, but Handley had them in superabundance, and yet he was never a huge success away from radio. He was radio's man and while 'ITMA' ran he was the king.

3

Comedy at War

'ITMA' apart, it must be admitted that by and large radio comedy during the 1939–42 period was of poor quality. The reasons are fairly obvious. The call-up had denuded the BBC of many of its bright young producers, writers and technicians. Censorship was strict and the authorities unwilling to sanction material 'damaging to morale'—that's to say, jokes about rationing, the blackout, poor conditions in the forces, and inadequacy and incompetence in high places. All these subjects were a natural source of humour and, in fact, later in the war were the very essence of such shows as 'Much Binding In the Marsh', 'Stand Easy', and Eric Barker's 'HMS Waterlogged'. These programmes were respectively the RAF, army and navy divisions of the highly successful series 'Merry Go Round' which blossomed in 1944–45. By then so much had changed. For one thing, the allies were clearly *winning* the war, whereas in '39–'42, they equally clearly weren't.

The BBC's dispersal didn't help much either, but the Variety department, functioning first in Bristol and later in Bangor, did produce some comedy shows that are worth remembering. One of the brightest was 'Garrison Theatre', starring Jack Warner. The show was really little more than a music-hall bill supposedly set in the theatre of an army camp. It was devised by Harry S. Pepper and Charles Shadwell, the conductor, whose infectious laugh made him for a time more famous than many of the comedians at whom he laughed. The programme was billed thus in *Radio Times* for January 6, 1940:

8.0 'GARRISON THEATRE'

Devised by Charles Shadwell and Harry S. Pepper

Famous artists have promised to appear (engagements permitting) at the Garrison Theatre tonight to entertain the troops.

Jack ('Tiny') Warner will be there

Garrison Theatre Orchestra conducted by Lieut. Charles Shadwell (late West Yorkshire Regiment)

Produced by Harry S. Pepper

Jack 'Tiny' Warner, better known today as the star of the TV series 'Dixon of Dock Green', had been a frequent radio performer before the war, and in 'Garrison Theatre' he was an instant and total success. Every week he delivered a monologue describing various arcane activities—for instance, one speech as a cockney rodent operative started, 'I'm a bunger-up of rat holes', and ended, 'But as long as there are rat holes, there'll be bungers-up of rat holes, so it looks as if I've got a job for life.' And, every week in another spot on the show, he read 'a letter from my brother, Sid', an infantryman stationed somewhere in England, which always ended with a postscript such as: 'P.S. I can't say where we're stationed, but if Hitler invades, we'll pelt him with Margate rock.' Warner's catchphrases—'Mind my bike', 'little gel', and 'blue pencil'—became famous. 'Mind my bike' was a cheerily inconsequential remark which cropped up almost by accident when Warner, seeking a new and aural way of making an entrance, thought of the sound of a bicycle bell, and the phrase 'Mind my bike' to go with it. 'little gel', his reference to Joan Winters (Charles Shadwell's daughter) who was also in the programme, depended for its effect on Warner's cockney accent which was picked up by listeners and much imitated. 'Blue pencil' referred to the strict censorship of the time, when all mail from servicemen home was read by their officers to make sure it contained no information likely to give comfort to the enemy. The censors literally used a blue pencil to make the deletions, and the phrase came to mean also the censorship of vulgarities in comedians' scripts. Thus the phrase 'blue pencil' became a synonym for very basic Anglo-Saxon—the 1940 version of 'expletive deleted' which gained currency after the Nixon tapes débâcle of the mid 'seventies. So, when Warner said 'Not "blue pencil" likely!' everyone knew what he really meant, and the phrase was used everywhere and by everyone.

The series ended in May 1940 when, like 'Band Waggon', 'Garrison Theatre' was acquired by impresario Jack Hylton and disappeared from radio to become a big success 'on the halls', never to return to the air.

(Popperfoto)

The 'ITMA' cast: l. to r., Jack Train, Carleton Hobbs, Mary O'Farrell, Michele de Lys, Tommy Handley, Clarence Wright, Lind Joyce, Fred Yule, Jean Capra, Hugh Moreton and Charles Shadwell, 1945.

Francis Worsley, Ted Kavanagh and Tommy Handley

(Popperfoto)

(Radio Times Hulton Picture Librar

Sound effects boy John Ammonds provides the sound of diver's bubbles with a pipe in a bowl for an 'ITMA' show from Bangor, 1941. Also pictured: Tommy Handley and Horace Percival

Jack Warner in 'Garrison Theatre'
(Radio Times Hulton Picture Library)

Vic Oliver (BBC)

Pat Dixon, 1942 (BBC)

The 'Stand Easy' gang: l. to r., Ramon St. Clair, Len Marten, Charlie Chester, Ken Morris and Arthur Haynes

(Radio Times Hulton Picture Library)

'Much Binding in the Marsh': l. to r., Sam Costa, Richard Murdoch and Kenneth Horne (Popperfoto)

'Heigh Ho!': l. to r., Charmian Innes, Maurice Denham, Charles Maxwell (producer), Kenneth Horne, Nell Ballantyne and Peter Waring (BBC)

Jack Hylton's gain was undoubtedly radio's loss, for the engaging and gifted Jack Warner wasn't to broadcast again in a major series until 1953 when 'Meet the Huggetts'—a saga of a working-class family, developed on radio from a series of popular films—started a long and successful career. During the 1950s Jack Warner made many films, from one of which—*The Blue Lamp*—the 'Dixon of Dock Green' series was developed.

If 'Garrison Theatre' was the biggest success of that long winter of the Phoney War, as cynics dubbed the period from September 1939 to May 1940, 'Danger—Men at Work!' ran a fairly close second. It had started its long life on May 11, 1939 and was originally written and produced by Max Kester and Anthony Hall. By 1940, Kester was being given a solo credit as writer/producer, and of the original cast of Doris Nichols, Jacques Brown and Van and Allan, only Nichols and Brown remained, Van and Allan having been replaced first by Jack Train and George Moon, and subsequently by Haver and Lee, a music-hall double-act who adapted quickly and easily to radio. Doris Nichols played Mrs Ponsonby, a wealthy widow, who was 'humourless, gullible and ready to be shocked and outraged by anything that happened to her'. Jacques Brown played Nikolas Ridikoulos, who could be described as a wandering Greek whose anarchic interruptions gave the show its drive.

Reading the scripts now, the show seems to have been fashioned on the lines of the Marx Brothers films—a string of loosely-knit anecdotes with Mrs Ponsonby in the Margaret Dumont role, Haver and Lee playing the Chico and Harpo characters, and Jacques Brown as a kind of Mediterranean Groucho. The following extract is from the show broadcast on November 8, 1940. Mrs Ponsonby has insisted on singing, to the dismay of Haver and Lee and the disgust of Nikolas Ridikoulos, who has decided on a little light sabotage:

NICHOLS (*sings*) Oh, like a bird in the sky I would fly, And I'd flutter with the butterflies and birds on high.
Ah. . . . . !
BROWN Puss puss puss puss!
HAVER Quiet there!
BROWN Puss puss puss puss!
NICHOLS (*sings*) Bear me, oh bear me, on your breast, And waft me to the skies . . .
BROWN Puss puss puss puss!
NICHOLS Oh, waft me to the skies.
Ah. . . . !

BROWN Puss puss puss puss!
HAVER What's this 'puss puss' business?
BROWN I've lost my cat.
LEE Stop singing a minute, Mrs Ponsonby.
(*Doris Nichols stops singing*)
LEE Do you still think you've lost your cat?
BROWN Yes. Puss puss!
LEE Go on, lady, it wasn't you.
NICHOLS How dare you interrupt my song looking for a cat!
BROWN Well, I got to find it.
HAVER What's the idea, bringing a cat to a broadcast?
BROWN She likes queer noises.
HAVER She'll come back after the broadcast.
BROWN She won't come back till somebody holds up a mouse.
HAVER Anybody got a mouse in their pocket?
LEE I've got a mouse. Look.
NICHOLS Oh, put that mouse away!
BROWN Puss puss puss puss!
TOM* Mrs Ponsonby, will you go on with your song. They're wondering what's happening at Broadcasting House.
NICHOLS Put that mouse away! Oh, it's climbing up my skirt.
TOM Please, Mrs Ponsonby, sing!
NICHOLS (*With the mouse climbing over her, sings*) Oh, like a bird in the sky I would fly, And I'd flutter—OH!—Flutter—OH! . . .
HAVER Where is the mouse, lady?
NICHOLS (*sings*) Ever so high . . . Oh!
BROWN My cat'll find it.
LEE It's run up her sleeve.
NICHOLS (*sings*) Oh, like a bird in the sky I would fly, And I'd . . . (*laughs*) . . . you're tickling! Ah!
LEE Here it comes.
NICHOLS (*sings*) Ah!
BROWN Got it!
NICHOLS (*hits top note*) Ah!
BOTH What a woman!

John Simmonds, who is now senior producer (radio) and has among his many production credits 'Round The Horne' and 'Beyond Our Ken', worked on 'Danger—Men At Work!' when he was a studio

* 'Tom' was the producer Tom Ronald, subsequently famous for such programmes as 'Life With The Lyons', who at that time in 1940 was standing in as announcer.

manager. Technically, it was a tough show full of sound effects and musical cues, and John Simmonds's task—mixing speech, music and effects—wasn't made easier by the fact that the show was live. Over the years since the war, Max Kester had become fairly casual in his approach to the production of 'Danger—Men At Work!', adding gags and extra pieces of radio 'business' as rehearsals progressed, so that an accurate timing of the show was virtually impossible. This naturally caused John Simmonds a great deal of mental anguish as he is, I know from personal experience, the most meticulous of men. However, on one particular occasion the ad lib additions and subtractions had made the show a positive minefield for the sweating technicians, and as scene followed scene and cue followed cue, it became apparent that the show was going to underrun by some ten minutes—a fairly appalling state of affairs in a live broadcast in front of a studio audience. Apparently the unflappable Kester took the news calmly. Having 'twirled his long ginger moustache and thought about it', he walked out of the control room, down the stairs and onto the stage where the show was proceeding on its merry way. Simmonds remembers: 'I saw Max whispering something to Jacques Brown, but from the control room, of course, I couldn't hear what was being said. I was fairly close to panic and wondering what on earth was going to happen.' What happened was that the show *did* finish ten minutes early and after the closing announcement, when disaster seemed imminent, Jacques Brown, as the result of Kester's whispered message, calmly walked up to the microphone and said, 'Well, listeners, for the benefit of those of you who tuned in late and missed the first ten minutes of our programme, we will now do it all over again.' And so they did, with John Simmonds and his assistants frantically scrambling on the floor of the control room looking for the right pages of their now discarded scripts.

This incident happened many years after 1940 when every script had to have the OK from the censor before it was broadcast, and when no improvisations or ad libbing were allowed. This censorship factor may well account for the apparent dullness of much radio in 1939/40, and if the BBC wasn't getting hot under the collar about it, the listeners certainly were. A letter written to *Radio Times* by a Mr. B. L. Twin on February 9, 1940, is fairly typical:

> 'Our entire family of six adult persons summarise their criticism of your average morning's broadcasts tersely as follows—Thank heaven for Hilversum. Please take a leaf out of their programme book.'

Take a look at the back numbers of *Radio Times* for the period, and you'll sympathise with Mr Twin. A typical morning's broadcasting in

February 1940 went as follows: 7 a.m. News followed by Sea Shanties. Followed by 'Lift Up Your Hearts'—a thought for the day. Followed by 'Up In The Morning Early'—physical exercises for men. 7.45 a.m. Classical violin solos. 8.15 a.m. The Metropolitan Police Central Band. 8.45 a.m. A ballad concert with Felton Rapley at the organ. 9.40 a.m. The Kenilworth Octet playing light music . . . and so on.

No wonder people turned to the Dutch radio station, Hilversum, or to Lord Haw Haw (William Joyce), who broadcast daily from Hamburg. The success of this Irish American ex-member of the British Union of Fascists worried the government no end, particularly as he seemed to have a network of spies in England giving him accurate and detailed information which he often broadcast before the BBC announced it. The BBC retaliated with Vera Lynn and the result was a draw until, with the victories of El Alamein and Stalingrad and the disintegration of Nazi Germany under the nightly bomber raids on Berlin, Hamburg, Essen and the rest, Haw Haw was first ignored and then forgotten until his capture, trial and execution after the war.

May 1940 was hardly an auspicious time to launch a new comedy show with Europe collapsing like a deck of cards under the Blitzkrieg, Churchill growling his defiance, and 'we shall never surrender' becoming the watchword for the whole nation, but 'Hi Gang', starring Bebe Daniels, Ben Lyon and Vic Oliver, started a long and successful run on May 26. At that time, Vic Oliver was married to Sarah Churchill and was thus Winston Churchill's son-in-law. It strikes me as incongruous that while Churchill was dominating the world scene, his son-in-law was topping the bill at the Hackney Empire and swapping jokes with Bebe Daniels and Ben Lyon in radio's 'Hi Gang', but such is the stuff of democracy. Here is an extract from the very first 'Hi Gang' programme:

LYON As this is the first programme, I feel it my duty to our listeners to interview you and learn a few facts about your past life, and so on. . . . Now tell me, Vic, where were you born?

OLIVER I was born on a train between Liverpool and Dublin.

LYON You mean, *boat*.

OLIVER Maybe . . . I was too young to remember.

LYON Where did you get married?

OLIVER I really don't know. . . . I really don't know.

LYON You mean to tell me you don't know where you got married?

OLIVER Oh, I beg your pardon, I thought you said, 'Why did you get married?'

LYON Do you like dogs?

OLIVER I do, I have a dog.

LYON What's its name?
OLIVER Corset.
LYON Why Corset?
OLIVER Because I tie him up during the day and let him out at night. Ha ha! What a joke. I am colossal!
LYON What is your profession?
OLIVER Profession? I like that—I am an actor!
LYON Yes, I know. But how do you make a living?
OLIVER I am an inventor.
LYON An inventor? That sounds interesting. . . . What do you invent?
OLIVER I've invented luminous pyjamas.
LYON Luminous pyjamas?
OLIVER That's for people who walk in their sleep in the blackout. . . . Also I invented bottomless birdcages. Birdcages with no bottoms at all. . . . That's for canaries you can trust.

And so it went, wisecracks, put downs, simple, effective, and, in 1940, just what was wanted. Bebe, Vic and Ben helped morale enormously during the war, particularly Bebe and Ben, who, as American citizens, didn't have to stay in Britain at all. At a time when many British stars had gone to the States, there was something very heartwarming about the two Americans staying on through the bombs and shortages to entertain us.

Even so, 'Hi Gang' and its successor 'Bebe, Vic and Ben' weren't universally popular, and indeed John Watt, who was Director of Variety at the time, came in for a lot of criticism for the poor quality of much of the home-grown Light Entertainment. In 1941 the Board of Governors deplored 'the low standard of music hall' and the research unit found that up to twenty per cent of the listeners interviewed regretted the vulgarity of many Variety programmes. In 1942, Watt sent his assistant, Pat Hillyard, to the USA to buy, beg, borrow, or at any rate acquire American writers and stars to lift the prevailing standard of British radio comedy. Hillyard enlisted the cooperation of the USO (United Services Organization) whose job it was, like its British counterpart ENSA, to entertain the troops. Soon recordings of American shows began to arrive, and things improved somewhat. Paradoxically, by 1944 there were complaints of too much 'Americanization' of Variety, but by then native talent had begun to emerge in the persons of Kenneth Horne, Richard Murdoch, Charlie Chester, and Eric Barker. However, 1942 and 1943 were undeniably the years when the best of Britain's radio comics were American. Their slickness and energy were a revelation, and though they hadn't the same tang as their warmer, if clumsier English counterparts, their influence on the post-war generation of British funny men was marked. By 1943, British listeners could hear 'The Charlie MacCarthy Show', 'The Bob Hope Show', 'The Jack Benny Hour', and Fred Allen, who in 1943 capped a long and successful radio career in the States with his invention 'Allen's Alley', which in shape and style was reminiscent of 'ITMA'. Allen, like Handley, was the sane man in an insane world, and his alley was peopled with eccentrics.

All these shows were recorded on disc, which not only allowed the stars to stay in Hollywood and entertain world-wide, but enabled the BBC to build up a stockpile of programmes that could be repeated whenever required. The war accelerated the development of recording, for although it had been a practical proposition for many years, the BBC engineers had been worried about the quality of both tape and disc, and more shows had been live than recorded. There was an artistic reason for live shows too, the rationale being that performances would be better for that added tension felt by actors and comedians when faced with the now-or-never situation of the live transmission. Deryck Guyler, after serving with the RAF Police, was invalided out in 1942 and joined the BBC Repertory Company. He had a horror of recording: 'One fluff at the end of those massive fifteen-inch discs and the whole thing was ruined. The advantage of being live was that the sense of theatre was stronger, the adrenalin flowed, and like any performance, you were braced to get through it.'

The Drama Repertory Company was called on to do many things—Greek drama, Variety, documentaries—even newsreading on the overseas service, remembers Deryck Guyler, who was once landed with four pages of script announcing one of the advances on the Russian front: 'There were about forty or fifty Russian names in this bulletin and I could never have pronounced them, even if I'd had hours to prepare. As it was, they just put it in front of me, the red light went on and I had to read it—live. I did the only thing I could do—I just made up the names as I went along. It must have been the strangest bulletin ever read but nobody seemed to mind—after all, it *was* a victory!' On another occasion, Guyler had to fill in in an emergency and was rushed into a studio at the last minute, where he read a scene from *Julius Caesar* in a raincoat, an Anthony Eden hat and holding an umbrella—to the amazement of Marius Goring, who was playing Brutus. Happily, Deryck Guyler survived these hazards to become one of the most sought-after character actors in the history of broadcasting. To date, he's clocked up over six thousand appearances on radio alone, at one period broadcasting on thirty-three consecutive days—surely a record.

At the time when Deryck Guyler, Bebe Daniels, Jack Benny and the rest were bringing comfort to wartime listeners, and John Watt was being chided for the vulgarity of his department's output, a young man named Peter Eton was invalided out of the navy. Eton's effect on both radio and television in the years to come was to be massive—it was he who 'made' 'The Goon Show'—but for the time being he was an ex-matelot with a knee full of shrapnel acquired at Dunkirk by courtesy of the Luftwaffe, and a deep irritation with the BBC. 'I wrote to them and said, "Really, your programmes are rotten, and I'm sure I could devise better ones. I've got ideas—and surely you must employ *somebody* with ideas." ' Eton was duly sent an application form—'You know the sort of thing—"Parents (if any)", "size of collar", and all that sort of rubbish.' He was interviewed and was given a job with the London Transcription Service, a propaganda outfit run partly by the Foreign Office and partly by the BBC. At first he was an announcer, but then a childhood stutter recurred and he became a producer. After a spell as a propagandist, he moved to the BBC Gramophone Department and started writing. 'I'd scribble amusing pieces between gramophone records. It was there I met Charles Maxwell [later to produce 'Take It From Here', among many other things], who had a group of actors under his wing—people like John Slater, Ian Sadler, Gwen Day-Burroughs, and Cécile Chevreau. They were known irreverently as "Charles Maxwell's Lavatory Players", and I wrote short comic sketches for them to perform between discs.' After a spell with the Features and Drama Departments, the Light Entertainment Department, based at Aeolian Hall in Bond Street, became Peter Eton's stamping ground. His attitude was typical of the young, iconoclastic, intolerant and irreverent broadcasters who made British broadcasting in the 1950s the adventure playground it was, and who in the 'forties, along with Maxwell, Kester and the rest, were preparing the ground for the 'Golden Age'.

Between 1944–45, the business of educating, informing and entertaining had really moved into top gear, with shows by and for the forces having a special place in the schedules. There were 'Shipmates Ashore', 'Navy Mixture', 'Forces' Favourites', 'War Office Calling The Army', 'Strike A Home Note' ('for Scottish servicemen and women overseas'), 'Welsh Half Hour' (for Welsh servicemen and women), 'S.E.A.C.' (a newsletter for forces in South East Asia), 'Hello G.I.'s' (for the American forces in Britain), 'War Review', and perhaps the most important historically, 'Mediterranean Merry Go Round' ('home forces entertainment for men and women serving in the Mediterranean area'). This latter was a magazine programme containing a mixture of songs, sketches, a quiz, and dance music provided in rotation by the army, the navy and the RAF, and mainly written and performed by men and women in the three services. The shows were actually recorded in London and could call on the many servicemen stationed in Britain, and although they really came to their peak in the post-war years, it was Leslie Bridgmont who, in 1944, started it all going.

Now, the BBC has always been a breeding ground for eccentrics, and one of the most eccentric was undoubtedly Leslie Bridgmont. Edward Taylor (today Asst. Head of L.E. (Radio)) described Bridgmont as 'almost a Dickensian character—his starting points were obscured in the mists of memory although he himself produced extraordinary statements like "When I was duelling with Baron von Richthofen in the First World War . . ." He'd been in the Royal Flying Corps, and he'd presumably been on those dawn patrols, so it's conceivable. At other times he said he'd trained as a medical student and only the chicanery of the British Medical Council, who couldn't face competition of his calibre, kept him from the top of the profession. If ever we met a friend who had cancer or something like that he'd say, "If only they'd listened to me. I could have put paid to cancer in 1938." His cancer cure was all rather involved but as he explained it, it all seemed rather clever. By 1955 he was beginning to feel that perhaps he'd done enough and shouldn't drive himself so hard, and he often didn't bother to come into the office. He would normally record a show on Sunday, and often decide to take Monday off in compensation. Then, round above five o'clock on Monday, Leslie would ring and say, "Has anybody asked for me?" and if we said no, he'd say, "Right, I didn't take the day off for compensation. I was *in*. I'm taking tomorrow off for compensation." And he would absent himself each day until he needed to actually use the excuse. He sometimes wouldn't appear until Friday. The writers would decide who should be in the show, and Leslie's secretary would book things, and Leslie would scarcely know about the show until he went to the studio. During one series of "Much Binding" Dickie Murdoch and Kenneth Horne noticed that Leslie pretended he knew a lot more about their script than he actually did, so in collusion with the secretary, they worked out a little wheeze. They gave her about ten pages of absolutely filthy material. (This was in the days when you couldn't say "knickers" and had to say "underwear".) The secretary typed and duplicated these pages along with the real script and then put the awful pages onto the front of the script and gave it to Leslie on the day of the recording. Leslie started off by getting a furrow in his brow and then riffled back through the pages to see if what he thought he'd heard was really in the script. At about page nine he said, "Look here, what's going on? We can't do this." And Dickie and Ken pretended they didn't think there was anything shocking about it. They gave him a very worrying half hour before they finally dissolved into laughter.'

Bridgmont had started his BBC career in the 'thirties in West Region where he produced outside broadcasts of dance bands, and then drifted into studio productions. In 1940 he devised and produced a satirical revue called 'Howdy Folks', starring Nan Kenway, Douglas Young, Eric Barker and Jacques Brown, and in 1944, he produced 'Mediterranean Merry Go Round', undoubtedly the greatest of all his many contributions to radio.

The army's contribution to this programme became the province of Charlie Chester with 'Stand Easy'. The following is an excerpt from 'Merry Go Round' (Army Edition) No. 121, featuring Charlie Chester, Arthur Haynes, Len Marten, Louise Gainsborough and Ken Morris. The producer, of course, was Leslie Bridgmont.

Audience with piano and rhythm: fade in whistling 'Army, Navy and Air Force'

ANNOUNCER	(*over*) Here's 'Merry Go Round' going round the services week by week, bringing music and fun to boys and girls in khaki and two shades of blue—to all you servicemen and women wherever you are. This week the predominating colour is once again—khaki.
ORCHESTRA	*Music up and finish*
GAINSBOROUGH	Yes, it's Cheerful Charlie Chester and the happy gang of other cranks from 'Stars in Battledress', with the Blue Rockets Dance Orchestra under the direction of Eric Robinson—which means, of course, that it's 'Stand Easy'.
CHESTER	Having studied the Lunar and the Zodiac in conjunction with the laying down of the no standing instructions, as opposed to the Order of St. John—there is only one way to eliminate disaster. . . . As Scorpio said to Saturn as he scarpered, 'That's tore us' —and we must stand as a body . . . and give ourselves a leg . . . up with the wages . . . and down the hatch . . . I stand for the public . . . I don't care about the people . . . Don't forget that Ras Prince Monolulu warned us with those words: 'Never push your Grandma while she's shaving.'
FX	*Motor horn*
MARTEN	Oi, what does Bernard Shaw do with his old razor blades?

CHESTER He cuts up a side turning and flogs 'em.

ST CLAIR I say, what is a theme?

CHESTER A theme, sir? Well, a theme is the thing that runs up the thide of your trouthers.

MORRIS Look here, I think I'm overworked.

CHESTER Well, what do you do?

MORRIS Oh, this and that.

CHESTER When?

MORRIS Oh, now and then.

CHESTER Where?

MORRIS Oh, here and there.

CHESTER Blimey, you need a holiday.

HAYNES You silly man, you're talking out of the back of your neck.

CHESTER I thought there was a draught—oh, it's the band. Take it away folks.

In racehorse terms, 'Stand Easy' might be said to be out of Leslie Bridgmont by the War Office, though, in fact, it was the creation of Charlie Chester—or more properly, Cheerful Charlie Chester—who had first thought of the show when he was transferred from the Royal Irish Fusiliers to 'Stars In Battledress' in 1943.

'Stars In Battledress' was conceived by the War Office in order to harness the talent of former professional entertainers and musicians serving in the army, and to supplement the efforts of ENSA, whose ranks were filled with those who, for reasons either of age or of health, had not been called up, and whose companies could, on occasion, be diabolically bad. Cynics at the time said that ENSA stood for Every Night Something Awful—perhaps unfairly—but the big names like George Formby and Tommy Trinder couldn't be everywhere at once, and ageing concertina players and sopranos weren't entirely to the taste of the tough young servicemen. 'Stars In Battledress' solved the problem. Here were serving soldiers and members of the ATS entertaining their own age group, and what they lacked in experience and polish they made up in youth and energy. The outfit was run by George Black Jnr., son of the impresario, and himself a stage producer of skill and imagination. When 'Stars in Battledress' was formed in 1943 he sent at once for Charlie Chester, whom he'd known as a comedian and writer before the war, and gave him the job of organising his fellow soldier-thespians into groups capable of going anywhere and entertaining the troops.

It was while he was doing this that Sergeant Chester conceived his idea for a radio show—a gang show, which he called 'Punchinello Parade'. As a title it may have left something to be desired, but the show was the authentic parent of 'Stand Easy'. Towards the end of the war, Bridgmont's 'Merry Go Round' was getting good contributions from the RAF and the navy, but the army segment lacked a proper identity. Bridgmont tackled Chester's colonel, and Chester's colonel tackled Chester. Or, more exactly, with the epic phrase, 'Chester, you will write a hit comedy show', he ordered him to save the army's radio face. Chester was shrewd—or foolhardy—enough to make it a condition that he run the show and select the cast. The colonel agreed, and 'Stand Easy' was born. It had catchphrases (it seems, looking back, that it was all catchphrases), and it was exactly the kind of show that the British soldier could identify with. When peace came, the programme had a hypnotic effect on listeners. There was a point where the topical chant it always featured had bookies laying odds on what the subject of that week's particular chant would be. The chant always related to an event of the day, a typical one being 'Down in the jungle living in a tent, Better than a pre-fab—no rent.'

Chester hand-picked his cast, and they responded by turning themselves into headliners—even, in Arthur Haynes's case, into a bigger star than Cheerful Charlie himself. But at the beginning Chester made them rehearse 'mike technique' with a mophead stuck between two chairs and virtually drilled them into becoming radio performers.

'Stand Easy' relied for its effect chiefly on its amazing puns and colossal speed, the formula that had worked so well for 'ITMA'. Indeed, 'Stand Easy' could be said to be a working-class 'ITMA', and even at one time topped 'ITMA' in the popularity ratings. After the war, 'Stand Easy' continued on its wisecracking way, with the addition of a new subtitle: 'The Civvy Street Rag'. The following extract is from the programme transmitted on Monday June 10, 1946. Interestingly, on the original script the two 'topical chant' gags are written in pencil.

ANNOUNCER It's look out for laughter in the next half hour, for here's Cheerful Charlie Chester and his crazy gang, including Arthur Haynes, Ken Morris, Len Marten, Louise Gainsborough, and Ramon St. Clair, with the Blue Rockets Dance Orchestra directed by Eric Robinson. Presenting 'The Civvy Street Rag . . . STAND EASY'!

BOYS (*sing*) Stand Easy . . . and this, you will know, is 'The Charlie Chester Show'.
Audience applause

ORCHESTRA *Intro music*

CHESTER	'The Amazing Adventures of Whippit Kwick, the Cat Burglar'. Taking refuge in the heart of the dreaded jungle of Jhansibulla, seeking his fortune in the treacherous province of Japonica, and still escaping the long arm of the law is the world's most notorious crook (*music call sign*) Whippit Kwick. Together with the master brain is Whippit Kwick's faithful friend, Ray Ling—the Chinese fence.
FX	*Gong and piano*
RAY LING (HAYNES)	(*Chinese patter*)
CHESTER	What was Ray Ling trying to say?
RAY LING	Trying to say? I said it, didn't I?
CHESTER	You said what?
RAY LING	How are the cigarette shops in London?
CHESTER	Aw shut up.
WHIPPIT KWICK (MORRIS)	Yeah—they might as well be.
CHESTER	Who said that?
WHIPPIT KWICK	It was me and I want a fag. (*Music call sign*) Cork tipped.
CHESTER	There in the merciless tropical heat, they were anxious to get away from the shack—the shack in which there still lay a body. . . . They lumbered ungracefully onward, skilfully guided by Stabu, the elephant boy.
STABU (MARTEN)	Skilfully guided, me foot! I can't get this blinkin' elephant out of third gear.
CHESTER	As they made their way down the jungle path, Whippit Kwick shot a glance to the right.
FX	*Gun shot*
	And then shot a glance to the left.
FX	*Gun shot*
CHESTER	Say, what's all this shooting?
WHIPPIT KWICK	I can't help it. It's my eyes, they're bloodshot.
CHESTER	Aw shut your face.
WHIPPIT KWICK	O.K.
FX	*Door slam*
CHESTER	In the distance the natives could be heard droning their medieval chant—
BOYS	Went to the Derby, saw them sprint, Who'd have thought of Airborne*—we're skint.

* A horse called Airborne, an outsider, won the Derby in 1946.

CHESTER Suddenly the elephant began to sense that all was not well.

ORCHESTRA *Chord*

CHESTER Stabu the elephant boy was softly coaxing the animal. He spoke in his native tongue to soothe the elephant.

STABU Git up there, you wall-eyed son of Satan, or I'll tie your trunk in a knot.

CHESTER Oh no, you'll not.

ALL Oh yes, he will.

CHESTER Aw shut up! Where were we?

WHIPPIT KWICK Still in this stinkin' jungle.

CHESTER Ah, that's right. Slowly the terrified elephant began to slow up.

FX *Very heavy crash*

CHESTER Sorry—the elephant pulled up dead.

FX *Gong*

RAY LING (*Frantic Chinese patter, muffled*)

CHESTER What's the matter with you, Ray Ling?

RAY LING I don't know about the elephant pulling up dead, but if you don't pull him off my face I'll be dead.

ORCHESTRA *Chord*

CHESTER Look out!

ORCHESTRA *Chord*

CHESTER That was what scared the elephant—it was a wild boar.

VOICE Gee, I'm so mad I could bite my nails to the quick. (*Music call sign*) Clip it, quick.

CHESTER And from the distance came the incessant chanting of the natives.

BOYS Victory celebration—nothing in the pub, Got a flag to wave but—no grub.*

CHESTER As they continued on their way, suddenly something in Whippit Kwick's mind struck a chord.

ORCHESTRA *Chord*

CHESTER How's that?

WHIPPIT KWICK Nope, t'ain't the right chord.

ORCHESTRA *Chord*

WHIPPIT KWICK That's it. Ray Ling, quick.

RAY LING All right, all right.

* We'd won the war, but in 1946 the acute food shortages continued. The government policy was to feed starving Europe before releasing surplus food on the home market, a source of much complaint at the time.

WHIPPIT KWICK	Where's the envelope you picked up?
RAY LING	Here 'tis.
CHESTER	Whippit Kwick took the envelope. He began to tear it open, his excitement was mounting.
FX	*Siren whistle (slowly up) then crash*
CHESTER	Mounted a bit too high. Look, as Whippit Kwick tore the envelope open he recognized the handwriting within—Humpty Gocart's!
ALL	Humpty Gocart's?
WHIPPIT KWICK	It's impossible. I left him in charge in New York.
CHESTER	What was the answer to this latest riddle? How did a letter from Humpty Gocart in America get to the jungle? Where was Humpty—was he alive or was he . . . ?
WHIPPIT KWICK	No no, not that!
CHESTER	And with all these questions to be answered, while the sun sinks in a golden glow, we reluctantly bid again farewell to the world's most amazing criminal—(*music call sign*)—Whippit Kwick.
ORCHESTRA	*Music to finish*

The naval contribution to the wartime 'Merry Go Round' was 'HMS Waterlogged', starring Eric Barker, his wife Pearl Hackney, Jon Pertwee, Humphrey Lestoq, and Harold Warrender, who was the quiz master. Here is an excerpt from 'Merry Go Round' (Naval Edition) No. 119, again produced by Leslie Bridgmont:

Audience with piano and rhythm: fade in whistling 'Army, Navy and Air Force'

ANNOUNCER	(*over*) Here's 'Merry Go Round'. This week the predominating colour is once again—navy blue.
ORCHESTRA	*Music up and finish*
CROW*	Ship's Company of HMS Waterlogged, Sinking In The Ooze—tut, now where's he gone? Messenger!
PERTWEE	'Ullo?
CROW	Go and tell the Ship's Company he's wanted.
PERTWEE	Oh, I can't.
CROW	Why not?
PERTWEE	I feel so silly, talkin' to meself.
ORCHESTRA	*'All the Nice Girls Love a Sailor'*

* George Crow, the bandleader.

BARKER Carry on smokin'. As you know, I went up to town yesterday to attend an important Admiralty Conference, and when we were in the pictures she suddenly—I mean, this Conference was to decide the future of HMS Waterlogged. I had to see a Sea Lord. I don't know which one. Apparently there's only one there on Fridays. Blimey, if I were a Sea Lord, I know one that wouldn't be there on *Thursdays*—however, he's got a very nice office, this Sea Lord, equipped with everything a man could want. As a matter of fact it was one of the pieces of equipment that he didn't want that I went to the pictures with.

The RAF gave the world 'Much Binding In The Marsh' with Squadron-Leader Richard Murdoch, Wing Commander Kenneth Horne, Sam Costa, and the Sydney Torch Orchestra. At the time, both Murdoch and Horne were stationed at the Air Ministry in Kingsway, London, running a small department concerned with shipping Spitfires to Russia. They weren't desperately overworked, as not that many Spitfires were actually sent to Russia, and in any case it was a fairly routine operation. With a lot of RAF time on their hands and not a great deal of RAF work to do, they naturally improved the shining hour by spending their days writing the scripts for 'Much Binding In The Marsh', which their WAAF assistant duly typed. One day, panic set in when they heard that the Air Officer Commanding was approaching at speed to make an unscheduled inspection. They had to make their office look busy and proceeded to do it with the skill and aplomb they brought to their script writing. Within minutes typewriters were clattering, telex messages were being sent to Archangel, and a suitably harrassed Murdoch and Horne were frantically telephoning the Spitfire factory, the docks, the Ministry of Aircraft Production, and Moscow. The AOC arrived, inspected, and was so impressed by the activity that he promptly decided that the office was under-staffed and posted two extra members of the Women's Auxiliary Air Force to help cope with the volume of work!

'Much Binding In The Marsh' was based on a fictitious RAF station consisting of one officer, one 'other rank', and Horne as Air Officer Commanding. The whole concept had a sort of Monty Python silliness, with Horne as a naïve, boring and foolish Senior Officer (the opposite of what he was in real life), Murdoch as the quick-thinking, amusing and gentle CO (a character very like himself), and Sam Costa as the archetypal grumbling aircraftsman, brighter than his 'betters' and unhappy with his lot—a lovely piece of character work from this former dance band singer and early member of the 'ITMA' team. Today Sam Costa thrives as a disc jockey, Richard Murdoch divides his time between theatre and radio, and alas, Kenneth Horne is dead. This is how they spent Christmas at Much Binding in 1945:

ANNOUNCER As you can imagine, Christmas at Much Binding in the Marsh is being a very gay affair. Christmas dinner is over; both the officers have waited on the 'other rank'. Plans are afoot to give everybody a really bright evening, and details are now being discussed by the AOC and the CO in the Officers' Mess.

PIANO *Much Binding Theme*

HORNE Well, that was a wizard lunch, Murdoch.

MURDOCH I am glad you enjoyed it, sir.

HORNE By Jove, yes! One of the nicest sandwiches I've ever had. What was in it, Murdoch?

MURDOCH Well, there was— er— have you read any good books lately?

HORNE I thought it tasted something like that. By the way, Murdoch, what did you think of my waiting?

MURDOCH Well—I couldn't help feeling that in some ways it was a pity that you insisted on serving the soup in a colander.

HORNE Yes, I suppose it was a bit wasteful, but still, I think the airman preferred clear soup. By the way, you were lucky to get hold of that goose, Murdoch.

MURDOCH Well, sir, it wasn't exactly a goose, if I might be so frank. I happened to be by the Thames at Henley, and I saw a most graceful white bird floating downstream, and there was nobody about, so I put some salt on its tail and some rope on its neck.

HORNE Didn't it mind, Murdoch?

MURDOCH No, sir. Never said a word. It was so full of emotion that the words stuck in its throat.

HORNE The chap seemed to enjoy eating it. By the way, what did you use for the stuffing.

MURDOCH I didn't have to, sir—it was full already.

In 1946, RAF Much Binding In The Marsh closed down and the personnel were demobbed, but happily they reassembled soon after, in 1947. Maurice Denham and Marilyn Williams joined the cast and Murdoch and Horne returned to 'Much Binding' itself. This is how they made the transition from RAF to civilian life, in the recording of January 2, 1947:

FX *Footsteps*

MURDOCH I hear they've been having snow up in Yorkshire.

HORNE Ah, it's a small world, isn't it. By the way, where can I get in touch with you?

MURDOCH I'm in the phone book, sir. And you, of course, will be at the Wash and Brush-up, Platform 15, Euston. Keep in step, sir. Oh, by the way, I don't have to call you 'sir' any longer, do I, Kenneth?

HORNE No, Dickie, you don't, do you? I say, I'm sure you left the light on in your office. We could probably see from here.

MURDOCH No, sir. I—I couldn't look back.

HORNE The hedges look a bit bare at this time of the year, don't they?

MURDOCH Yes, sir, it's probably the lack of foliage. Well, here are the crossroads, you take that one to the Spagthorpe bus stop and I shall go this way and hitch-hike from Sprantfield Abbot.

HORNE Yes, that's the idea. Well, goodbye, Dickie.

MURDOCH Goodbye, Kenneth.

FX *Tramp, tramp*

ORCHESTRA *'Much Binding'—minor—up to finish*

ANNOUNCER That was February 1946. The scene changes to one of London's busiest railway stations. January 1947. And who is this, fighting his way along the platform with a brown paper parcel in one hand and a meat pie in the other? I think it looks like the former CO of Much Binding in the Marsh. It is! Richard Murdoch!

AUDIENCE *Applause*

ORCHESTRA *Normal 'Much Binding'—and fade*

FX *Station noises in background*

MURDOCH Porter, porter, does this part of the train go to Sprantfield Abbot?

PORTER Where, sir? Never heard of it.

MURDOCH Well, before you get there you have to change at Spursley Junction.

PORTER Never heard of that either, sir.

WILLIAMS (*station announcer—hollow*) The train now arriving at Platform 2 comes as a bit of a surprise to us. On the other hand, the train now standing *on* Platform 3 will, we hope, in due course be moved back onto the lines. The train now standing at Platform 4 is the through train to Crewe and Plymouth. The rear carriage is the through train to Possingbridge Halt, calling at Sprintsworth, Flike, Doodling M'Travers, Stench, Market Groping, Duckets Bottom Holiday Camp, Nape, and Jittery St. Tolhurst.

MURDOCH Oh dear, what a pity—not Sprantfield Abbot.

WILLIAMS Don't be so impatient. Passengers for Sprantfield Abbot should change at the slightest provocation.

MURDOCH (*pushing his way through*) Excuse me, sir, thank you, madam. . . .

PORTER Here's an empty compartment for you, sir.

FX *Moos, baas, etc. after door opens with creak*

MURDOCH Well, it's practically empty.

FX *Door shuts*

MURDOCH All right, porter, I like this one next door better.

FX *Door opens*

MURDOCH Thank you very much. That's very good of you. I'll drink your health at the next stop.

FX *Door slams*

WILLIAMS (*station announcer*) Will the passengers who have taken the 4.15 train from Platform 8 to Ponders End please bring it back again at once. Here is another announcement: will the passengers on Platform 7 kindly stand aside and make way for the former Air Officer Commanding Much Binding in the Marsh—Kenneth Horne.

AUDIENCE *Applause*

HORNE Excuse me, porter, does this train go to Sprantfield Abbot?

PORTER Yes, sir—just the last carriage here, and if you want a bit of company I should pop into this compartment and join that gentleman. He's going there, too.

HORNE Oh, thank you. Oh—it is kind of you. D'you mind if I keep the change?

FX *Door opens*

HORNE Good morning.

MURDOCH Good morning. Stuffy, these carriages, aren't they?

HORNE More than these seats are.

MURDOCH Excuse me, sir, this is a smoking carriage, d'you mind if I don't light up?

HORNE Of course not. Don't have one of mine.

MURDOCH Thanks. I shan't mind if I don't. (*Pause and cough*)

HORNE Use this train much?

MURDOCH No—only for travelling.

HORNE Oh. (*Hums, etc.*) Going far?

MURDOCH My agent doesn't seem to think so. (*Pause and cough*)

HORNE } The test match result was most . . .
MURDOCH } Railway travel isn't what it was . . .

MURDOCH I beg your pardon, carry on.

HORNE No, *you* go on, please.
(*Both pause and cough*)

MURDOCH } I was only going to say that those trains . . .
HORNE } What I really meant was the bowlers . . .
(*Both pause and cough*)

MURDOCH By the way, sir, I was interested in what you were saying just now about the monastery on St. Olaf's Island.

HORNE I didn't mention it.

MURDOCH Oh, didn't you? Well, it takes all sorts to make a world.

HORNE I suppose it does. Mind you, when I was in Sidi Barrani . . .

MURDOCH Good heavens! I know a chap who always used to say that.

HORNE Oh, who was he?

MURDOCH Oh, rather a pompous old poop—RAF type. Mind you, I must confess that if it wasn't for your moustache you would be quite like him.

HORNE But I haven't got a moustache.

MURDOCH Good heavens, then it must be—I say, sir, surely you remember me? I used to be under your command.

HORNE Why, of course, it's Corporal Spenlove-Enthover.

MURDOCH Not exactly, sir. I'm Murdoch.

HORNE Well, aren't I a silly old fossil?

MURDOCH Yes, sir. You haven't changed a bit.

HORNE Nor have you, Murdoch. I would have recognised you anywhere.

MURDOCH So would I. I suppose you've seen it?

HORNE Yes, I came across it at my dentist's yesterday. Have you got yours with you?

MURDOCH Yes.

HORNE Read it out will you?

MURDOCH Certainly, sir. 'To be sold by auction at Much Binding in the Marsh, Jan. 2nd: Quantity of redundant RAF property and equipment including one shed almost large enough for aeroplane hangar, several miles of barbed wire, sentry box, pigeon cote, windsock (slightly darned), an out tray, one tender fire crash, coffee percolator standing in its own grounds and three files marked 'Top secret not to be read by anybody'. Messrs. Lumley Chesterfield and Triggett, Auctioneers and Valuers, established 1812—messages can be taken at the greengrocers.'

HORNE That's exactly the same as mine, Murdoch, except that mine says 'Massages can be taken at the greengrocers.'

MURDOCH Really, Sir? I expect that's a misprint.

Though in Civvy Street, their characters remained the same and the catchphrases lingered on—Horne's 'Not a word to Bessie' (Horne's fictional wife), Murdoch's 'Read any good books lately?' (his invariable question when confronted by the unanswerable), Horne's 'Did I ever tell you about the time I was in Sidi Barrani?' (a prelude to a boring story), Sam Costa's 'Good morning, sir, was there something?', and his exit, mumbling something about 'Emily and her twinges', and the Much Binding Song with which Murdoch and Horne invariably ended their show, with new lyrics every week. The following example is from a 1947 recording, but is typical of those idiotic and delightful songs:

At Much Binding In The Marsh,
Today we've had a tricky job in finding
At Much Binding In The Marsh,
The nineteen-forty-seven Miss Much Binding.
The one we most admired was Mrs Plackett's daughter Toots,
Her hair was really lovely, it was hennaed at the roots,
And she'd have looked still better if she'd taken off her boots—
At Much Binding In The Marsh.

At Much Binding In The Marsh,
Just like the bathing costume he was wearing,
At Much Binding In The Marsh,
Sam Costa's dive was neat as it was daring.
In six months' time we hope he'll show no signs of the event,
But on the swimming bath itself some money must be spent,
The concrete at the bottom got a very nasty dent—
At Much Binding In The Marsh.

At Much Binding In The Marsh,
The sideshows at the club are most attractive.
At Much Binding In The Marsh,
The fortune teller's plain but very active.
She's really rather wonderful, your future she divines,
She gazes at the palm and then she makes some mystic signs,
I found it rather awkward when she read between my lines—
At Much Binding In The Marsh.

At Much Binding In The Marsh,
The fashions here today have been astounding;
At Much Binding In The Marsh,
Miss Goodbody's creation was dumbfounding.
She said it was a model that a Paris firm had done,
It had a sequin farthingale which glittered in the sun,
And on the back a label which said 'C.C. 41'—
At Much Binding In The Marsh—

HORNE *Turn the hem up!*
At Much Binding In the Marsh—

MURDOCH *Mine's a gussett!*
At Much—two—three—four—Binding In The Marsh.

Ah—happy days!

4

The New Wave

When Britain staggered dazed and exhausted into peacetime the one thought on everyone's mind was that there was going to be no return to the bad old days of the 'thirties. A massive Labour victory at the General Election rammed home the message. It had been a people's war and it was going to be a people's peace, in broadcasting as in everything else.

Already the atmosphere of radio comedy had become less elitist, and more in tune with ordinary people, and the progress in this direction made during the war was to continue and extend as more and more of the new wave of entertainers were demobbed. Many of the wartime shows continued in peacetime settings however. As we've seen, 'Stand Easy' made the transition with the addition of a subtitle—'The Civvy Street Rag'; RAF Much Binding In The Marsh was adapted for peaceful purposes, as a Country Club, 'ITMA' went to Tomtopia—and 'HMS Waterlogged' became 'Waterlogged Spa'.

One way or another, the stars were on their way, but in 1945 they weren't there yet. Spike Milligan, Harry Secombe, Tony Hancock, Jimmy Edwards, Frank Muir and Denis Norden and the rest, saw the world from the point of view of ex-servicemen fresh from North Africa or Iceland, from Monte Cassino or the skies over Germany. They'd entertained their fellow soldiers, sailors and airmen, they'd joined concert parties, they'd founded—without knowing it—a new show-business tradition. They moved unconsciously as a group, aspiring to the same things, with the same targets and sharing the same background. When these 'NAAFI entertainers' returned to civilian life, they could not forget the magic of having made other people laugh, and of holding audiences—albeit captive audiences—enthralled. Harry Secombe's recent novel, *Twice Brightly*, recalls the period vividly. It's partly autobiographical, but the story of the just-demobbed would-be comic struggling to find a niche in the competitive world of Variety entertainment, with new ideas and new and different material, could apply to many of the young post-war comics. Michael Bentine, for instance, did an act with a motor tyre inner tube, a chair and a sink plunger. Harry Secombe himself did an act demonstrating how different people shaved and was 'paid off' at Bolton, the manager commenting: 'In future he can shave in his own bloody time.' Peter Sellers, in Variety at Coventry, despaired of getting any laughs and went on stage one night with a record player and a Jimmy Shand recording of eightsome reels, which he solemnly played in place of his own act. 'I just sat there and played this record—both sides,' he says. 'Then I bowed and walked off—and the thing was that it got more applause than *I* usually did!'

The catch 22 question as far as entertaining is concerned is, 'How do you get started in the first place?' Typically, a comedian says to an agent, 'Can you book me?' The agent says, 'Yes, if I like your act. Where can I see you working?' The comedian says, 'I can't work until you book me.' And the agent says, 'Well, I can't book you until I've seen you working.' In the immediate post-war period there were three ways to break this vicious circle. One was to appear at the Windmill Theatre, another was to appear at the Nuffield Centre, and the third was to get to know Jimmy Grafton.

The Windmill Theatre was a small place in Great Windmill Street, off Shaftesbury Avenue, which specialised in nudes. In those days the nude performers had to keep absolutely still, and the nudity was of a very discreet nature, heavily 'artistic' and about as aphrodisiac as an hour's brass-rubbing. Between the nude scenes and dance numbers, Vivian van Damm, the proprietor of the Windmill, would put on comedians. It was a tough training for the would-be comic as it was the nudity that the audience came for, not the jokes, and they did six shows a day, starting before noon. Van Damm held regular auditions and if he liked you he'd employ you, and you thus had a 'showcase' where agents, managers and BBC producers could see you at work. (Incidentally, it's interesting to note that the ranks of those who failed the audition include Spike Milligan, Benny Hill, Roy Castle, and the late Ken Tynan, the internationally-celebrated drama critic and literary adviser to the National Theatre, not to mention creator of the explicitly sexual revue, *Oh! Calcutta!* Perhaps the germ of the idea was born as he stood awkwardly on the Windmill stage imagining what it would be like to be surrounded by all that bare flesh!)

However, among the many comedians who did start at the Windmill and subsequently went on to radio glory, are Eric Barker, Tony Hancock, Harry Secombe, Peter Sellers and Dick Emery; and it was at the Windmill that Frank Muir met Jimmy Edwards, who was also on the six-shows-a-day treadmill. At that time, Muir was writing for an extraordinary character named Peter Waring, a 'sophisticated' comedian who had achieved a big success at the Windmill Theatre, and had become a regular broadcaster in 1946. Charles Maxwell, later the producer of 'Take It From Here', remembers Peter Waring as 'a complete mystery man. The front that we were shown was not the real Peter at all. He'd been a conjuror but then he acquired the mannerisms ot a man-about-town, the language, the long cigarette holder and so forth, and we planned a series with him and Kenneth Horne, Charmian Innes and Maurice Denham, called 'Heigh Ho'. We were all set to record the first programme when I got a call from Pat Hillyard [the then Assistant Head of Variety] saying he wanted to see me rather urgently. Apparently, they'd just discovered Peter Waring was an ex-jailbird who used to work for the BBC in the accounts department before absconding with the funds. I said, "Well, we're all set to do the first show. Do you want it cancelled?" Hillyard said, "No—but tell the girls to keep an eye on their handbags!" We did the show and it was very good. We only did six because by then they felt they couldn't employ this man. It was a tragic waste of talent.' Frank Muir was still in the RAF when he started writing for Waring, and remembers him as 'a comedy conjuror in those days but he later dropped the conjuring and concentrated on the comedy. Then he got this radio series, 'Heigh Ho', and asked me to write it. It wasn't very good but it didn't stand a chance anyway after they discovered that Peter was a thumping crook.' Waring subsequently went to prison for fraud and committed suicide there.

This is an extract from 'Heigh Ho' transmitted on October 25, 1946, which is interesting as an example of the early Frank Muir:

ANNOUNCER Ladies and gentlemen . . . (*lazily*) . . . 'Heigh Ho'.

ORCHESTRA *'Heigh Ho' fading for:*

ANNOUNCER Once again we invite you—at your own risk—to come with us to that flat at Number 6, Somerset Mews, where off to work we go with Peter Waring, Kenneth Horne and Charmian Innes.

ORCHESTRA *Music up to finish*

WARING (*singing*) I'm biding my time,
'Cos that's the kind of guy I'm . . .

INNES — I wish you'd stop that awful noise, Peter. Why choose that song anyway?

WARING — It's my new theme song, darling. I was thinking of joining the building trade.

INNES — Do you think you could be any good at it?

WARING — With the Ministry's help I might get a roof on before Christmas.

INNES — Do you know anything about the work? I mean, what exactly will you do?

WARING — That's the trouble—I shall have to start at the bottom and work downwards. I expect they'll make me carry bricks up a ladder on my shoulder—you know, darling, all the hod jobs.

When Peter Waring left the scene, Muir and Edwards became a formidable partnership. 'Jimmy and I made a very happy combination,' says Frank Muir, 'because Jimmy was an ideal mouthpiece for what I wanted to write.'

The Nuffield Centre started in the bombed-out shell of the Café de Paris in Coventry Street. The War Office requisitioned the building and The Nuffield Trust for the Forces of the Crown financed its rebuilding and later paid for new premises in Adelaide Street off the Strand. It was a services club for 'other ranks', and a lady called Mary Cook was in sole charge of entertainment from 1943 until long after the war. She developed a flair for spotting new talent and was to help many aspiring comedians, including me, during her long reign. The twice-weekly shows varied in quality—sometimes Gracie Fields appeared, but at other times the bill was devoted to unknown and untried servicemen. Mary Cook had a specially soft spot for these unknowns, helping them through bouts of stage-fright and gently advising them on how to improve their material. She didn't think that all her geese were swans, but if she saw someone she believed to be outstanding she would contact the BBC and make sure that the newcomer was seen and heard by producers. Michael Bentine, Alfred Marks, Frankie Howerd, Peter Sellers, Harry Secombe and Jimmy Edwards all owe their start in some measure to Mary Cook.

The third of the post-war trio of talent-helpers was Jimmy Grafton. In 1946, Grafton, a newly-demobbed infantry major, took over the family pub, Graftons, in London. At the same time he started writing for various comedians, among them Alfred Marks, Dick Emery and Robert Moreton, who was to become Archie Andrews's first tutor in the series 'Educating Archie', and whose catchphrase 'Oh, get in there,

Moreton' was at odds with his lugubrious stage persona. Grafton also wrote for the first compère of the new 'Variety Bandbox' programme, Derek Roy.

Grafton's pub soon became the haunt of up-and-coming comedians, and in 1948 Michael Bentine introduced Harry Secombe into the circle. Shortly after, Spike Milligan and Peter Sellers joined the group. Grafton began to write with Milligan who, he says, 'was largely illiterate at the time but had great comic vision and originality'. In fact, Milligan's character, Eccles, first appeared (though not under that name) in a Derek Roy series, 'Hip Hip Hooroy', co-written by Grafton and Milligan. By then the quintet (Milligan, Secombe, Bentine, Sellers and Grafton) had taken to calling themselves Goons, and their humour Goon humour. Grafton, as befitting an ex-major and publican, was nicknamed KOGVOS, 'Keeper of the Goons and Voice of Sanity'. They made a trial recording privately of a show they called 'Sellers' Castle' in which Peter Sellers played an impoverished peer, and the BBC showed interest. A pilot show was made, with Jacques Brown producing, but the planners found it too advanced for their taste. Later, on the advice of Pat Dixon, the guru of Light Entertainment, the team was given another chance. This time the producer was Dennis Main Wilson, and the programme was scheduled for a series. The Goons wanted to call it 'The Goon Show', the BBC wanted to call it 'The Junior Crazy Gang', but eventually they all agreed on Grafton's compromise, 'Crazy People', and on May 28, 1951, 'The Goon Show' was born. Though it started as a group effort, it soon became associated in the public's mind with Spike Milligan, whose influence on its development was undoubtedly profound.

In 1975, in a television interview with Milligan conducted by David Dimbleby, in which Jimmy Grafton and Peter Sellers also participated, Grafton remarked that 'Spike looked at the world and decided it was peopled with idiots and therefore he'd create his own parallel world of idiots. If you think of the characters in "The Goon Show", you have Grytpype-Thynne, who is a supercilious idiot; Henry and Minnie Crun, who are ageing, doddering idiots; you have Moriarty, who is a teeth-gnashing, incompetent, frustrated, plotting idiot; you have the child idiot, Bluebottle, the constant victim; and you have Eccles, who is the nearest thing to what you might say is Spike's own id—a very simple, uncomplicated idiot who doesn't want to be burdened with the responsibility of thinking and just wants to be happy and enjoy himself. I think that fundamentally is Spike. I've always thought that Eccles is the true Milligan and that the rest is just a cover . . . Spike achieved a reputation for eccentricity and has become, by his own choice, a sort of court jester. You begin to wonder to what extent in some circumstances the eccentricity is involuntary and to what extent it's deliberate. He can always get out of trouble by going a little mad. Is this deliberate or is it something that he can't help?' Peter Sellers theorised that Milligan 'used to like people but he found a great deal of disillusionment in that area and began to take more to plants and animals. I think he's frightened of people. Basically he's a romantic.' Milligan's own explanation of himself and his behaviour was as follows: 'I was trying to shake the BBC out of its apathy . . . I had to fight like mad, and people didn't like me for it. I had to rage and bang and crash. I got it all right in the end, and it paid off, but it drove me mad in the process . . . I'm unbalanced. I'm not a normal person and that's a very hard thing to have placed upon you in life. I have no control over it. I certainly don't organize my personality so that I can extract myself from situations by suddenly going berserk. I face up to life. I fight a lot of battles against authorities. You cannot fight them by being mad.'

There are times when I have a suspicion that Spike believes he is the only sane person left alive, and although he is in many ways a self-perpetuating myth, I sometimes have a nervous feeling that he may be right.

In the days when 'The Goon Show' was still called 'Crazy People', Milligan shared the credit for the scripts with Larry Stephens (an ex-marine commando) and Jimmy Grafton. The original line-up of 'Crazy People' was Peter Sellers, Harry Secombe, Spike Milligan, Michael Bentine, The Ray Ellington Quartet, The Stargazers, Max Geldray, and The Revue Orchestra with Robert Busby. The format of the show consisted of five sketches interspersed with musical items. Here is an extract from programme 7, transmitted on July 9, 1951:

ANNOUNCER This is the BBC Home Service.

SECOMBE It's the Goon Show.

ORCHESTRA *'Goon's Gallop'* (*up and under*)

ANNOUNCER Here once again is the show for young dogs, bollweevils, and hairy sinews; featuring the unsmiling severity of Judge Jeffreys, Nell Gwyn, Guy Fawkes and Arnold Fringe; together with the tone deaf cacophony of Gunga Din and his quartet, the Coldstream Guards, Adolf Hitler, and the Black Prince with his unstrung anchors. So away with your warming pans and listen to—

SECOMBE THE GOONS!

ORCHESTRA *'Goon's Gallop' up and out*

SELLERS And here is the only man who has successfully swum the Bakerloo Line—our beloved author—J. D. Quirkleback de Mountford Splunt.

SECOMBE My name is Jones.

SELLERS Mmm.

SECOMBE I first wrote this show on the deck of my yacht in the Mediterranean.

SELLERS And you . . . er . . . submitted it to the BBC?

SECOMBE No.

SELLERS Why not?

SECOMBE Have *you* ever tried to get the deck of a yacht into Broadcasting House?

SELLERS (*cracked laugh*) But what were you doing in the Mediterranean?

SECOMBE I went there for my wife's health.

SELLERS And did it improve?

SECOMBE But yes. She wrote to me every day from London.

SELLERS So you travelled alone?

SECOMBE Oh no. (*Laugh*) I hired a little French secretary.

SELLERS (*laugh*)

SECOMBE (*laugh*)

SELLERS Blônde or brunette?

SECOMBE I don't know. He was bald.

SELLERS (*under laugh*) Hmm . . . of course, of course! (*As laugh ends*) It must have been Thursday.

SECOMBE Yes. But one night off Monte Carlo, a great storm blew up. The yacht shivered and rolled—great waves crashed over the decks. The crew rushed for the lifeboat; but I knew that as captain it was my duty to stay where I was.

SELLERS And where was that?

SECOMBE In the bar of the Ritz Hotel.

By the second series it was being billed as 'The Goon Show', with the same cast and writers as previously; however, by the third series, Michael Bentine and The Stargazers had left, the orchestra was now being conducted by Wally Stott, and, most significantly, the show was being produced by Peter Eton. Spike Milligan did not appear in six of the twenty-six episodes because of illness and his place was taken by the comedy actors, Dick Emery and/or Graham Stark, both noted for their facility for comic voices. By the fifth series, Larry Stephens had been replaced as co-writer by Eric Sykes—better known today as a TV star (both writer and performer)—for twenty of the twenty-six episodes, with Milligan writing the balance solo. Stephens was back again in the seventh series, contributing to all but two of the programmes. The majority of programmes in this series was produced by Pat Dixon, who was followed in the producer's chair by Jacques Brown, Charles Chilton, Roy Speer, and Tom Ronald. New writers, John Antrobus and Maurice Wiltshire, joined Spike Milligan and Larry Stephens for occasional episodes. The ninth and tenth series were produced by John Browell, and the show ended its run on January 28, 1960.

'The Goon Show' was a stupendous achievement in broadcasting; it became a hit mainly because it echoed the mood of disenchantment that was then current, and stood the supposedly real world on its head. Thanks to the teamwork of its producers, writers and stars it was brave and adventurous and fast-paced, and nothing captured the imagination in quite the same way until the emergence of 'Monty Python's Flying Circus' on television in the late 'sixties.

One of the things that made the Goons so special was their imaginative use of sound effects. FX (as they are described in the script) had always been an important part of radio, and in comedy had usually consisted of exaggeratedly loud bangs, heavier than normal footsteps, and so on, but with 'The Goon Show' they reached their full flowering eminence. They became almost a show within a show, huge, lengthy, and above all, funny. Vernon Lawrence, now a TV producer, served his apprenticeship with the BBC as a sound effects boy. After his training, which included a spell at Bush House as an announcer on the World Service, he asked to be transferred to the Variety Department, where his official title was assistant studio manager. The studio manager had two assistants, one (the senior) in charge of the gramophone desks, the other doing spot effects, so-called because they were literally done on the spot, next to the artists. In some shows they were discreetly hidden behind a curtain, but in 'The Goon Show' they were 'full frontal', the FX man being almost as important as the actors and therefore entitled to perform his complicated rituals in front of the audience. In a typical script Vernon Lawrence would see: ' "Henry Crun hits Min on head. Her teeth rattle. Henry hits her again." The first sound of that sequence we got by hitting an anvil with a shovel. The sound of teeth rattling we got by shaking a bag of beads. The second and ultimate clout was achieved by hitting the anvil again, but this time with a large stage weight.' On the actual recording, feeling every inch a star as the sound effects provoked gales of laughter, Lawrence overreached himself and brought the stage weight down on the anvil with such force that the weight shattered into fragments and Lawrence found that he'd punched the anvil with his fist. He stood there in excruciating agony, his hand swelling visibly, with gales of laughter beating round his ears.

Not all his experiences were so painful, however, and, confessing to being a bit of a ham, he preferred the tricky business of spot FX to the calmer job of grams operator. These two jobs often linked up: 'Supposing the scene was about the French Revolution with the hated aristos being guillotined. To establish the atmosphere, the grams operator would have sorted out a disc of crowd noises. Then, for the actual effect of the guillotine blade descending, I'd scrape a sword down a sheet of metal; then, for the blade decapitating the victim, I'd cut a cabbage in two, and knock the half cabbage into a basket. Then the grams man would bring in a disc effect of crowds cheering their appreciation.'

The BBC had not only a library of effects gramophone records but a library of spot effects too: a room full of cubby holes, each containing the appropriate prop—tea cups, knives, anvils, bird warblers, swanee whistles, trays of gravel for footsteps, large sheets of tin which, when rattled, passed for thunder, and so on. During its life, 'The Goon Show' not only used all the props already in the library but added considerably to its range and number. Ever after when a writer asked for a special sound effect, he would invariably be told: 'Oh, you want the one like the Goons did in . . .' followed by a detailed description of what the Goons had done and how they'd done it.

All really great shows leave an indelible impression on their listeners. They become folklore, but like all folklore, the truth is often blurred by the myths that spring up. What were the origins of 'The Goon Show'? What was it like in reality? As studio manager and producer, John Browell probably spent more time with the Goons than anyone else. Unlike Ronnie Waldman, he does not feel that the order of priority in the make-up of a successful show is first, producer, second, writer, and then the actor. In his opinion, the writer comes first: 'It's his skill that primes the pump as it were, and without that spark nothing of any great quality can emerge. After that it's the cooperation between producer, writer and performer that's going to end up on the listener's ear as something good or something indifferent. I'm convinced that the producer must not inflict his own obsessions on the programme. He must study the performer and allow him to blossom, only protecting him from the self-inflicted wounds of a bad or below par performance. He is there to create the atmosphere in which the talents of writer and artist can flourish. Many performers are insecure; they need affection and sympathy, but not to the point where it becomes ridiculous. Being a radio producer is to be constantly exercising your judgement.'

Browell walked the tightrope of 'The Goon Show' with great success. He had first worked on it in 1951 as studio manager. 'I'd been on quite a number of programmes in the comedy line and it so happened that I was allocated to *this* show. It was in a pretty chaotic state. Scripts were never finalised. There were four inventive geniuses working on the show and throwing in ideas right up to the last minute, which meant very often that the performances were ragged and undisciplined, and people went round in a state of near insanity. I didn't like it. I didn't enjoy it. I thought it was a load of rubbish at the time, and I left it as soon as I could.' His next connection with the show came when Peter Eton became its producer: 'I think the chaos had got to such a state that a drastic change was necessary. With Eton in control the show started to take more of a story line, although it was still following the old formula of a three spot show. It even had catchphrases! I was sorry to see Michael Bentine go, as he was a very inventive gentleman, but I think there were just too many inventive geniuses together.'

Peter Eton mourned the passing of Bentine, too, convinced that if only they could have harnessed the two sorts of imaginations—Milligan's and Bentine's—the show would have been sensational; but in fact they worked against each other and Spike needed somebody like Larry Stephens, a totally different personality, to work with. Eton was a good, solid, professional producer; he understood the Goons' humour and was extremely sympathetic to it and, in fact, furthered it as much as possible. But he himself was not a Goon. He stood outside their imbecilities, and controlled and directed them with his own sense of what was apt. Under Eton, 'The Goon Show' prospered.

When John Browell took over, he took the same line as Eton and under his firm hand the show reached its peak. It is commonly believed that Spike Milligan was the sole writer of 'The Goon Show', but, as we have seen, many other writers were involved. Browell recalls that 'the more inventive and fantastic scripts came from Spike. The cleverer scripts were Eric Sykes's because he was an extremely intelligent writer and he could write in Goon idiom, but also bring a sensible storyline to bear and add a logical conclusion. Larry Stephens could do this, too. You would find a much more rational plot in a Larry Stephens script than you would in one of Spike's. Milligan tends to be anarchistic. If he hadn't got an idea for the ending of the programme he would blow it up. This has always been part of his thinking—when in doubt, blow it up. You can see this at the end of the BBC's 50th Anniversary Goon Show—in spite of many long arguments with Spike on the subject, he wished to have a chaotic end. He's not a comfortable person to work with, but I admire him. He's certainly a genius, there's no doubt about it. But one mustn't forget Peter Sellers's contribution— his absolute flair for characterization was marvellous; and it could not have worked without the catalyst of Harry Secombe—the great central figure, the rock-like character that held all of us together through our stormy scenes of trouble.'

The following extract is from one of Milligan's scripts, 'The Terrible Revenge of Fred Fu-Manchu', produced by Peter Eton (December 6, 1955):

SEAGOON Now to organise the defence. Who'll volunteer?

BLUEBOTTLE I will, my capitain. Enter Balloonbottle, son of the regiment, with cardboard water pistol and own water in empty lemonade bottle.

SEAGOON Noble lad! Bluebottle—from the right—number!

BLUEBOTTLE Sixty-three.

SEAGOON Curse! Sixty-two deserters. Oh, if we only had some more idiots to make up the number.

ECCLES (*approaches, singing*) Twenty tiny fingers—twenty tiny toes—and I've got 'em all.

SEAGOON You! From the right—number!

ECCLES One!

SEAGOON Form fours!

FX *Squad forms fours*

SEAGOON Let's see them do that on television! Now, Bluebottle, take this stick of dynamite.

BLUEBOTTLE No. I don't like this game.

SEAGOON Shut up!

ECCLES Shut up!

SEAGOON Shut up, Eccles!

ECCLES Shut up, Eccles!

SEAGOON Now—if you see Fu-Manchu come up that road, light the fuse, count scramson and throw it under his car. Understand?

ECCLES No.

SEAGOON Good! Farewell!

FX *Whoosh*

BLUEBOTTLE Eccles!

ECCLES Yup?

BLUEBOTTLE *You're* going to light the nice stick of dynamite, aren't you?

ECCLES Yeah, yeah.

BLUEBOTTLE How many have you got to count up to before it explodes?

(Popperfoto)

Spike Milligan, Peter Sellers and Harry Secombe rehearsing 'The Goon Show', 1952

Peter Eton, 1952

(Popperfoto)

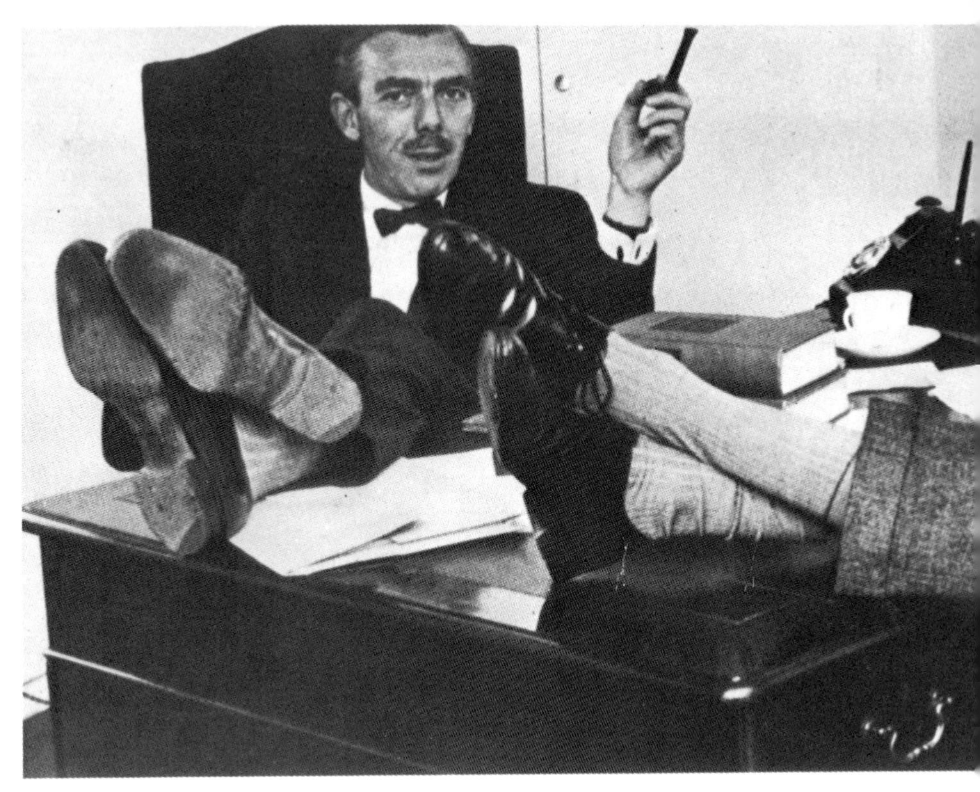

Frank Muir and Denis Norden, 1963

'Take It From Here': Jimmy Edwards, Joy Nichols and Dick Bentley, 1949

(Popperfo

(Popperfoto)

'Bedtime with Braden': Pearl Carr, Bernard Braden, Benny Lee and Barbara Kelly, 1953

(Popperfoto)

(Popperfoto)

1952: BBC Variety producers meet to discuss Coronation plans under their boss, Variety Director Pat Hillyard (foreground). Front row: Charles Chilton, Miss Absalom, Con Mahoney, C. F. Meehan, Miss Steavenson; Second row: Alistair Scott Johnston, John Hooper, Gale Pedrick, Bill Worsley, Tom Ronald, Audrey Cameron; Third row: R. H. Alexander, Roy Speer, Peter Titheridge, Frank Hooper, Pat Newman, Peter Eton; Fourth row: Leslie Bridgmont, Dennis Main Wilson, Gwen Potter, Joan Clark, Bill Sullivan; Back: Geoffrey Riggs, Gwen Morris

Dennis Main Wilson, 1958

(BBC)

ECCLES Um . . . oh . . . um . . . I dunno.

BLUEBOTTLE Well, you'd better light it and count how long it takes. Then you'll know, won't you?

ECCLES Oh, yeah. I'll light it now.

BLUEBOTTLE No, not yet. Wait till I get behind that tree.

FX *Whoosh*

BLUEBOTTLE (*shouting off*) All right!

FX *Match struck and fizzle continuing under—*

ECCLES Um . . . one . . . two . . . three . . . er . . . four . . . five . . . six . . . it's getting difficult here . . . ah! . . . seven. Good job I went to High School.

BLUEBOTTLE (*off*) What are you waiting for, Eccles?

ECCLES (*shouting*) What comes after seven?

BLUEBOTTLE (*shouting off*) What did you say? I can't hear you.

ECCLES (*shouting*) I said, 'What comes after seven?' Come over here and tell me.

BLUEBOTTLE (*shouting off*) No. You're not going to get me coming over there. Now then, what is it?

ECCLES Well, I—

FX *Explosion*

Pause

ECCLES Ooooh! (*Calls*) Bluebottle! . . . Bluebottle! Ooooh . . . what's this custard on the wall?

BLUEBOTTLE Don't touch me, you rotten swine. Scrape me off and take me home.

'The Goon Show' came to an end because Milligan had become fed up with it. He was constantly arguing with the BBC about what was and what was not possible to broadcast, and in the end the BBC reluctantly agreed that there would be no more. Until the BBC's 50th Anniversary in 1972, that is, when in front of an audience liberally sprinkled with royalty they did it 'one more time'—and the show proved as popular as ever!

Three collections of 'The Goon Show' scripts have now been published in book form, and the gramophone records of the programmes continue to sell in large quantities. Whenever 'The Goon Show' is repeated on radio it draws a huge listening audience, and the programme's popularity shows no sign of waning. Perhaps it's because today we feel the same sort of uncertainty we did in the early 'fifties, and we turn again to the totem for reassurance.

5

The Ubiquitous Muir and Norden

While Milligan and company were busy storming the barricades of BBC prejudice and apathy, they failed to notice that a breach had already been made by two gifted young men who, with a breathtaking combination of skill, shrewdness and talent, had almost by stealth changed broadcasting forever: they were Frank Muir and Denis Norden. In 1947, Muir and Norden were both working on Charles Maxwell's production 'Navy Mixture', with Muir writing a weekly spot for Jimmy Edwards called 'You May Take Notes', and Norden writing solo routines for Dick Bentley. Joy Nichols, a talented Australian actress and singer, was the programme's commère. Maxwell had the idea of making the five into a team, with Muir and Norden to write, Joy Nichols, Dick Bentley and Jimmy Edwards to star. The result was 'Take It From Here'. It wasn't at first a healthy infant, and barely survived its first six programmes, but with a bit of luck and a lot of faith from Charles Maxwell and Michael Standing, the Director of Variety, it weathered the BBC's initial lack of interest and went on to run for eleven years—325 programmes in all.

Far more than just a hit radio show, 'Take It From Here' was probably the most influential show ever made. When one listens to old recordings or reads the scripts, that statement might seem hard to justify, but the truth is that we have now so thoroughly assimilated Muir and Norden's innovations, that 'Take It From Here' no longer seems the strange and remarkable programme it was. The reason why it was so influential was that it called upon the listener's intelligence—but without losing its mass appeal. Great play was made of Jimmy Edwards being an MA and an ex-bomber pilot, but Wallas Eaton's plaintive cry, 'Come 'ome, Jim Edwards' suggested that Edwards had a very humble background and quickly deflated his stage pomposity. Dick Bentley was pictured as old and vain; 'Ah, Bent, old man,' Jimmy would say, 'and I *do* mean bent old man.' Muir and Norden were the first writers to use the performers' actual personalities, and to weave real incidents (Jimmy Edwards's engagement, for example) into the dialogue. The cast commented on the action, and fact and fiction were delicately mixed to give the listener a glimpse of the *real* Nichols, Bentley and Edwards amid the fantasy projection of themselves. All this was new, and once the initial strangeness wore off, made for deeply-satisfying listening.

The extract which follows is from programme 161, first transmitted on April 6, 1953, and subsequently repeated on April 9, 12, 19, 21, 24 and 25, 1953—an eloquent testimonial to its popularity.

ANNOUNCER So we come to the TIFH Film Award: the TIFH Oscar.

EATON Look at those highly successful films, 'Goodbye, Mr. Chips', 'The Good Earth', and 'Limelight'. Each one is a *biography*—of a schoolmaster, an ignorant farmer and a tatty music-hall comedian.

ANNOUNCER So one film producer thought he must be on a cert if he filmed the autobiography of somebody who has been *all* these things. Strangely enough, there *is* such an autobiography . . . .

EDWARDS And I am prepared to sign copies at a very nominal charge.

EATON Yes, Jimmy Edwards, schoolmaster, ignorant farmer and tatty music-hall comedian—all rolled, rather untidily, into one.

ANNOUNCER Ladies and gentlemen, we present the Edwards biography, *From Non-Stop Nudes To The BBC* or *The Naked And The Dead.*

ORCHESTRA '*Oh Lucky Jim*'

BENTLEY Ah, ragtime! Yes, it all seems so terribly dated and ridiculous nowadays. But remember—it's very likely people will be laughing at *us* in thirty years' time.

EDWARDS Do you think we can wait that long? Joy, I'm still hanging about waiting to be born!

NICHOLS Jimmy Edwards was born in Barnes. Which probably explains why he never shuts the door behind him. That wet Saturday was an anxious, tense time for the Edwards

	family. They sat around the drawing-room, huddled in tight little groups.
ALL	(*sing*) Roll me over, roll me over, roll me over, wish me luck, we're at it again.
FX	*Knock on door*
EATON	Hang on—that'll be young Doctor Bentley. I'll go.
FX	*Door opens*
BENTLEY	Good evening. I want plenty of hot water.
EATON	What for?
BENTLEY	To sip. I've got the indigestion again. I missed my lunch. I had to deliver a bicycle.
NICHOLS	(*motherly, kind*) Oh, Doctor, I'm Mrs. Edwards' sister-in-law from Number 91.
BENTLEY	Charmed.
NICHOLS	What's that necklace you're wearing, Doctor? It's pretty.
BENTLEY	It's a stethoscope.
NICHOLS	Oh, yes. What's that?
BENTLEY	It's a sort of telescope for looking into people's chests with your ears. Now, where's my patient?
NICHOLS	Then came 1926.
EATON	1926! *Ragtime*!
ORCHESTRA	'*Varsity Rag*'
EDWARDS	Time for Jim to go to school. Time for Jim to have a speech. I don't mind talking about myself. None of your potty little private schools for me. I went to a school so exclusive you could only go there on the recommendation of a judge or magistrate. It was here, at this school, that I learned the one thing that has stood me in good stead all my life. *Bullying*!

When a new series of 'Take It From Here' was scheduled in November 1953, Muir and Norden were asked to preview it in *Radio Times*. Eschewing the 'Gosh folks, it's a lot of hard work but it's a barrel of laughs' approach, they wrote the following:

> 'Come, man, out with it. You did not summon us here merely to pass the time of day.'
>
> Charles Maxwell did not reply at first. He remained with his back to us, staring sombrely through the French windows at the bleak Buckinghamshire landscape painted on the garage wall. When he finally turned, his face was grey.
>
> 'Gentlemen—' His voice was low, but then, he only stands five foot one at the best of times. His hands shook a little as he poured

himself a whiskey and soda from the bottle of whiskey and soda on the walnut whatnot. 'Gentlemen, they—they are bringing back "Take It From Here".'

Although it was warm in that library a sudden chill seemed to descend. That this should happen yet again in our lifetime. . . .

'Are you—are you certain beyond all reasonable doubt?'

'Quite certain. The chancellories of Europe have been agog with the rumour for some time. This morning it was confirmed by a telephone call from A Certain Lofty Personage.'

'What did Lofty say?'

Choosing his words carefully, Maxwell recounted to us the whole bitter story. A story which it would need the pen of a Liddell Hart to record. In truth, it would need more than the pen of Liddell Hart. It would need ink as well.

When he had finished speaking, he rose and climbing onto a chair, placed his hands impressively on our shoulders.

'So you see, men, we are fighting not for a mere principle but for "TIFH" itself!'

An amused chuckle caused us to spin round. Leaning negligently against the door jamb was the tall, smiling figure of Dick Bentley, eyes reckless at the scent of danger, a cigarette drooping lazily from behind his ear.

'Bentley!' Maxwell cried. 'You were listening? You heard?'

Bentley's teeth showed white as he opened his gold cigarette case. It has long been one of his foibles to carry his teeth in a gold cigarette case.

'Yes,' he said. 'I heard. So these devils want "Take It From Here" back, do they! By St. George, we'll show 'em the stuff we're made of!' His voice rang out, a challenge, a waving banner, a trumpet blast. 'They won't find me afraid,' he cried, and quietly slipped to the carpet in a dead faint. We looked aghast at his prostrate form. What to do?

'Leave this to me,' said a new voice. 'Here, old friend. Sniff this.'

It was Jimmy Edwards, efficiently coupling up a length of gas tubing. He took Bentley's head into his hands as tenderly as a Welsh fly-half picking up a pass.

Now that Edwards was here, everything seemed, somehow, less sinister. Quietly he took command. Opening Bentley's cigarette case, he forced brandy between his teeth. Bentley stirred. 'I'm sorry, chaps,' he gasped, 'I came over funny.'

Ignoring this wild boast, Maxwell began to outline the plan of campaign for the long gruelling weeks that lay ahead. 'Fortunately,' he said, 'we shall not be alone in this struggle. I am disposing Wallas Eaton on the right flank and the Keynotes will enfilade in echelon. In addition, there are'—he flushed with embarrassment—'two girls. June Whitfield and Alma Cogan.'

'Girls?' said Bentley, thickly, lurching to his feet. 'Where?'

'Steady on!' muttered Edwards, twisting his engagement ring nervously. He addressed himself to Maxwell. 'I think, Guv'nor, you know by now that we'll never let the BBC down as long as there's money in it.'

'Sentimental old ass,' said Maxwell uncomfortably. 'I knew I could rely on you two. Our only weak link is—'

The three of them turned and looked at us through narrowed eyes.

'Frank and Denis,' said Maxwell soberly. 'The script is our last line of defence. Can you make the script of this forthcoming "Take It From Here" a landmark in radio? Can you write us a script that will not only be funny in itself but, by the acuteness of its observation and the satiric pungency of its comment, reflect our times in the distorting mirror of laughter?'

We answered him with quiet confidence. 'No.'

And, by thunder, we've been as good as our word.

June Whitfield and Alma Cogan came into the show to replace Joy Nichols, who had decided to return to her native Australia and capitalize on her tremendous radio success in the theatre. So highly was she regarded by the BBC that she was replaced not by one but by *two* girls, one to take over her acting roles, the other to handle the song spot. With this new arrangement, 'Take It From Here', if anything, got better, and scenting that in June Whitfield they had an infinitely versatile character actress, Muir and Norden revived an idea they'd toyed with in the previous series, rearranged the parts and called it 'The Glums'. It was a hideously funny saga of working-class family life, with Dick Bentley playing the moronic son, Ron, June Whitfield as his doting fiancée, Eth, and Jimmy Edwards as the coarse and ignorant father, alternately bullying and wheedling, cursing and cajoling. The writing was of scalpel sharpness, and all gave memorable performances. Here is a typical Glum script first transmitted on March 14, 1956. 'Boy announcer' David Dunhill sets the scene.

DUNHILL This week we find Ron and Eth in a bedroom. Ron is lying on his back on top of the bedspread, hands behind his head, gazing up at the ceiling. Eth is sitting guiltily on the edge of the bed. So let us go, straight away, over to the Glums.

ORCHESTRA *'The Glums'*

WHITFIELD Oh Ron. . . . I don't think we should be doing this.

BENTLEY I don't care. I like it, Eth.

WHITFIELD But Ron, this is the Ideal Home Exhibition. People keep filing through and staring at us. Beloved, you're just supposed to walk through and *admire* this Regency bedroom, not lie down on the bed and take your boots off.

BENTLEY My feet hurt, Eth. (*Blows three times*)

WHITFIELD Now what are you doing, sweetheart?

BENTLEY Blowing on me big toe.

WHITFIELD Oh, take it away from your mouth, Ron, do. You're not the only one whose feet hurt, remember. I've also walked miles and miles. That's the worst part of these exhibitions, they—

BENTLEY (*tragedy*) Oh! Oh, Eth! Oh!

WHITFIELD What is it, Ron?

BENTLEY I've sat on me free samples.

WHITFIELD Ron, if you eat any more of those free samples, you'll be physically ill. Just what have you eaten so far, Ron?

BENTLEY (*savouring the memory of them*) A handful of jelly crystals, bit of Danish smoked herring—a tiny pot of apricot jam—a carton of cooking fat—some hot kidney soup—a swig of vanilla sauce—a slice of South African gorgonzola—twenty-eight frozen peas—a tiny little brown loaf and a tin of chocolate spread.

WHITFIELD A tin of chocol—Ron! That was brown boot polish! Don't tell me you ate the whole tinful.

BENTLEY Yes, Eth.

WHITFIELD What are you going to *do*?

BENTLEY (*pause*) I'll have to clean me boots with spit.

WHITFIELD Oh come on, Ron, we'd better move on. Though, I don't know. It's ever so nice sitting in a nice room like this. Oh, beloved, wouldn't it be wonderful if this bedroom was really ours. What would you do if it *was* really ours, Ron?

BENTLEY I'd take me boots off and blow on me toe again.

WHITFIELD There's so many lovely things here. Look at that Regency wardrobe. It's all hand carved. By hand. I'd love to see what's inside it. Do you think I dare open the wardrobe door, Ron?

BENTLEY Go on Eth.

WHITFIELD Righto, here goes.

FX *Door open*

WHITFIELD (*little scream*) Ron! *Look*!

EDWARDS 'Allo, 'allo, 'allo!

WHITFIELD Mr. Glum! What are you doing inside that Regency wardrobe?

EDWARDS To be absolutely honest, Eth, I can't recall. My last clear recollection was passing a stand where a gentleman was inviting people to come up and taste various Empire wines. It was round about Southern Rhodesia the labels began to blur a bit.

BENTLEY Dad.

EDWARDS Yes, son?

BENTLEY I've got a tiny little loaf.

EDWARDS Well, don't worry about it, Ron. It don't notice with your hat on.

WHITFIELD A small brown bread, Mr. Glum. Ron's been going round the exhibition collecting samples.

EDWARDS Yes, that's what all the family's been wandering round doing, Eth. Mrs. Glum's here, you know. I left her by the kitchen section. She was watching a man whipping eggs and cake mixes and electric irons.

WHITFIELD Electric irons! How do you whip an electric iron?

EDWARDS Just wait till the salesman isn't looking. Oh, he's got this Ideal Home Exhibition taped, has Uncle Charlie. You got to take your hat off to a man who can walk out through a turnstile concealing a *loft ladder*.

WHITFIELD It is fascinating here, Mr. Glum. But I find it's sort of frustrating. I mean, seeing those lovely things being displayed then having to go back to what you've got at home.

EDWARDS I know. I get the same feeling when I see a Marilyn Monroe film.

When scripting 'Take It From Here' Norden felt that they were writing not so much for the public as for the producer, Charles Maxwell, with whom they often disagreed, but who, they felt, was 'the customer'; in the process they learnt not to take their own sense of humour for granted. Maxwell was an important influence on them both. He had trained for the law in his native Scotland, but was a keen amateur actor and, in his own words, 'escaped from the legal profession in 1936 to become an announcer for Radio Luxemburg'. From announcer he became a producer, making shows which starred Gracie Fields and George Formby. With the coming of war, Radio Luxemburg closed down and Maxwell joined the BBC. He went into the RAF, was invalided out, rejoined the Corporation and stayed with them for thirty-one years. Of 'Navy Mixture'—just one of the many successful programmes to his credit—he says: 'I tried to introduce new things. I brought in Peter Brough. He was completely new and had just invented Archie Andrews. Peter said to me, "I can get the best scriptwriter in the business, Ted Kavanagh." So he paid Ted to write a guest spot for him on the first one and everything went wrong—he dropped the script and goodness knows what else, and it wasn't a very good script. But we tried again, and Ted said that it really wasn't his cup of tea but "There's this bloke from the air force, he's a good writer. His name is Sid Colin." So Sid, who was still in uniform, wrote most of the Archie Andrews spots. Having had success with a ventriloquist, we thought why not a conjuror, and we got Sirdani, whose catchphrase "Don't be fright" became a national slogan for a time.' When told that he'd been accepted for the show, Sirdani asked, 'How much money?' Maxwell said, 'Oh, I never talk money. Our contracts people will be in touch to arrange your fee.' 'No,' said Sirdani. 'How much money do I have to pay *you*?' It's typical of that time—1944—that such a misunderstanding could exist. Later, Maxwell was to engage Jimmy Edwards, Joy Nichols and Dick Bentley, and, as we have seen, with the addition of script-writers Muir and Norden, 'Take It From Here' was born.

Today, of course, Muir and Norden are better known for their own appearances on radio and television, though in fact even when they were writing they did some performing. The billing of 'Take It From Here' included the name Herbert Mostyn, Herbert being Frank's middle name and Mostyn being Denis Norden's. They popped up in most programmes they wrote, doing the odd voices that couldn't be handled by the rest of the cast. Muir always enjoyed performing more than his co-writer and, in fact, in the late 'forties appeared regularly on television, only giving it up when their writing commitments became too heavy. He had gone into the RAF as a photographer in 1940 and almost immediately joined the station concert party. The entertainments officer was Arthur Howard, later to create Mr. Pettigrew, the nerve-wracked assistant headmaster in Muir and Norden's television series, 'Whacko', which starred Jimmy Edwards. After eighteen months with the RAF in Iceland, during which time 'Whenever we had a camera they never had a plane in which to use it, and when they did provide a plane the camera was somehow missing,' Muir returned to RAF Henlow. While waiting to be demobbed, he again joined the station concert party, and to his surprise found that the officer in charge of entertainments was still Arthur Howard. Denis Norden remembers

Muir as 'a very good comedian with a throwaway type of humour'. Frank Muir recalls that Norden as a performer was 'always much better than he thought he was—he almost had to be driven to it'.

Both of them had always wanted to write; Frank Muir says he can't remember a time when he wasn't writing. At school he had written regularly for the school magazine—'turgid pieces with titles like "The Condemned Cell" '. Norden, on the other hand, wanted to be a foreign correspondent— an ambition which he feels may have been due to seeing Joel McCrea in a film called *Foreign Correspondent*, in which McCrea wore a trench-coat that, to the young Norden, somehow made the job seem that much more dangerous and exciting. He could speak French and Spanish fluently and while still in his teens worked as an interpreter for refugees from the Spanish Civil War. At sixteen, he nearly *did* become a foreign correspondent, thanks to the patronage of Sefton Delmar of the *Daily Express*, but his parents, understandably enough, didn't want their teenage son traipsing round Madrid in a trench-coat.

If the young Norden couldn't be a newshawk, he was still determined to do something 'different', and he became a boilerman at the Gaumont State Cinema, Kilburn. Actually, he was a protégé of the owners of the cinema and theatre chain and eventually, in 1941, became the manager of a Variety theatre in Watford. While chatting to the theatre's musical director, Sidney Kaplan, who'd been at the Holborn Empire before it was bombed, Norden conceived and wrote a six-part history of the Holborn Empire, illustrated by gramophone records, which was bought by the BBC and duly broadcast. He joined the RAF as a wireless operator but soon started writing for the station concert party, 'to get off guard duties'. He landed in Normandy on D Day and soon after was involved in troop shows alongside Bill Fraser (later to become famous as Sergeant-Major Claud Snudge in Granada's popular television series, 'Bootsie and Snudge'), and Eric Sykes, the writer/performer, among whose later achievements were 'Educating Archie' for radio, and his own series, 'Sykes', for BBC television. They must have made a formidable trio. On demob, Norden became, in Frank Muir's phrase, 'a comedian's labourer', writing solo acts for radio comics—163 of them in all—a ghastly if instructive apprenticeship.

'Take It From Here' wasn't the only show that Muir and Norden wrote in the 'fifties. In fact, back numbers of *Radio Times* reveal that at one time in 1954 they were involved not only with 'Take It From Here' but also with 'In All Directions', starring Peter Ustinov and Peter Jones, and 'Bedtime With Braden', starring the Canadian actor and funny-man Bernard Braden; and they were appearing on television in the panel game 'The Name's The Same'.

'In All Directions' and 'Bedtime With Braden' were both produced by Pat Dixon, a man whose work and personality are still remembered with respect and, indeed, awe, by those who knew him. When Con Mahoney, after a distinguished career in the army, joined the Variety Department in Aeolian Hall, just after the war, he received a curt welcoming note from Pat Dixon. It said simply, 'Dear Mahoney, Welcome to the cesspool with the velvet lid.' Dixon was deeply contemptuous of the seamier side of the Variety and pop music world of those days, and being a man of complete integrity, could not bear the wheeling and dealing that was the norm of the Variety world. Con Mahoney described him as 'the most unlikely inhabitant of Aeolian Hall that could be imagined. He was not of the old school of Variety producers who'd learned their business in the rough and tumble of the theatre. Pat was not a producer by instinct or experience, but a theorist who approached his work in an academic way.' His father, H. Macneile Dixon, was an eminent philosopher and Dixon himself had the manner of an Oxford don. He had a passion for innovation and was always looking for something new to put on the air. His judgement of writers and writing was said to be impeccable but, though his type of producer was not uncommon in the talks or drama departments (where, for instance, George Orwell and Louis McNeice had both worked), he was an oddity in the more down-to-earth world of Variety. Apart from Michael Standing, who was himself more a thinker than a doer, Pat Dixon had little respect for other members of the BBC hierarchy, and wouldn't hesitate to short circuit the chain of command and go direct to the top brass to make a point or get a show on the air. Denis Norden saw him as a rebel: 'He had a Confederate flag on the wall of his office and was really an early hippie. In those days BBC producers dressed like bank clerks, but Pat went to extremes to dress casually.' This casualness was at odds with his tall, stooping academic figure—'A caricature of an Oxford don.'

However, with all his scrupulous honesty, Dixon was not averse to helping others to be midly unorthodox. Denis Norden remembers when 'the travel allowance was twenty-five pounds, except that if you went abroad for business purposes you could get a bit more. Both Frank and I wanted to have a weekend in Paris, so we said to Pat, "If we tell the Bank of England we're going to Paris to do research for a programme, would you support us if they query it?" He said, "Certainly." So we told our bank managers and they said "Ah, but we must have it in writing." So we rang Pat and he said, "Well, the best thing is for you to write to me and make a suggestion about a programme and I'll write back and say by all means." So we wrote: "Dear Pat, we have an idea for a programme to be called 'Ça, c'est Paris', which would be a picture in sound of Paris. The chestnut trees in blossom, the traffic along the Bois, the taxi cabs, and so on. Would the BBC be interested in it?" He replied, "Dear Frank and Denis, yes, we would be interested providing it was authentic and you had done the proper research." We then took the letters to our banks, and put in for the extra business allowance for our travel—it was only about a fiver's difference anyway—and that was the last we thought about it. But about eight months later we had a phone call from Pat, who had this rather drawling voice, saying, "Boys, I'm afraid I made a mistake. I put your correspondence in the *correspondence* file and it went through channels, and planners are now asking what happened to that programme 'Ça, c'est Paris'." We went cold. We said, "What can we do?" He said, "Well, it's got to be proceeded with." We told him we couldn't possibly do it. He said, "Do you mind if I take it over?" And, of course, we said "Please do." In the end, Pat got six weeks in Paris at the BBC's expense and there was a one and a half hour gala programme called "Ça, c'est Paris" in which Eric Barker played an English tourist in Paris, and it included Chevalier, Piaf, Jean Sablon, and every big name of the time, and it had the noises of the taxi cabs, the traffic along the Bois—and the sound of the chestnut trees in blossom as well.'

Dixon, who could go to such lengths to further the interests of people and shows, seemed quickly to lose interest in them once they were on the air, rarely staying with programmes he'd been instrumental in creating. He had a passion for American humorous writers, he read them all and was able to quote from them widely. Denis Norden remembers: 'When we were doing "Bedtime With Braden", we gave lines to Nat Temple whose band was on the programme. Nat was very funny if used sparingly, and one day Pat came to us—he'd been reading some New York Jewish humorist and he said, "Can't you give Nat some yiddish words to say?" I said, "It's no good, Pat, because nobody will understand them," but the next week he came in and said, "Look, can't he call somebody a 'gonif'? It means a scamp or ne'er do well." ' [According to Leo Rosten's book, *The Joys of Yiddish*, the word means a thief or a crook, albeit a nice one—hardly the same thing.] 'The only time Frank and I ever saw Pat completely floored was when we were discussing the possibility of doing "In All Directions". Pat had taken us all to the Caprice for lunch and in the course of the meal, Peter Ustinov chose to use the accent of a typical American film producer, discussing a multi-million dollar deal—it was hilarious. When we came out of the restaurant he hailed a taxi and, switching accents, said to

Pat in his Morry Grosvenor voice (that is, Petticoat Lane Jewish): "Well, thank you very much for lunch, but I must dash. I've got to get back to the showrooms. We're trying to shift a pre-war Austin 12." Then he got into the cab and left Pat absolutely speechless.'

Pat Dixon had a taste for good living and his happy hunting grounds were The Ivy and The Caprice. Not for him the Grosvenor Arms and the other pubs in the Bond Street area frequented by BBC types. He was a strange, difficult and gifted man; but as Norden says, it was as if his whole experience of life was at second hand. He had a patrician manner, and was never on intimate terms with his staff. Throughout a whole series working with John Browell as studio manager, he never said more than 'Good morning', and then after the programme, 'Goodnight, Browell, thank you'. Browell was consequently amazed that when the next series came up, Dixon particularly asked for him: 'I thought he couldn't bear the sight of me but it turned out that he was just shy.' Con Mahoney explains: 'He'd have absolute confidence in the person he'd recognised as a craftsman—and then he left them to it. He was never good with people in the generally accepted sense of the phrase, but he was greatly loved by the few people who got to know him well, and will always be remembered as one of the leading creative figures of BBC Light Entertainment. He was certainly much loved by Muir and Norden, who felt that with Dixon they could write in a more sophisticated style than was acceptable elsewhere.

The following extract is from 'Breakfast With Braden' (the forerunner of 'Bedtime With Braden'), transmitted on July 1, 1950. The cast were Bernard Braden, Benny Lee and the singer Pearl Carr, with Nat Temple and his orchestra, and the script was written by Muir and Norden, with Eric Nichol. Pearl Carr played an ingénue given to gauche adoration of Braden, as this typical extract shows:

MUSIC *'Aintcha Glad'* (*Benny Lee*)

BRADEN That was 'Aintcha Glad' sung by Benny Lee, who can be heard nightly singing in the Penicillin Room at the Streatham Cash Chemists. Now we turn again to our Household Hints Department. Look at this new atomic toaster which automatically burns the toast, scrapes it, butters it, dabs on marmalade and, unless watched closely, eats it. This toaster can be installed at practically no cost, provided you already have a cyclotron in the basement. And for housewives whose hubbies drop cigarette ash on the carpet, here is a unique gadget—a fingerprint-proof revolver, which will—

CARR Hello, Mr. Braden.

BRADEN Well, hello, Pearl Carr. You're looking mighty spruce this morning, Pearl. That a new outfit?
CARR It's an old suit, but I'm wearing a man's shirt.
BRADEN Really? Anybody I know?
CARR No, no, it's mine. It's the way you wear yours. I . . . I was trying to look like you.
BRADEN Congratulations on a brilliant failure, honey. But how come this urge to look like me?
CARR Well, somebody told me that you were in love with yourself, so I thought that perhaps if I dressed as you do I might remind you of you.
BRADEN But, Pearl—you're wearing high heels.
CARR Yes, they said—
BRADEN It's a lie!
CARR Oh! I've been silly again, haven't I, Mr. Braden? I keep thinking I can attract you to me by the way I wear my hair, by my clothes, and all the time your mind is turned to higher things.
BRADEN Well, maybe your skirt *could* be a *bit shorter*, Pearl.

This breakfast-time comedy show was very much a Pat Dixon conception, and although today's top radio shows are at times when television is either not transmitting or is at least transmitting a specialist subject, in 1950 to do a comedy programme at 8.15 a.m. was, to say the least, an innovation. To be accurate, there had been another morning comedy show, 'It's A Pleasure', but it didn't catch on; it needed the combination of Dixon, Braden, Barbara Kelly (Braden's wife), Muir and Norden to create an audience for the 'esoteric' breakfast laughter show.

Muir and Norden have never been able to resist a challenge. An early morning comedy show—a panel game—advertising—they are willing to have a go at anything. They are chiefly known for their appearances on the panel game 'My Word', where their main contributions are mind-splitting puns which Jack Longland, the show's first chairman has described as 'a form of language surgery'. In each programme, they are asked to give their versions of how a well-known quotation or saying came to be used. This is a fragment of what Denis Norden made of 'A nod's as good as a wink to a blind horse':

'In 1942, I was a Wop. Before I get either a reproachful letter from the Race Relations people or a Welcome Home card from the Mafia, let me explain that term. In 1942, a "Wop" was the RAF

> abbreviation for "Wireless Operator", and that was what Daddy did in World War Two. (Oh, come on, child, you've heard of World War Two, it starred Leslie Banks.) I was 1615358, Wireless Operator U/T: U/T being another ingenious RAF abbreviation. It stood for "Under Training". About that training. The RAF had calculated that the maximum period necessary to transform even the most irresolute of civilians into a red-hot Wireless Operator was three months. At the time we are considering, I had been Under Training for a year and a half.'

A long and involved story follows in which Norden explains that a 'Wop' had two different tests, aural and visual. Being short-sighted, he couldn't read the Morse flashed on an Aldis lamp—but a fellow Wop would prod him in the back—softly for a short blink, hard for a long blink. The story concludes:

> '. . . even today, RAF trainees who have trouble making out what visual signals are being shone into their short-sighted eyes, are being rescued by that same system of dig-in-the-back simultaneous translation. The lads have even adapted a proverb to cover the situation: A prod is as good as a blink to a shined Morse.'

Frank Muir is still faintly surprised that although both he and Norden are so in tune, the style of their respective stories is so different, and it's true that you could not mistake one for the other. Norden is the more deadpan of the two, letting the words do their work, while Muir uses the vaguely foppish quality of his voice to enhance the bizarre nature of his stories. What they do share is an intense delight in words and their order. This is Muir getting his teeth firmly into the quotation 'So he passed over and all the trumpets sounded for him on the other side':

> 'A few weeks ago, the publisher Mark Bonham Carter was walking in Hyde Park when he heard someone calling his name, "Mark! Mark!" He turned and there was nobody there. He walked on a little and again he heard a small rather querulous voice call, "Mark! Mark! Mark!" Then he looked downwards and there at his ankles was a small dog with a hare lip. I mention the incident as a demonstration of the peculiar quality which names have for being other things. . . . Take Strip Tease. Were you aware that Strip Tease was named after the man who imported it into this country at the fag end of the last century, Phineas Stripp? Well it was. . . . He had heard tell from travellers that a new form of entertainment was sweeping the halls of Calais and Dieppe—to the inflammatory music of Offenbach, girls stood on stage and proceeded to unbutton their dresses. . . . It had no name in France

> but when Phineas imported the idea he hired a theatre in London in between the matinée and the evening performance and served tea while the ladies divested. These became known as Stripp Teas, and the name stuck.'

The story rambles on, but finally Phineas decides to get to France by means of an ingenious self-propelling combination of a pair of bloomers stuffed with camphor balls:

> 'Phineas found that by moving his feet this way and that, they made a pair of fine rudders, giving him perfect steering control. He straightened up and, to a muffled cheer from the beach, settled down to a steady eight knots on a course of roughly SE by S. . . . So he passed Dover, and all the strumpets undid for him on the other side.'

Ouch! (Both these stories are taken from Muir and Norden's collection, *You Can't Have Your Kayak And Eat It*, published by Eyre Methuen.)

Muir and Norden's most important achievement has been to make comedy script-writing a respectable occupation. Before they came along, it had been assumed that producers would also write, and when they ran short of ideas, they would employ joke-writers to pad out the script—for instance, Ray Galton and Alan Simpson (of 'Hancock's Half-Hour' and 'Steptoe And Son') began their careers that way, selling jokes at five shillings a time to Derek Roy. It was Frank Muir and Denis Norden who, building on the bridgehead created by Ted Kavanagh, made writers the most important element of a comedy show (that's to say a *good* comedy show), and the principle they established back in the 'fifties still stands today.

6

Taboos

As well as big stars, brilliant writers and distinguished producers, radio has brought to light many able administrators, of whom Michael Standing was undoubtedly one of the most gifted. His father was Sir Guy Standing, whose many activities included that of starring in films; his sister is the well-known actress, Kay Hammond, and Standing himself became very well known as a BBC interviewer with his regular live interlude, 'Standing On the Corner', in the pre-war 'In Town Tonight' programme. He joined the BBC in 1935 and worked in most departments before becoming Head of Outside Broadcasts during the war and, incidentally, a war correspondent.

He became Director of Variety in July 1945 after the former director, John Watt, had left abruptly over a policy dispute. When he took over the Variety department, he found himself flung in at the deep end of a very unfamiliar world: 'I had been involved in the BBC's affairs in a number of ways and I knew quite a lot about broadcasting, but I did find the people in the Variety department were rather a different kind of community to the kinds that I'd been hitherto involved with. Their morale was very low and they'd had some crushing blows with programmes that had blown up in their faces—but I remember addressing the department in Aeolian Hall and telling them that the task of finding successful Variety formulae and producing effective Variety programmes was something that was infinitely worthwhile. I pointed out that success in doing so would have to compensate for the very small salaries that they then received and reminded them that giving pleasure was something that very few people had the opportunity of doing on the scale that broadcasting could do it, and if they'd awakened a laugh in an unhappy household they'd done a great thing which they could look back on with enormous satisfaction.'

The Variety department at that time had a heck of a job to do. Standing told me: 'I think I once reckoned that the number of spaces that we filled in all the services of the BBC were 240 a week. That included repeat programmes, and of course in those days the Variety department was responsible for Sandy MacPherson and all the theatre and cinema organ programmes, dance music, jazz, a proportion of "presented" light music with singers and so on, feature programmes like "Scrapbook", "Monday Night At Eight", and purely laughter programmes like "Music Hall", "Take It From Here", and "ITMA". I used to reckon to work about fourteen hours a day, and as often as not, seven days a week. I liked to put in an appearance at the studios and see what was going on. Lots of things were recorded on Sundays, and indeed were broadcast *live* on Sundays.' It is hardly surprising that under that kind of pressure, Standing developed TB and was out of action for a year. On his return, Con Mahoney became his personal assistant, and Standing continued to improve the standards and enlarge the scope of his department.

He found himself fighting a continuing battle with the seamier side of the dance music and variety world, he said. 'The thing that worried me most when I went to Variety was the sense one felt of corruption impinging on the department from the outside. You were surrounded by people who regarded the giving of presents as an absolutely fair and orthodox way of behaving. Song plugging was rife, and the practice of the entertainment business giving expensive presents was widespread. I had been in the job for less than three months when someone who shall be nameless—and is anyhow now dead—sent me a large silver cigarette box, with an inscription: "To Michael, with very best wishes etc. etc. from X." It was something which in those days must have been worth forty or fifty pounds, nowadays probably five or six hundred. I sent it back. I'd never even met the person. But he rang up, astonished that I'd sent it back, and I said, "It's very kind of you but I really can't accept it, and please forgive me for returning it to you." He sent it back again. This time I sent it back with a much more severe note and he shut up. Subsequently we became perfectly good friends—he was a celebrated figure in the field of radio and he continued to do a lot of broadcasting. He never offered me anything again, and he was always exceedingly careful and circumspect in his attitude towards me, but I wondered then to what extent his success depended upon his largesse. So, of course, I kept an eye on his programme activities. Another time, within a fairly short time of being in the job, I interviewed a band leader about a broadcast, and when he'd gone I had occasion to shift the blotter on my desk and found twenty pounds there. So he didn't do any broadcasting for quite a time after that.'

I feel, and I'm sure Michael Standing would agree, that it was the BBC's lack of understanding of the nature of Variety that allowed these abuses to creep in. The practice of song plugging ended during Standing's reign: 'In 1948 there was an anti-song plugging agreement in which I was greatly involved. I think that this was the first time in history that the music publishers had really come together and agreed on a single line of policy. I think it had the immediate effect of stopping money passing, but before very long some publishers found ways of favouring people who could influence the commercial success of their songs. After the song-plugging agreement the situation improved immeasurably and our people concentrated much more on the medium of broadcasting. You see, in those days salaries in the BBC were shockingly low, and married producers with children had a very difficult time in making ends meet at all. They had to go out and meet artists who lived on a totally different scale, all the important figures in the business, and it was often very difficult indeed for them to resist what seemed to be a perfectly friendly offer, a loan for this, a holiday there—and occasionally things went wrong. I don't believe that there was so much actual corruption, but in the odd cases that did come to my notice one saw unfold a story of fatuous stupidity.'

In his eight years as Director of Variety, Michael Standing undoubtedly did more than anyone in the history of broadcasting to improve the standards of Light Entertainment. Post-war radio had become much more outspoken than it was in the 'thirties. Jokes were broader, and the humour of the barrackroom became more and more the commonplace of the air. There had, of course, always been tasteless broadcasters and old music-hall comics who knew how to put one over on young and inexperienced producers, using words and oblique references that weren't recognised as being dubious until too late—Max Miller, for instance, had been 'banned' for telling a joke that overstepped the mark. By 1949, it was felt that for everyone's sake a general guide should be issued and standards enforced that applied to all. Thus the famous *Green Book* was issued; a book that became a legend among broadcasters and an unintended source of mirth among programme producers. Though today it reads in places more like a comedy script than a policy document, it was necessary and important at the time. It puts the official BBC point of view, outlining the task of setting 'a standard that will be accepted by most rational people'.

Michael Standing wrote most of it himself, collecting memos and documents from various sources—guides that had been issued over the years either to individual programmes or producers. Having assembled this mass of material, he turned it into one comprehensive guide. Surely he must have had a chuckle when he was writing it? 'Yes, indeed,' says Standing, 'and many of the things in it must today seem absolutely ludicrous, but nonetheless public standards at that time were very different from now.'

Here is the *Green Book*, warts and all, and I'm most grateful to the BBC for allowing the document to be reprinted in full for the first time here.

PRIVATE AND CONFIDENTIAL

BBC VARIETY PROGRAMMES POLICY GUIDE
FOR WRITERS AND PRODUCERS

PREFACE

This booklet is for the guidance of producers and writers of light entertainment programmes. It seeks to set out the BBC's general policy towards this type of material, to list the principal 'taboos', to indicate traps for the unwary or inexperienced, and to summarise the main guidance so far issued of more than a short-term application. It is however no more than a guide, inevitably incomplete and subject of course to supplementation. It cannot replace the need of each producer to exercise continued vigilance in matters of taste.

GENERAL

The BBC's attitude towards its entertainment programmes is largely governed by the fact that broadcasting is a part of the domestic life of the nation. It caters in their own homes for people of all ages, classes, trades and occupations, political opinions and religious beliefs. In that respect it has no parallel among other media of entertainment and the argument, frequently advanced, that the BBC should be ready to broadcast material passed for public performance on the stage or screen is not valid. The Corporation must have its own standards moulded in the light of its own circumstances. The influence that it can exert upon its listeners is immense and the responsibility for a high standard of taste correspondingly heavy. Its aim is for its programmes to entertain without giving reasonable offence to any part of its diversified audience. It must therefore keep its programmes free from vulgarity, political bias, and matter in questionable taste. The claims of sectional interests to special consideration need constantly to be weighed but at the same time the BBC must not be at the mercy of the cranks. On more or less controversial issues the Corporation confines itself to what it regards as fair comment in the context. On matters of taste it has to set itself a standard that will be acceptable by most rational people.

These are the principal factors influencing BBC policy. The responsibility for enforcing it, since in normal times there are no official censors, is very largely vested in producers themselves and it is therefore of paramount importance that they should be aware both of the Corporation's general attitude towards the subject and of the detailed rules which have been drawn up during some 25 years' practical experience.

Producers are not asked to be narrow-minded in their approach to the problem but they are required to recognise its importance and to err, if at all, on the side of caution. Material about which a producer has any doubts should, if it cannot be submitted to someone in higher authority, be deleted, and an artist's assurance that it has been previously broadcast is no justification for repeating it. 'When in doubt, take it out' is the wisest maxim.

VULGARITY

Programmes must at all cost be kept free of crudities, coarseness and innuendo. Humour must be clean and untainted directly or by association with vulgarity and suggestiveness. Music hall, stage, and to a lesser degree, screen standards, are not suitable to broadcasting. Producers, artists and writers must recognise this fact and the strictest watch must be kept. There can be no compromise with doubtful material. It must be cut.

A. General. Well known vulgar jokes (e.g. the Brass Monkey) 'cleaned up', are not normally admissible since the humour in such cases is almost invariably evident only if the vulgar version is known.

There is an absolute ban upon the following:—

Jokes about—

- Lavatories
- Effeminacy in men
- Immorality of any kind

Suggestive references to—

- Honeymoon couples
- Chambermaids
- Fig leaves
- Prostitution
- Ladies' underwear, e.g. winter draws on
- Animal habits, e.g. rabbits
- Lodgers
- Commercial travellers

Extreme care should be taken in dealing with references to or jokes about—

- Pre-natal influences (e.g. 'His mother was frightened by a donkey')
- Marital infidelity

Good taste and decency are the obvious governing considerations. The vulgar use of such words as 'basket' must also be avoided.

B. Sophisticated Revue and Cabaret. A great deal of the material performed elsewhere in these types of entertainment is just not suitable to be broadcast. There can perhaps be a little more latitude in the editing of 'sophisticated' programmes which are billed and generally identified as such but not sufficient for them to reflect all the accepted characteristics of this kind of show. The fact is that radio revue and cabaret must be tailored to the microphone in much the same way as other programmes and deny itself many items technically suitable which do not conform to established BBC standards.

ADVERTISING

Advertising of any sort is not normally allowed and gratuitous publicity for any commercial undertaking or product may not be given. Occasionally, however, such references may be unavoidable where, for instance, a commercial firm is sponsoring a public event, e.g. the *Star* Dancing Championships, the *Melody Maker* Dance Band Contest. In such cases mention of the sponsoring body must not go beyond the proper courtesy and essential programme interest.

Otherwise mention of all firms, trade and proprietary names is barred.

N.B. The following trade names are now regarded as generic terms:—

Aspirin	Pianola
Bakelite	Spam
Cellophane	Tabloid
Gramophone	Thermos
Luminal	Vaseline
Nylon	Zip
Photostat	

The inclusion of any of these is therefore permitted in scripts but derogatory references to them must be avoided as constituting a form of 'trade slander'.

AMERICAN MATERIAL AND 'AMERICANISMS'

Various fairly obvious factors, such as American films and the fact that much modern popular music originates in America, tend to exert a transatlantic influence upon our programmes. American idiom and slang, for instance, frequently find their way quite inappropriately into scripts, and dance band singers for the most part elect to adopt pseudo American accents. The BBC believes that this spurious Americanisation of programmes—whether in the writing or in the interpretation—is unwelcome to the great majority of listeners and, incidentally, seldom complimentary to the Americans.

There is and always will be a place in programmes for authentic American artistes and material but the BBC's primary job in light entertainment must be to purvey programmes in our own native idiom, dialects and accents. The 'Americanisation' of British scripts, acts and performances is therefore most actively to be discouraged.

LIBEL AND SLANDER

Actionable references in Variety Programmes have been few since broadcasting began. Producers must, however, take all possible steps to ensure that defamatory material is not included in scripts. The three most likely forms for it to take are:

(a) an uncomplimentary gag by one artist about a fellow artist or other person
(b) an impersonation which may be taken as derogatory.
(c) the use in a fictional setting of a character identifiable with a living person (particularly, of course, if the character is 'bad').

Considerations of taste are usually a safeguard against (a) and (b), though the possibility of defamation makes caution on the producer's part more than ever necessary. Against (c) there can be no complete safeguard, but producers and writers must be scrupulously careful to see that characters in plays and sketches are not given names of living people whose circumstances are remotely similar to those in the fictional plot. In the case of titled people reference books must be consulted. In other cases all reasonable checks that are possible must be made.

BIBLICAL REFERENCES

This is by no means always easy, so many biblical phrases having long since passed into the language and being therefore for the most part admissible in any context. The criterion should, generally speaking, be whether a phrase or saying is still largely identified with the Bible. In that case it should not be used in a comedy setting—though it may be quite suitable in programmes of a more serious character.

Sayings of Christ or descriptive of Him are, of course, inadmissible for light entertainment programmes.

Jokes built around Bible stories, e.g. Adam and Eve, Cain and Abel, David and Goliath, must also be avoided or any sort of parody of them. References to a few biblical characters e.g. Noah, are sometimes permissible but, since there is seldom anything to be gained by them and since they can engender much resentment they are best avoided altogether.

RELIGIOUS REFERENCES

Reference to and jokes about different religions or religious denominations are banned. The following are also inadmissible:—

Jokes about A.D. or B.C. (e.g. 'before Crosby)
Jokes or comic songs about spiritualism, christenings, religious ceremonies of any description (e.g. weddings, funerals)
Parodies of Christmas carols
Offensive references to Jews (or any other religious sect)

POLITICAL REFERENCES

No precise general directive can be given since each individual case needs to be considered on its merits and the performer, the manner of delivery, and the context all need to be taken into account. General guidance is however given in the following quotation from a directive issued on 2nd July, 1948: 'We are not prepared in deference to protests from one Party or another to deny ourselves legitimate topical references to political figures and affairs, which traditionally have been a source of comedians' material. We therefore reserve the right for Variety programmes in moderation to take a crack at the Government of the day and the Opposition so long as they do so sensibly, without undue acidity, and above all funnily.

'Generally speaking, political issues should not be made the running theme of any light entertainment programme or item, and references should be no more than incidental. Occasionally, of course, a sketch or comedy sequence based on, e.g. the National Health Service, is permissible.

'We must guard against the over-exploitation of songs with a political theme. Usually these are MS numbers sung by comedians and are legitimate enough for one or two performances when strictly topical, but undesirable if "plugged" in many programmes.

'We must bar altogether:

(a) anything which we adjudge to go beyond fair comment in this sort of context on a matter of general topical interest;
(b) anything that can be construed as personal abuse of Ministers, Party Leaders, or M.P's, malicious references to them, or references in bad taste;
(c) anything which can reasonably be construed as derogatory to political institutions, Acts of Parliament and the Constitution generally;
(d) anything with a Party bias.

'To sum up, our approach to the whole subject should be good humoured, un-partisan, and in good taste.'

Members of Parliament may not be included in programmes without special permission. This permission will not be granted, whether or not the M.P. concerned is willing, for programmes in which the BBC considers it unsuitable or undignified for a Member of Parliament to appear.

PHYSICAL AND MENTAL INFIRMITIES

Very great distress can be caused to invalids and their relatives by thoughtless jokes about any kind of physical disability. The temptation to introduce them is the greater because in the milder afflictions they often represent an easy source of comedy, but, as a matter of taste, it must be resisted. The following are therefore barred:

Jocular references to all forms of physical infirmity or disease, e.g. blindness, deafness, loss of limbs, paralysis, cancer, consumption, smallpox.

Jokes about war injuries of any description.

Jokes about the more embarrassing disabilities, e.g. bow-legs, cross-eyes, stammering (this is the most common 'gag' subject of this kind).

Jokes about any form of mental deficiency.

DRINK

References to and jokes about drink are allowed in strict moderation so long as they can really be justified on entertainment grounds. Long 'drunk' stories or scenes should, however, be avoided and the number of references in any one programme carefully watched. There is no objection to the use of well-known drinking songs, e.g. 'Another Little Drink', 'Little Brown Jug', in their proper contexts. Trade slogans, e.g. 'Beer is Best', are barred. Remarks such as 'one for the road' are also inadmissible on road safety grounds.

EXPLETIVES

Generally speaking the use of expletives and forceful language on the air can only be justified in a serious dramatic setting where the action of the play demands them. They have no place at all in light entertainment and all such words as God, Good God, My God, Blast, Hell, Damn, Bloody, Gorblimey, Ruddy, etc., etc., should be deleted from scripts and innocuous expressions substituted.

IMPERSONATIONS

All impersonations need the permission of the people being impersonated and producers must reassure themselves that this has been given before allowing any to be broadcast.

Artists' repertoires of impersonations are usually restricted to:—

(a) leading public and political figures;

(b) fellow artists.

As to (a) the Corporation's policy is against broadcasting impersonations of elder statesmen, e.g. Winston Churchill, and leading political figures. Any others in this category should invariably be referred.

As to (b) there is no objection, but certain artists have notified the Corporation that no unauthorised impersonations may be broadcast. The present list is given below but should be checked from time to time with the Variety Booking Manager. A double check by producers as to permission is advisable in these cases:—

Gracie Fields
Ethel Revnell (with or without Gracie West)
Renee Houston
Nat Mills and Bobbie
Vera Lynn
Jeanne de Casalis (Mrs. Feather)
Harry Hemsley

Very occasionally the question arises of the *impersonation of people now dead.* There is, of course, no possible objection to the portrayal or caricature of historic figures of the remote past, but the impersonation of people who have died within living memory or whose relations may still be alive, should normally be avoided altogether. In any event only exceptional cases will be considered and the permission of surviving relations, if any, must always be obtained.

MENTION OF CHARITABLE ORGANISATIONS

Appeals for charity are normally confined to 'The Week's Good Cause'. No such appeals are allowed, save in the most exceptional circumstances, elsewhere in programmes. Veiled appeals in the form of incidental references to charitable organisations are also barred.

Special permission must therefore invariably be sought for the mention of a charity, whatever the context, in entertainment programmes.

'BRITISH' AND 'ENGLISH'

The misuse of the word English where British is correct causes much needless offence to Scottish, Ulster and Welsh listeners. It is a common error but one which is easily avoided by proper care on the part of writers and producers. At the same time we should not hesitate to use the word 'English' if it is the proper description.

POPULAR MUSIC

Virtually all newly published dance numbers are approved for broadcasting by the Dance Music Policy Committee before publication, and it is unnecessary to detail here policy considerations affecting the acceptance of such material. Two matters, are, however, worth noting:

(a) British Music
It is the Corporation's policy actively to encourage British music so long as this does not lead to a lowering of accepted musical standards.

(b) Jazzing the Classics
The jazzing by dance bands of classical tunes or the borrowing and adaptation of them is normally unacceptable. Any instances of this in MS material submitted for programmes must be referred by producers to a higher authority.

MISCELLANEOUS POINTS

Avoid derogatory references to:—

Professions, trades and 'classes', e.g. solicitors, commercial travellers, miners, 'the working class'
Coloured races
Avoid any jokes or references that might be taken to encourage:—
Strikes or industrial disputes
The Black Market
Spivs and drones

Avoid any reference to 'The MacGillicuddy of the Reeks' or jokes about his name.
Do not refer to Negroes as 'Niggers' ('Nigger Minstrels' is allowed).
'Warming up' sequences with studio audiences before broadcasts should conform to the same standards as the programmes themselves. Sample recordings should be the subject of the same vigilance as transmissions.

SPECIAL CONSIDERATIONS FOR OVERSEAS BROADCASTS

Humour in other countries, as in our own, is limited by social, political and religious taboos, and some sources of comedy legitimate enough for this country are not acceptable abroad. The majority of overseas audiences are not Christian by religion nor white in colour. Disrespectful, let alone derogatory, references to Buddhists, Hindus, Moslems, and so on, and any references to colour may therefore cause deep offence and should be avoided altogether. It is impossible to list in detail all potentially dangerous subjects but a few random examples are given here:
Chinese abhor the description 'Chinamen', which should not be used.
Chinese laundry jokes may be offensive.
Jokes like 'enough to make a Maltese Cross' are of doubtful value.
The term *Boer* War should not be used—South African War is correct.
Jokes about 'harems' are offensive in some parts of the world.

It can be seen from the foregoing that the strictures of 1949, although reasonable enough in themselves, were fairly sweeping. Were these regulations still in force today, the majority of television comedies would be unshowable. Not that I'm saying that they *are* showable, but one must agree with Michael Standing and note how much public acceptance, if not public taste, has changed in just under thirty years. I'm not sure that the new permissiveness is an improvement on the old standards of 'good taste', but I suspect that it's my age rather than my reason that dictates that point of view. I grew up in a broadcasting world where the use of swear words was unthinkable. I don't find them necessary in my work today, but, then, I didn't create 'Steptoe And Son' or 'Till Death Us Do Part', where swearing is an essential part of the characterisation, and I applaud such shows. It's my belief that people who want to censor television and radio are a greater threat to our freedom than the occasional cynical writer or producer who panders to his audience's lower instincts. Errors of judgement in matters of taste can be quickly rectified, while censorship, however well-meaning, is more difficult to combat and eventually becomes repressive.

The late Sir Charles Curran, when he was Director General, had to grapple with the elusive problem of taste on the air and was firmly on the side of reason. He told me: 'Hugh Greene [his predecessor] tried to establish the maximum freedom. I'm trying to consolidate on the basis of maximum fairness. Once freedom is established you must be sure you use it fairly.' As for satire, Sir Charles's view was that 'If satirical comedy is to be justified it must be based on an exaggeration of the *truth* and not an exaggeration of a *falsehood*.' These brief remarks, extracted from a long interview I conducted with Sir Charles Curran in 1975, seem to me to be so apt and so reasonable as to need no further comment. So much, then, for the principle. But, as the *Green Book* said in 1949, 'it cannot replace the need of each producer to exercise continued vigilance in matters of taste.'

7

Some Top Shows of the 'Fifties

When one surveys the radio comedy of the late 'forties and early 'fifties, it becomes apparent that in addition to the prodigious output and the remarkably high standards, the *variety* was staggering. Every taste was catered for, from the simple domestic comedies of 'Meet The Huggetts' and 'Life With The Lyons' to the anarchy of 'The Goon Show' and the sophistication of 'In All Directions'. The gentle urbanities of Eric Barker in 'Just Fancy' were as prized as the direct, jokey fun of 'Ray's A Laugh', and while some shows never achieved the Hall of Fame status of, say, 'Take It From Here', a great many were incredibly successful.

Let's look at 'Ray's A Laugh', which was one of the hit shows of its day. Story lines were crisp and direct, the jokes funny, the characters well-rounded if not over subtle. It was very much Ted Ray's show. He not only starred in it but master-minded the writing of Ronnie Hanbury, Eddie Maguire and George Wadmore. At the time it was on the air, Ray was one of Britain's leading music-hall comedians, appearing frequently at the London Palladium and as a bill-topper all over Britain. One of the many top comics who came from Liverpool, he possessed a style that was machine-gun fast and an ability to ad lib that was phenomenal—as his appearances on 'Does The Team Think?' proved. Ted Ray epitomised the best of the old Variety school. A most even-tempered craftsman, he was an off-stage wit who took his sense of humour on stage with him—and this is rarer than is generally thought, for the off-stage comic is rarely funny on, and the on-stage 'riot' can become a pain in the neck once out of the limelight. I remember an occasion when he was supporting Danny Kaye—who in 1947–48 was the biggest of big stars—at the London Palladium. Ted Ray entered, took in the full house seething with excitement and the expectation of seeing the great Kaye, and quipped, 'I always knew I could do it if I had the support!'

On radio in 'Ray's A Laugh' he had the best support going—in Peter Sellers, who played a variety of rôles; in Kitty Bluett, who played Ted's wife; in Bob and Alf Pearson, the singing duo; in Fred Yule, Kenneth Connor and Patricia Hayes, all brilliant radio performers. Ray deployed them with skill, allowing everyone a share of the laughs and keeping the show together with his own enormous zest and energy.

Patricia Hayes, who is today one of Britain's best known character actresses, was with 'Ray's A Laugh' for five-and-a-half years. She had started her broadcasting career as a child in 1922, and was working in feature programmes when one day Pat Dixon phoned and told her he thought she might do well in Light Entertainment. She began with Max Wall in a programme called 'Our Shed', and from there went to 'Ray's A Laugh'. She remembers needing the job badly because 'at the time my marriage had broken down and I had three children to bring up. During the five and a half years I worked with Ted, I was never out of the house for more than half a day a week.' That was how long it took to rehearse and record a comedy show, but the repeat fees turned that one half day's work into a respectable income. From 'Ray's A Laugh', Pat Hayes went from strength to strength, working with every top comedian on radio and television, but she still remembers 'Ray's A Laugh' with great affection and warmth.

If Patricia Hayes was fortunate in working with Ted Ray, Ray himself was fortunate in his producer, George Inns. Inns had the long experience and deft touch that one came across so frequently in radio in those days. He'd grown up in the BBC, having gone through the mill as messenger boy, sound effects lad and, subsequently, producer, whose biggest radio hit was undoubtedly 'Ray's A Laugh'. When he transferred to television, his immensely popular spectacular, 'The Black And White Minstrel Show', created a standard of presentation that was unrivalled in its day.

'Ray's A Laugh' combined many elements of variety and comedy, with domestic sketches and songs. One of the most successful devices was the use of Ray's 'conscience', his unspoken thoughts being turned into a character, chiding and mocking by turns. Each week, Ted Ray, as George, the owner of an Enquiry Agency, set out to unravel a mystery, meeting in turn the various spot characters the show had created. There was Soppy (Peter Sellers, using a voice not unlike Bluebottle's in 'The Goon Show'), Jennifer, an apalling little girl (played by Bob Pearson), Mrs. Hoskin and Ivy (played respectively by Ray himself and Bob Pearson), and many more, including the Duchess of Dillwater, also played by Peter Sellers.

Over the years it ran, the cast and the format changed, but here is an extract from the programme transmitted on November 23, 1950, which is typical of the style and content of 'Ray's A Laugh'.

PETER — We present Ted Ray as George, the Man with a Conscience—the man who runs the Cannon Inquiry Agency.

ORCHESTRA — *'George's Conscience'*

GEORGE — Have you finished your cup of tea, Miss Dobbs?

DOBBS — Yes, thank you, George.

GEORGE — Then let's get on with the letters. Now, Messrs. Burkham and Waily's Fairground, Pintable, Tilts.

DOBBS — Yes.

GEORGE — We are sorry to hear that you are having more trouble.

DOBBS — Yes.

GEORGE — When we found the missing Skeleton Man, you were the people who made no bones about it.

DOBBS — Yes.

GEORGE — And after all, he had had many a close shave before he married the Bearded Lady.

DOBBS — Yes.

GEORGE — But I was the one who told you that the Skeleton Man would make a rattling good husband. Now, have you got all that, Miss Dobbs?

DOBBS — No.

GEORGE — What?

DOBBS — Yes.

GEORGE — Very well. I don't know what the new trouble is with those circus people, but I'm going over to see Burkham and Waily right away.

DOBBS — Can I come with you, George?

GEORGE — Certainly not. You stay here and look after the office.

DOBBS — I wish I'd never taken this job.

GEORGE — Good heavens, why?

DOBBS — Because when I started here, my mum warned me.

GEORGE — Warned you?

DOBBS — Yes. She said, being alone with you, I'd have to be careful.

GEORGE Don't worry, Gertrude—I wouldn't dream of making advances.

DOBBS She told *me* to be careful, George—she's no right to order *you* about!

GEORGE Now then—none of your hanky panky!

DOBBS Oh, if you were half a man you'd take me to the circus.

GEORGE If I was half a man I'd be in it. Here I go.

ORCHESTRA *'George's Conscience'*

FX *Fairground noises and hurdy gurdy*

GEORGE Oh, Conscience—

CONSCIENCE Yes, what is it, George?

GEORGE This is grand—coming to the fairground—combining work with pleasure. It makes me feel like a lord.

CONSCIENCE Why don't you go into the big tent and you'll feel like a marquee.

GEORGE Oh shut up! I'd better find the manager's caravan. I'll ask this chap carrying the bucket. Pardon me.

SOPPY What do you want, Soppy?

GEORGE Where's the manager?

SOPPY He's around behind.

CONSCIENCE There must be an answer to that.

GEORGE Quiet you! Now, boy—are you employed by the circus?

SOPPY Not 'arf, Soppy, I assist Madame Phoebe Daniels.

GEORGE Phoebe Daniels? Who's she?

SOPPY The lion tamer.

GEORGE Oh yes.

SOPPY She's the bravest woman lion tamer in the world.

GEORGE She is?

SOPPY Yes—she goes into the cage with the lions—cracks the whip and makes the ferocious lions jump through the flaming hoops.

GEORGE Wonderful.

SOPPY Yes, Soppy, I wouldn't 'ave 'er job for anything.

GEORGE But you're her assistant—don't you have anything to do with the lions?

SOPPY No. All I do is comb their hair and brush their teeth.

GEORGE Well, I'm glad you're happy in your work.

SOPPY Yes, I'm much happier than when I worked with Madame Sally Volatally.

GEORGE Who was she?

SOPPY A tightrope walker. One day I went round to her caravan to ask her to show me the ropes.

GEORGE You did?

SOPPY Yes. After the show one night, I crept up to her caravan—my heart bursting with passion.

GEORGE What did you do?

SOPPY I got to her caravan—looked through the window—and then it happened.

GEORGE What happened?

SOPPY She took off her blonde wig and started smoking a pipe.

GEORGE Madame Sally Volatally?

SOPPY She was no madam—he was a deserter from the fusiliers.

ORCHESTRA *'George's Conscience'*

GEORGE I'll have to ask someone else.

JENNIFER Hello.

GEORGE Why, it's a little girl—what's your name?

JENNIFER Jennifer.

GEORGE That's a nice name. Tell me, Jennifer, what do you want to be when you grow up?

JENNIFER A woman.

GEORGE Ha ha, very good.

JENNIFER And I want to be tall when I grow up—not like my daddy.

GEORGE Isn't he very tall?

JENNIFER No—he's stopped growing at both ends and started growing in the middle.

GEORGE Your daddy sounds a jolly little man—I bet you've got a happy home.

JENNIFER Oh no—shall I tell you something?

GEORGE Yes.

JENNIFER Mummy and daddy haven't kissed each other for ten years.

GEORGE Why not?

JENNIFER Well, mummy won't kiss him when he drinks and *he* won't kiss *her* when he's sober.

GEORGE I see—well hadn't you better go home now?

JENNIFER (*crying*) Oh don't talk about home, kind sir—I don't want to go home.

GEORGE Don't want to go home—why not?

JENNIFER Well, we've got a new baby in our house and I get the blame for everything.

ORCHESTRA *'George's Conscience'*

CONSCIENCE The manager's probably over there in that beautiful cream and gold caravan.

GEORGE	Yes, I'll try there. Only the best people could afford to live in a caravan like that.
FX	*Door opens*
HOSKIN	It was terrible, Ivy—I've never known such a thing in all my life.
IVY	What happened, Mrs. Hoskin?
HOSKIN	I was fast asleep in bed and I had a shocking nightmare. I dreamt there'd been an election and another Government had got in.
IVY	Did they make you give your teeth back, Mrs. Hoskin?
HOSKIN	It wasn't only that, Ivy—I've got shooting pains all over my body.
IVY	Um—yes—you would, yes—I know—um . . .
HOSKIN	You've no idea, Ivy—so I sent for your cousin Charlie.
IVY	He's no good—what did he do?
HOSKIN	He said, Someone ought to bring this woman to.
IVY	And did he bring you to?
HOSKIN	Yes—but he drank them both himself. So I sent for Aunt Ada.
IVY	Did she make a cup of tea?
HOSKIN	Yes, but we'd no spoons so I couldn't stir.
IVY	No—you couldn't, could you—um—no, and were the pains still shooting, Mrs. Hoskin?
HOSKIN	Shooting? They were shooting like bullets, Ivy—so I got Dad up.
IVY	And what did he do, Mrs. Hoskin?
HOSKIN	He knocked back a large brandy and sent for Dr. Hardcastle.
IVY	Young Dr. Hardcastle—he's luvly, Mrs. Hoskin. He's LUVLY!
HOSKIN	Yes, well, he came over and then he did it!!
IVY	What did he do, Mrs. Hoskin?
HOSKIN	He told me to cover myself all over with a piece of paper and mark where the pains were with a pinhole.
IVY	And did that help him to find the trouble?
HOSKIN	No, but when we tried it on the player piano it played 'Enjoy yourself, it's later than you think'.
FX	*Door shuts*

In complete contrast there was 'In All Directions', starring Peter Ustinov and Peter Jones. Ustinov had been a child prodigy, acting with Will Hay in the film 'The Goose Steps Out', and writing successful

'Ray's a Laugh': Ted Ray, Charles Hawtrey, Patricia Hayes and Peter Sellers, 1953 (Popperfoto)

'In All Directions': Peter Jones and Peter Ustinov, 1953 (Popperfoto)

Beryl Reid, Archie Andrews and Peter Brough in 'Educating Archie', 1953 (Popper

'Just Fancy': l. to r., Deryck Guyler, Patricia Gilbert, Desmond Walter Ellis, Eric Barker, Harold Warrender and Pearl Hackney, 1951 (Popper

'A Life of Bliss': l. to r., George Cole, Colin Gordon and Diana Churchill (BBC)

The Lyons family: Ben, Bebe, Barbara and Richard (Popperfoto)

(Radio Times Hulton Picture L

The Huggett family:
Ethel (Kathleen Harrison), Joe (Jack Warner) and Jane (Vera Day), 1954

'The Clitheroe Kid': l. to r., Diana Day, Peter Sinclair, Jimmy Clitheroe, Leonard Williams and Patricia Burke, 1960

films and stage plays while still in his teens. Peter Jones was also an actor and playwright, and together they had developed the happy knack of improvising comedy on almost any theme. They performed in private and at parties and it now seems inevitable that sooner or later Pat Dixon should have spotted them and harnessed their talents for radio. At first the two Peters were dubious of their ability to sustain their inventiveness, and to reassure them, Dixon co-opted Muir and Norden to edit the programme. Muir and Norden would invent a situation and then Jones and Ustinov would ad lib the dialogue to fit it. It was worked out in advance in Muir and Norden's office, and the results of this ad lib session were transcribed into script form, and then recorded in a BBC studio with further ad libs contributed by Ustinov and Jones. Denis Norden remembers one particular source of inspiration: 'Our typist went on holiday and we had acquired, as a temp., a magnificent creature who possessed a wonderful sinuous body movement. We called her the Puma. She moved just like one. She wasn't the greatest typist, but we found that if the Peters' invention ever flagged during the ad lib sessions, we would just ask her to bring in cups of tea and immediately she started her movement across the room they would revive, and as long as she was in the room, they were magnificent. . . . It was an interesting writing job from our point of view as we were relieved of any of the strictures of finding pay-offs—we just had to think of situations.'

The best-remembered characters that Ustinov and Jones created were Morry and Dudley Grosvenor, a pair of Jewish fly-by-nights, always involved in dubious transactions and usually having to run for it with the law in hot pursuit. The theme of the series was the search for the mysterious Copthorne Avenue, and as Morry and Dudley wandered vainly towards their goal their encounters with various people along the way constituted the show. The following extract is from a typical episode of 'In All Directions', originally transmitted on October 25, 1952. All the parts are played by Ustinov and Jones:

ANNOUNCER This is the BBC Home Service

MUSIC *Signature Tune*

ANNOUNCER We present 'In All Directions', with Peter Ustinov and Peter Jones—some diversions on a car journey.

MUSIC *Up to finish*

ANNOUNCER And here is Mr. Peter Ustinov.

USTINOV Good evening. Did you ever read a grim little story—I think it was by Lord Dunsany—about a man walking at night along a country road towards a cottage which he can see about half a mile ahead? He walks on towards it at a brisk pace, but somehow it doesn't seem to get any nearer. A little uneasily he quickens his step—breaks into a run—but when he collapses, exhausted, the cottage is still the same short distance away. Then, to his horror, he realises what is happening. The road is *stretching*—like *elastic* . . . Now, I'm not saying that is what happened when Peter Jones and I set out in his car to find a place called Copthorne Avenue.

FX *Fade in car*

USTINOV All I know is, although everyone we asked told us we were right on top of it, we never seemed (*fade*) to get any *nearer* to it . . .

JONES It *can't* be far now . . . you look your side and I'll look mine.

FX *Car driving along*

JONES Look—over there! Quick, pull up!

FX *Car pulls up*

JONES That's the place to give us a route card. It's a Travel Agency.

USTINOV We didn't want to go *abroad* . . .

JONES No, this is one of those *local* travel agencies. See what it says—'London By Night Tours Limited. Theatre Tickets. Concert Bookings and Conducted Tours by our own Luxury Sleeper.'

USTINOV 'Under the personal supervision of Messrs. Dudley and Morris Grosvenor'. Think it's worth crossing the road to ask there?

JONES Perhaps not. They look too busy. Couple of people have just gone in—gentleman in a pastel coloured gaberdine suit accompanied by a lady festooned with cameras. . . .

MUSIC *Link*

AMERICAN Do I get any service around here?

DUDLEY Yes, just one moment, sir. I'll call my partner—Morry!

MORRY (*off*) Ten bob each way—right—2.30—right. You're on. (*Coming on*) I beg your pardon, sir. I was just fixing up Sir Miles Thomas with a return air ticket to Johannesburg.

AMERICAN Just arrived on the liner 'United States'.

MORRY An impressive vehicle, I'm told. A very impressive vehicle.

AMERICAN Doing Europe. Paris, Nuremburg, Rome. Back to US on Thursday. This is the first time we've been in London.

WIFE This is the first time we've been in London.

DUDLEY Well, you've come to the right place. What do you want to see? A theatre?

MORRY London, rich in theatres . . . all the critics concur . . . Ice show?

AMERICAN No, we have those in the States.

WIFE We have those in the States.

AMERICAN We don't like ice shows—we're on the extra-mural faculty at Yale. We make masks.

WIFE We make masks.

AMERICAN My wife is a professor of maskology.

DUDLEY Is she wearing a mask now?

WIFE Left my face pack on.

MORRY If you want something more intellectual, there's John Gielgud.

AMERICAN Is he a comedian? Like Danny Kaye?

MORRY Oh yes. Spitting image.

WIFE We don't like laughing.

AMERICAN Any Shakespeare on right now?

MORRY Well, there's the Open Air Theatre.

AMERICAN No roof at all? Not even a sliding roof?

DUDLEY 'Ad the bombing very badly round there. Very nice, though. A friend of ours has got a job there weeding the scenery. We can get you in through him. Through the bushes actually.

AMERICAN What's this 'London By Night Tours' you advertise up there outside the shop?

DUDLEY You'll never regret joining our tour. We have many popular attractions. First of all, we take you to Trafalgar Square to see the pigeons.

MORRY That's very nice—we'll wake up the pigeons and get them to *wheel* for you. It's a wonderful sight, that is, if the street lighting is still on.

DUDLEY Then we take you to Speakers' Corner in Hyde Park—show you the *exact spot* where the speakers were speaking during the day.

MORRY They're asleep in bed, actually, but you do see where they *were*.

AMERICAN Is that near Buckingham Palace?

DUDLEY It's adjacent really. Very adjacent.

MORRY From there we take you to Paddington Sorting Office.

AMERICAN Is that near the Palace?

WIFE Is that near the Palace?

DUDLEY They're all near the Palace. We go round and round it on the tour.

MORRY Paddington Sorting Office, very ingenious—post a parcel a few days before and see it actually arrive.

WIFE Tom, we'd better make up our minds. We're losing our advantage.

AMERICAN Sure, honey. Well, first we'll go to an Eatery—then a Nitery, then we'll go on this 'London By Night' tour. Now, how do we settle this up financially? I hate to talk about money.

MORRY Well, we don't. We rather enjoy it. Have you got any American dollars on you? In *cash*? Greenbacks?

AMERICAN How much is this tour going to cost?

DUDLEY (*mumbles with Morry*) Shall we say four hundred dollars?

WIFE That's cheap enough . . .

MORRY *Each*! Four hundred dollars *each*.

AMERICAN I thought there'd be a catch in it. Here's eight hundred dollars.

DUDLEY Then you'll want some English spending money.

AMERICAN Say, what's the rate of exchange?

DUDLEY A florin.

AMERICAN How much is that worth?

DUDLEY A dollar. If you and your wife will just wait in the shop sir, I'll go to the bank and get your florins for you.

MORRY I think, if you don't mind, I'll accompany my partner—help him carry the florins back. They weigh 'eavy in bulk. Won't be a minute.

DUDLEY (*confidentially*) Are they still there?

MORRY Yes, they're still in the shop—no. They've come out! They're coming after us. Dudley—

DUDLEY Yes?

MORRY Run for it!

The characters of Morry and Dudley had grown over the years from a private joke into a public institution, the two Peters rounding them out and adding facets as time went on. They even used the characters in a radio adaptation of Dostoevsky's *Crime And Punishment*, starring John Gielgud. Peter Jones had a slightly difficult time, for although he was well known, Peter Ustinov was a superstar of both theatre and cinema, a multi-talented and widely-acclaimed genius. However, as Denis Norden points out, 'Peter Jones really carried the weight of the show. He was the check and the balance, the brake and the steering wheel.' Jones says he was regarded as 'Ustinov's friend' and until the third series all the fees were paid to Ustinov's agent, much to Jones's chagrin. However much you like the other man, such a relationship must inevitably cause a certain amount of irritation, and on one occasion Peter Jones made his feelings known in a speech at a Press Association dinner in which he described a dream (concocted for the occasion): 'I dreamed I was in the Mall with a crowd of people waiting for a procession. The people had rattles and hooters and things and were all dressed up, and in front of them was a line of soldiers and beyond them a line of policemen, and they were all looking to the left towards the Palace, and after an interminable wait a huge cry went up. Then we saw the gates open and this huge, wonderful coach came trundling out with the eight Windsor Greys trotting ahead of it. It came towards us but after it'd gone about two hundred yards, a gasp went up. One of the Windsor Greys had slipped its bridle and the others were careering down the Mall, and the coachman fell off and the coach was obviously completely out of control and no one knew what to do. And as the coach came alongside, I leapt over the soldiers and the policemen and hurled myself at the leading horse and gripped it by the bridle, and with a tremendous muscular effort I twisted its neck and it came to a halt. The whole coach ground to a halt.

'People were cheering, and I can remember vaguely the Queen getting out of the coach, the Duke of Edinburgh behind her, Armstrong Jones and his camera taking photographs, and the Queen took Edinburgh's sword out of its scabbard and she touched my shoulder and she said, "Arise, Sir Peter"—and after that I passed out completely. And then the scene changes and it's all misty and I'm on a cloud and I realise what's happened and this is it—good heavens, what an extraordinary thing—and I look down and I see that the world is not entirely out of sight. I'm hovering over the West End, the Jermyn Street, Piccadilly area, and I find that like an astronaut I can slightly manipulate this cloud, and I'm fascinated and I go a little lower down and I get near to Piccadilly Circus and I see they're selling newspapers, and I think, "I must try and get a little nearer so that I can see what they're saying", because this story surely must have made the front page. And I get nearer and I see people are fighting each other to get newspapers. And I get near enough to read the placards of the *Evening Standard* and the *News*, and they say—"Peter Ustinov Bereaved".'

In the 'fifties there was room for all shades of comedy, and it would have been a cantankerous listener indeed who didn't find something to please him. During the course of a typical Thursday evening in the winter of 1953 you could hear 'Ray's A Laugh', 'Take It From Here',

'Life With The Lyons', and 'Educating Archie'. Over the years this latter programme became a barometer of success; more than any other radio comedy it was the showcase of the emerging top-liner. If you were in it you were either a star or on your way to stardom, and at one time or another Archie's supporting players included Tony Hancock, Harry Secombe, Robert Moreton, Max Bygraves, Ronald Shiner, Julie Andrews, Hattie Jacques, Beryl Reid (as the schoolgirl, Monica), Bill Fraser, Bruce Forsyth, and Ronald Chesney (with his 'magic harmonica'). Over the ten years of its life it was written at various times by Sid Colin, Eric Sykes, Ronnie Wolfe, Ronald Chesney, Marty Feldman, and many others. With that kind of line up, the show couldn't really miss. Its star, Peter Brough, was both a ventriloquist and a businessman, the owner of several woollen mills, and in his radio work as in his business he knew that top quality got results.

At the end of the first series, the show won the *Daily Mail* Award. In his book, *Educating Archie*, Peter Brough states: 'We were well aware that our surprise victory had not been too well received in certain quarters. There were those who felt and murmured that the prize should have gone to one of the longer-running comedy shows, and there was acute jealousy that a team of youngsters in age and radio experience should have triumphed. This meant that in our second year the knockers and critics were ready to pounce at any sign of falling off, either in script or performance, and we had to tread with care.'

Here are some moments from 'Educating Archie' over the years. First, Archie with Monica (Beryl Reid), from the programme first transmitted on October 15, 1953; script by Eric Sykes, Ronnie Wolfe, Len Fincham and Lawrie Wyman:

ANDREWS Now, Monica, have you ever cleaned a car before?
MONICA Once I cleaned Miss Oglethorpe's car. I polished it beautifully.
ANDREWS Could she see her face in it?
MONICA I think so. She gave me sixpence to dirty it again.
ARCHIE Let's start by getting some water.
MONICA Water? Ughh . . .!!
ARCHIE Don't you ever bath?
MONICA No. I just wait until I'm nicely caked with dirt—then I have a good scrape around with a hockey stick.
ARCHIE The windscreen's mucky. Monica—take this bucket of water and throw it at the window.
MONICA Right ho.
FX *Glass smash*

ARCHIE Oh Monica—not the bucket as well. Perhaps we'd better just polish the car—have you got a rag?

MONICA I've got a tatty old blouse I keep for cleaning my bike.

ARCHIE Can we use it?

MONICA Yes—wait a minute, I'll take it off.

ARCHIE Spare my blushes—let's use our hankies.

FX *Grunting, groaning, hard breathing*

ARCHIE I'm fed up with this.

MONICA Me too—all this hard work makes you feak and weeble.

The following is a sequence from the transmission of December 5, 1956 written by Ronald Wolfe, George Wadmore and Pat Dunlop, and featuring Max Bygraves and Ken Platt.

PLATT I suppose you don't know this fellow coming in with the big head.

ARCHIE Big head? Yes, of course I know him. Hello, Mr. Bygraves.

BYGRAVES 'Ello, son, I've arrived and to prove it I'm here. Here, let me look at you, Archie. You've put on some weight, haven't you?

ARCHIE Have I?

BYGRAVES Yes, you're getting fat. Are you sure some squirrels haven't been stuffing nuts down your earole?

ARCHIE No, I'm just growing up. And between you and me I've had quite a few girl friends since the old days.

BYGRAVES Yes, I've heard the rumours. They say you've been going steady with a broom handle. Here, Arch, who's your friend —this layabout with his hands in my pockets?

ARCHIE Oh, this is Mr. Platt. Mr. Platt, this is a very famous singer of cockney songs.

PLATT Oh, would you be Billy Cotton?

BYGRAVES Not if they paid me a pension! I'm Max Bygraves.

The transmission of 'Educating Archie' on September 25, 1957 featured Dick Emery, Pearl Carr, and Warren Mitchell. The writers were Ronnie Wolfe, George Wadmore, and David Climie. Peter Brough and Archie return from Australia to be greeted by Dick Emery as Lampwick, a pressman.

BROUGH (*pompously*) Hello everybody—we're back—we're back!

LAMPWICK Well, 'op it again.

ARCHIE Eh? Who are you? We're expecting the Press.

LAMPWICK I am the Press. I am the foreign correspondent of the *Clapham Confidential*. Here's my card—Arnold Lampwick, D.B.T.C.

ARCHIE What does that stand for?

LAMPWICK Don't bend the card.

BROUGH Just a minute. You can't be the only reporter here. Where are all the others? Where are all my fans—don't they remember me?

LAMPWICK Yes—that's why they haven't turned up.

ARCHIE (*disappointed*) What a reception.

BROUGH Yes—and to think everywhere else we were wined and dined. In Sydney it was champagne. California champagne. New York—more champagne. . . . Now, what have you got to welcome us with?

LAMPWICK Here's me bottle of cold tea. You can drink down to the pencil mark.

BROUGH What? Is that all I get? Me? *Peter Brough*?

LAMPWICK What's he so famous for, then?

ARCHIE He's got a ventriloquial aptitude.

LAMPWICK Well, you'd better take him to the doctor and get some ointment slapped on him. Now, let's get on with this interview. What sort of reception did you get when you arrived in Australia?

ARCHIE Well, as we sailed into Sydney Harbour we were given full honours.

LAMPWICK Did they fire a twenty-one gun salute?

ARCHIE Er—not exactly.

LAMPWICK Oh, you mean they gave you the ten-gun salute?

ARCHIE Not quite.

LAMPWICK What did they do then?

ARCHIE They got an old age pensioner to crack his knuckles.

In 1958 the show was produced by Jacques Brown, and the cast included Bernard Bresslaw, Gladys Morgan and Dick Emery. The writers were Ronnie Wolfe, Ronnie Chesney and Marty Feldman. Here's a snatch from the transmission of October 5, 1958. Dick Emery played Grimble.

BROUGH Wake up, Archie, wake up!

ARCHIE (*coming out of sleep*) Ye-e-es?

BROUGH (*alarmed*) I just heard a horrible noise. It woke me up.

ARCHIE (*now fully awake*) So did I.

BROUGH What was it?
ARCHIE You—shouting 'Wake up, Archie!'
BROUGH Oh really! Someone must have heard that noise. (*Start fade*) Let's wake Grimble and search the house.
FX *Urgent rapping on door. Door opens*
GRIMBLE (*Snoring sounds*)
ARCHIE Grimble. Wake up!
GRIMBLE (*talking in his sleep*) Oh Gina . . . I love you. Oh, loll a little longer, my little Lolla. Oh Gina. My darling loved one.
ARCHIE Get up or I'll throw a bucket of water over you.
GRIMBLE (*still sleepy*) No, Gina . . . not again!
BROUGH (*fiercely*) Grimble! Stop dreaming.
GRIMBLE (*becoming fully awake*) Oh, it's you, Mr. Brough.
BROUGH (*dramatically*) Grimble! Did you hear a strange noise?
GRIMBLE *I* didn't, but I'll go back and ask Gina. (*Snores*)
BROUGH Wake up, you idiot. There's something peculiar . . .
FX *Door opens* (*over speech*)
GLADYS Ah, there you are. It is nice to see you.
BROUGH Mrs. Morgan, did you hear a strange noise?
GLADYS You mean a noise like someone playing a trumpet—then some heavy, clumping footsteps—then a door slammed—some more footsteps—and another door slammed?
BROUGH (*eagerly*) Yes.
GLADYS No! I didn't hear it—but I knew it was going to happen, so I put this cotton wool in my ears.

'Educating Archie' changed enough during its run to keep it fresh, and although I doubt whether Peter Brough would claim to be the world's greatest ventriloquist—the late Jimmy Wheeler said of him, 'Blimey, his mouth moves more than the dummy's does!'—Brough can accept such quips with a smile. When 'Educating Archie' was on the air it held its own with the best, it made stars of many and it entertained vast audiences every week for the three hundred-plus shows it ran.

'Just Fancy', which Charles Maxwell not only produced but also occasionally appeared in, was written by and starred Eric Barker. Having started out as a writer, Barker had become a comedian at the Windmill Theatre before the war. Thanks to Leslie Bridgmont, he broadcast regularly from 1939 on, and while in the Royal Navy he created the naval segment of 'Merry Go Round' which centred on the almost imaginary HMS Waterlogged. Eric Barker confesses in his autobiography, *Steady Barker*, that he loathed the strictures of naval discipline and was delighted at the end of the war to be demobbed and return to his cottage in Kent, and regular broadcasting. He says, 'Michael Standing offered me a two years' writing and performing contract at a figure I had not considered possible in my wildest dreams. I was to present "Merry Go Round" weekly.' There were 252 'Merry Go Round' programmes altogether, and in its time it was top of the ratings. After this arduous grind, Barker wanted a change of pace and direction. He invented 'Just Fancy' which was whimsical, ironic and observant—just like Eric Barker himself, in fact. He could have found no better producer than Charles Maxwell to take the show off the paper and into the mind. Here is an extract from 'Just Fancy' which was transmitted on September 4, 1959. The cast was Eric Barker, Pearl Hackney, Deryck Guyler, Ruth Porcher and Frederick Treves.

ANNOUNCER	Have you that listless, purposeless feeling that tomorrow will do? Good. The next half hour won't disturb your plans at all, because it consists of 'Just . . . Fancy'.
ORCHESTRA	*Signature tune—'Just Fancy'*
BARKER	Hello and welcome yet again to this . . . programme, I suppose you'd call it. I felt I must just mention for the benefit of those who write in and ask for seats in the audience of this show that, of course, we have no studio audience. This is not to say that we don't try to assess the effect our show has on its particular, or as some would say not *too* particular public, but—just for an experiment our producer, Charles Maxwell, than whom Anstruther, Fife has bred no bigger, has just gone out into Bond Street where our studio is situated, to bring in a stray couple of people who have never been into a BBC studio before, and ask for their opinion.
VOICES	(*Approach*)
BARKER	Ah! Charles!
MAXWELL	Well, here we are—may I introduce Eric Barker—Mr and Mrs Aigburth of Liverpool.
ALL	(*Ad lib greetings*)
MAXWELL	They've never been in a BBC studio before.
BARKER	Well done.
MAXWELL	Well, if you'll excuse me, I must go and get in the box. (*Goes off on this*)
MRS AIGBURTH	He's going to get in a box?

BARKER I wish he were, then we could saw it in half. No, Mrs Aigburth, it's the Control Box—that aquarium in the wall there.

MR AIGBURTH Then what would all the others in there be doing, Mr Barker?

BARKER They might be doing almost anything, Mr Aigburth, although they're always there. And you've never been to a BBC show before?

MR AIGBURTH No, although I had a cousin that was in 'Have A Go' at West Warmsley in County Down. What was that question he asked her, Bernadette?

MRS AIGBURTH The longest river in Mesopotamia.

BARKER Good gracious! I didn't even know they had a river out there.

MR AIGBURTH She said the Mersey, quick as a flash, and our Wilf—oh, how he laughed, and the monks.

BARKER The monks?

MR AIGBURTH Aye, it was in a monastery. But we've always wanted to come into a studio and listen to a show.

BARKER Have you ever heard 'Just Fancy'?

MRS AIGBURTH I may have done. We hear so many, you know. We love our radio.

MR AIGBURTH Billy Cotton's put on a bit of weight, hasn't he?

BARKER That's Peter Akister.

MR AIGBURTH How do you do?

MRS AIGBURTH And these ladies and gentlemen are all the turns, are are they?

BARKER Well—yes—now you two sit here on these two chairs and you'll be able to hear and see everything.

MR AIGBURTH Mr Maxwell said you didn't want us to laugh or clap, is that right?

BARKER No, because there's no one else in the audience, you see.

MR AIGBURTH We don't mind havin' a go.

BARKER No, no. Really.

MRS AIGBURTH We nearly got turned out at Blackpool—laughing so much.

MR AIGBURTH Hylda Baker!

MRS AIGBURTH She knows, you know!

BOTH (*Scream with laughter. They finish*)

MRS AIGBURTH Oh, I'm sorry.

MR AIGBURTH Are we holding you up?

BARKER — Not at all. First of all we'd like you to listen to Peter Akister and his very talented group of experts playing Peter's arrangement of 'Alouette'.

MR AIGBURTH — That'll be grand. We love a good brass band.

ORCHESTRA — '*Alouette*'

The most famous creations of 'Just Fancy' were Eric Barker's and Deryck Guyler's two old men living out their retirement in a residential hotel. Here is a short extract from a typical script:

BARKER — In the late autumn of life, what more can you ask than a comfy chair by the long radiator under the window at the Cranbourn Towers Hotel?

ORCHESTRA — *Old Gentlemen Theme*

BARKER, GUYLER — (*Both asleep. Wheezing*)

GUYLER — (*waking*) Oh, my word. Oh, that was a lovely forty winks. (*Pause and chuckle*) What does he look like? Rupert!

BARKER — (*waking*) Oh—ha. I must have had forty winks, I think. Did you drop off?

GUYLER — Yes, I think I did. It was a good lunch today.

BARKER — Lunch? Yes, not bad at all. What's the time? Good gracious, it's seven o'clock.

GUYLER — That clock always says seven o'clock, doesn't it?

BARKER — Oh yes, so it does. Where's my hunter? It's gone!

GUYLER — What?

BARKER — My hunter! It's gone! I always kept it in this pocket, as you know . . .

GUYLER — Now, now. Let's be calm about it. Now, when did you last have it?

BARKER — Let me think. I went to the jewellers this morning. Of course. I left it there to have the chime repaired, didn't I? Oh dear. I must be getting old, I think.

GUYLER — (*chuckling*) The times you do that sort of thing lately. And you get so excited.

BARKER — Yes, I know.

GUYLER — That time you lost your glasses and they turned up—where did they turn up—er—

BARKER — Yes.

GUYLER — Down the back of the chair. (*Laughs*)

BARKER — It's not turned out much of a day after all has it?

The two old buffers were cunningly written and so beautifully characterised by Barker and Guyler that the listener was hardly aware that they were fiction. It takes real skill to write about trivialities in such a way as to make them sound meaningful and touching, and this Barker managed to do.

Radio in the 'fifties was not only the quickest way to national fame; it was also extremely well paid. The *initial* payments were never that high, but the number of repeats both at home and overseas rapidly brought the money up to high levels. A good character man working on two hit series could pick up around £700 a week. Peter Sellers, working simultaneously on 'Ray's A Laugh' and 'The Goon Show', and Harry Secombe, working on 'The Goon Show' and 'Educating Archie', must have been in that bracket, and with a successful series running at a minimum of twenty-six programmes a year and frequently more, a top-class radio 'voice man' could earn in the region of £20,000 per annum. Not that everybody reached those levels, of course, but many did. It's ironic to think that a senior BBC producer during the early 'fifties received a salary of about £700 a year. These figures may not be totally accurate, but even if you were pessimistically to halve the artist's fees and optimistically to double the producer's salary, the differential was still enormous. What's more, the producer was all-powerful, and it's small wonder that the occasional whiff of corruption was discernible in the corridors of Aeolian Hall. The unfortunate Roy Speer, the producer of 'Educating Archie', was accused of accepting bribes, was tried, and found innocent. Leslie Bridgmont, overhearing a slack-witted newspaperman suggest in a pub that Bridgmont himself was about to be arrested on a bribe charge, sued the reporter for slander and won an out-of-court settlement not unadjacent to his yearly salary.

At this time a famous American radio producer on a courtesy visit to Britain was entertained by the BBC and was staggered to hear of the poor payment producers received. He himself commanded a salary of over £20,000 a year. Ah, said the Voice of the BBC, we don't pay large salaries because we wish to attract people who are *interested* in radio. The American's response: 'For £20,000 a year, *anybody* would be interested in radio.'

8

Three Domestic Comedies

There is something about domestic comedy—stories of family or community life—that has always had immediate audience appeal. In the early days of radio, John Henry and Blossom acted out domestic tiffs and misadventures. Mabel Constanduros' creation, the Buggins Family, was immensely popular, and the Plum family was another pre-war favourite. Nothing much *happened* in domestic comedy, but the listeners could identify with the fictional family or group and were at once soothed and reassured. Here were people on the air behaving very much like the listeners themselves; moreover the situations were immediately recognisable, if exaggerated, and there's something comforting about the idea of other people feeling and *acting* in the same way as us.

Post-war radio produced many excellent domestic comedies; 'Meet The Huggetts', starring Jack Warner and Kathleen Harrison, 'Life With The Lyons', with Bebe Daniels, Ben Lyon and their children, Richard and Barbara, 'The Clitheroe Kid', starring Jimmy Clitheroe, and 'A Life Of Bliss' (with David Tomlinson starring in the first series and subsequently George Cole) being perhaps the best.

'A Life Of Bliss', which started its radio life in 1953, was not, strictly speaking, a domestic comedy in that it wasn't the story of a family; however, it was domestic in atmosphere and concerned the doings of a day-dreaming bachelor, David Bliss, over whom the question of whether or not he would ever marry hovered permanently. It was produced by Leslie Bridgmont and written by Godfrey Harrison in a style of easy, effortless charm. That's to say, it was easy on the ear and seemed effortless, but it was apparently torture for Harrison to write. The show professed not to contain 'jokes' but to be essentially 'comedy of character', that most elusive of phantoms in the Light Entertainment field. It is extremely difficult to be funny without recourse to actual jokes and gags, but Godfrey Harrison managed to do it week after week. The trouble was that he needed a crisis situation to make the adrenalin flow and give him the necessary inspiration. Edward Taylor, who is now a senior producer, was at the start of his radio career in 1955 when, to use his own words, he was put to study in Leslie Bridgmont's office. There he learnt his craft and, incidentally, saw 'A Life Of Bliss' at close quarters. He recalls that Godfrey was not just late with his scripts, nor very late but very *very* late: 'In fact, his scripts turned into the posthumous—most of them weren't finished until the audience had gone. This I can witness. The cast would turn up on Sunday afternoon at 3.30 at the Playhouse in the traditional manner for recording a show, but they'd only have five pages of script, because Godfrey wouldn't have started till the Saturday. He'd have tried Monday, Tuesday, Wednesday, Thursday and Friday but nothing would have come. The cast would read these five pages while the Sound Effects people upstairs tried to line up the sound effects for the five pages. Well, of course, five pages doesn't take long to rehearse so there'd be long, long gaps all through the afternoon and Eleanor Summerfield and George Cole would play "Battleships" and tremendous theatrical gossip would be going on.

'By the time the audience came in at half past seven, Godfrey, who was in one of the dressing-rooms, supported by a number of peculiar-coloured tablets and a devoted wife called Jo, would be lurching about like a juggernaut under the influence of the tablets, spewing out words, and Jo would be taking them down and duplicating them page for page. And by the time they started at half past seven they'd have got seven pages, so they'd do the warm-up in the traditional manner and Leslie Bridgmont would think, "This audience is in for a shock but let's not let them have it until the last possible moment. At least we'll have a good opening scene." So they had the warm-up and said, "Right, we'll go ahead with 'A Life Of Bliss' in ten seconds from now", and ten seconds passed and the announcer said, " 'A Life Of Bliss', etc. . . . Today George finds himself in trouble with his boss." Then you'd hear the scene of George with his boss and it would go along, lovely stuff, and get laughs. Then after about four and a half minutes the artists ran out of pages and they would just go and sit down, and Leslie would come on as if this had never happened before and say, "Ladies and gentlemen, we have a slight problem this week in that we haven't got a complete script, owing to technical reasons. The rest of it should be arriving shortly, so if you'd just like to relax, we'll try and entertain you." Then there would follow an hour of most extraordinary events. Percy Edwards was on the show playing Psyche, Bliss's dog, and he would come on stage with his whole gamut of bird and animal impressions. Most people enjoy five minutes of that kind of thing but after forty-five minutes, when he'd imitated the lesser Abyssinian warthog, people were beginning to stir uneasily in their seats. Then Pet Clark, who was in the show as the girlfriend, would come forward and sing unaccompanied. By this time you could hear the tipping of seats as most of the audience tiptoed out. Then, on a good night, perhaps Godfrey would really get steam under way and words would pour out of him and Jo would be taking them down, and perhaps by eleven o'clock they'd have a full script and then they'd record the rest of it with only three people and a dog left in the audience, and Leslie would dub in audience reaction during the week. There was one particular time when I'd left at midnight and Leslie told me the following day how the cast had stayed there till one a.m. and then finally said, in effect, they'd had enough and were not waiting any longer. And they all marched off down Northumberland Avenue with Godfrey in his shirt sleeves running after them shouting "Traitors! Traitors!" '

The BBC were not keen on the reports they were getting of this apparently eccentric method of production, but Leslie Bridgmont fought for the show and it ran for over one hundred programmes and was very popular. There was never a bad show and they were quite often outstandingly good, which, considering the circumstances, is little short of a miracle. Here is an extract from a typical 'A Life Of Bliss', recorded on January 29, 1956. The cast included George Cole as David Bliss; Barry K. Barnes as Mr Hood, Bliss's boss; and Eleanor Summerfield as Bliss's secretary, Jennifer. The announcer was Kenneth Kendall, better known nowadays as a noted newsreader.

KENDALL And now over to his office to start yet another episode in the life story of David Alexander Bliss.
GRAMS *Bliss Theme. Cross fade to:*
FX *Telephone. One short ring*
Receiver lifted
DAVID Yes, Jennifer?
JENNIFER (*distort*) 'His Nibs' is on the line.
DAVID His Nibs?
JENNIFER Mr Hood.

Michael Standing (BBC)

Ray Galton and Alan Simpson

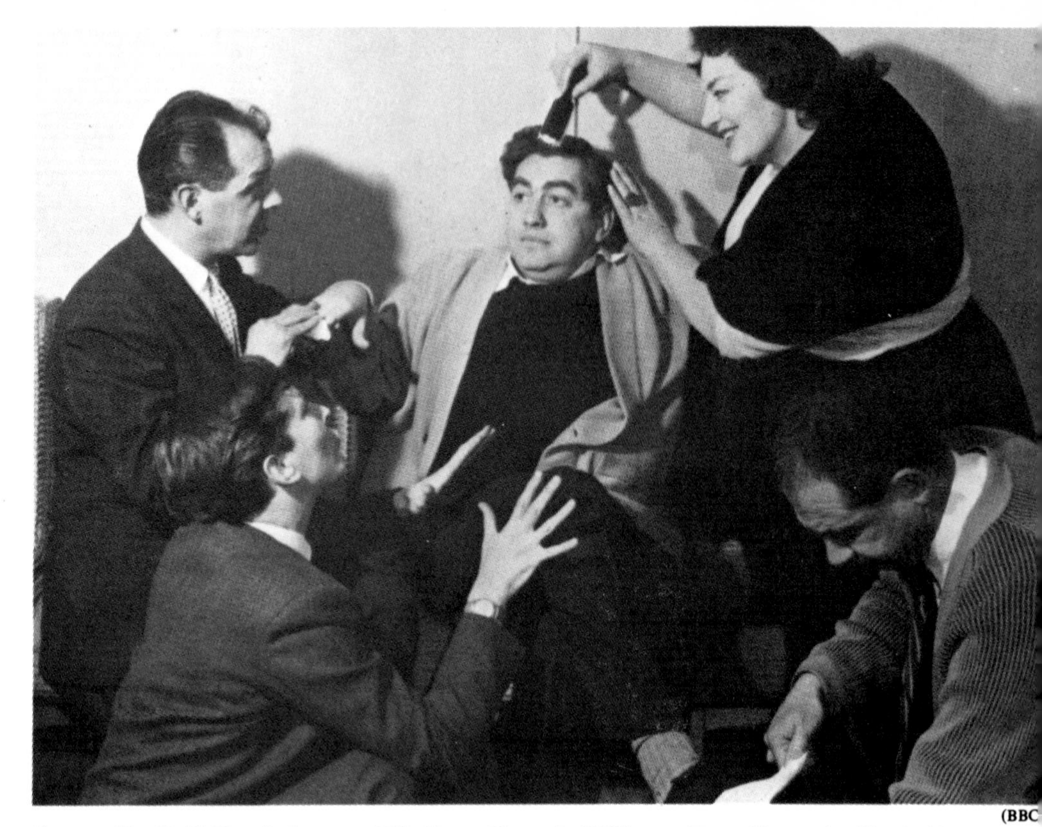

(BBC

'Hancock's Half Hour': l. to r., Bill Kerr, Kenneth Williams, Tony Hancock, Hattie Jacques and Sidney James, 1958

(Radio Times Hulton Picture Library)

Frankie Howerd, 1952

DAVID I say, steady on. Mr Hood's our General Manager. You mustn't say things like that. Would you put him through.

JENNIFER Yes, of course. Sorry. (*To Hood*) I'm putting you through.

HOOD (*distort*) Hello.

DAVID Oh hello, sir.

HOOD What's the matter with that girl of yours? She never seems to know who I am.

DAVID I think she does, sir. She must have known this time because she came through and told me so.

HOOD Told you what?

DAVID Mr Nibs was on the line.

HOOD Mr . . .?

DAVID Mr Hood was on the line. Sorry—I was thinking of somebody else. One of our clients.

HOOD (*not fooled for a second*) Now that's very odd. I've never heard of anyone called Nibs.

DAVID Perhaps it's just a 'pen' name. I mean . . .

HOOD I'm not in the mood for jokes, Bliss. While we're on the subject of your secretary, the letter you sent me yesterday contained no fewer than four mistakes.

DAVID Yes, I know, sir.

HOOD If you knew you should have made her do it again. Or did that never occur to you?

DAVID It did, actually.

HOOD But you still chose to send it?

DAVID Well, yes—it was the obvious choice. The other two were worse.

HOOD Oh, for heaven's sake, what made you engage the girl? Kindness of heart?

DAVID I suppose it was in a way. She's doing her best, sir.

HOOD She'll have to do better—for your sake. I know they say kindness costs nothing but it might cost you your job. Now then, listen carefully—Head Office is contemplating an investment in a firm called Lovelace and Co. You'd better make a note of the address.

DAVID Oh, right.

HOOD Lovelace and Co.—Hungerford Road.

DAVID (*making notes: to himself*) Lovelace and . . .

HOOD (*overlapping his 'notes'*) I want you to write to the Managing Director—T. S. Peregrine—and arrange a preliminary discussion.

DAVID (*to himself as he notes it down*) T. S. Preliminary . . .

HOOD (*sarcastically*) Peregrine Discussion!
DAVID (*oblivious*) Peregrine Dis . . .
HOOD Idiot! Suggest meeting at an early date. Have you got that?
DAVID Yes, I think so, sir. And if he agrees to the meeting, what then?
HOOD Give him a good lunch and sound his reactions.
DAVID (*noting down*) Good lunch. Note sounds.
HOOD Another joke?
DAVID Joke, sir? Oh—note *reactions*. Sorry.
HOOD You'll find him rather a difficult cuss to deal with.
DAVID You've dealt with him before?
HOOD 'Dealt with him' is right. He imagines he's all kinds of a businessman but he met his match for once.
DAVID Look, sir—wouldn't it be easier if *you* dealt with him this time? After all, you can speak to him in his own language.
HOOD Meaning what?
DAVID Talk the same language. You know—from one difficult cuss to another . . . one businessman to another.
HOOD So can you, surely?
DAVID Not so surely. So surely as you, I mean. I'm just beginning.
HOOD Yes, beginning with T. S. Peregrine. Give me a ring in the morning and I'll go into details. I haven't got the file by me at present. Better make a note of that too.
DAVID A note of what, sir?
HOOD Ring His Nibs in the morning!
DAVID (*oblivious*) Ring his . . . (*realising*) Gosh!

Kenneth Kendall also remembers the lateness of the scripts, but feels that though getting a page of dialogue out of Godfrey Harrison was like squeezing water out of a stone, he was nonetheless one of radio's cleverest writers of dialogue. Kendall's problem was that in addition to announcing 'A Life Of Bliss' at the BBC's Playhouse Studio in Northumberland Avenue, he had to read the news from the television studios at Alexandra Palace, some miles away. He would do the opening announcement, and then, if the script was clearly not forthcoming, the closing announcement too. He would then leap into a waiting car for a lightning dash to 'Ally Pally': 'If I'd waited till the thing was done right the way through I'd never have been in time for the news.'

Godfrey Harrison died suddenly in 1975, a loss to the writing profession. His death was a sad reminder of the tensions to which a talented comedy writer is prone.

'Life With The Lyons' was a fantasy projection of the real-life Lyons family—Bebe and Ben, Barbara and Richard—plus neighbours, the 'daily', and whoever else was needed to convey the story of a mildly eccentric American family deep in the heart of suburbia, whose biggest problem seemed to arise when the boss came to dinner. The writers were Bob Block, Ronnie Hanbury and Bebe Daniels herself. The writing was as disciplined as Godfrey Harrison's was undisciplined, but the end product was much the same in terms of skill, humour and popularity. The differences lay in the fact that 'Life With The Lyons' did not scorn jokes, and its tempo was much faster. Ben Lyon was cast as the fall-guy imposed upon by the rest of the family, the neighbours and Aggie the maid (played by Molly Weir). Tom Ronald was the producer; the following extract comes from a show called 'Three Blind Dates', first transmitted on May 12, 1954:

DANIELS	(*coming on*) Richard, why did you drag those old boots into the living-room?
RICHARD	Because I want to polish them. Barbara and I are going riding with Mary and Derek.
DANIELS	Well, that's nice.
ROBIN (RICHARD BELLAERS)	Who's lending you the horses?
RICHARD	Violet Hemmingway's going to let me have hers.
ROBIN	You mean the four of you are going to ride one horse?
BARBARA	Of course not, silly. Derek's getting the other three from the Marble Arch stables.
LYON	Well, be careful. Some of those animals can be pretty wild.
DANIELS	Your father's right. When I was a little girl I was thrown off a horse and knocked senseless.
LYON	(*chuckles*) And you can see how long it's lasted.
DANIELS	Well, it's only been—Ben!
ROBIN	Mommie, I didn't know you could ride.
DANIELS	Oh yes, I used to own my own horse, and what wonderful times I had galloping across the prairie.
ROBIN	Did you ever take a five foot jump?
DANIELS	No dear, my legs were too short.
BARBARA	Mother, he means did your *horse* ever take a *fence*?
DANIELS	Oh no, he was very good natured.
LYON	Give up, kids. If you want to know anything about horses, ask me. I used to do a lot of riding.

BARBARA I'll bet you looked wonderful on a horse, Daddy.

LYON I'd be too modest to say that myself, but you're quite right.

RICHARD What kind of a saddle did you use Pop, English or Western?

LYON Neither.

RICHARD You mean you rode side-saddle?

LYON Don't be ridiculous.

AGGIE (*coming on*) Oh Mr. Lyon, you're wanted on the telephone.

LYON (*going off*) Thanks, Aggie. It's probably my office.

FX *Door closes*

ROBIN Aggie, did you know Barbara and Richard are going riding?

AGGIE No, I didn't. Where are you going, Master Richard?

RICHARD Well, I'm not particular, but Barbara insists on a row along Rotten Ride.

AGGIE (*chuckles*) Ach, you mean Rotten Row, not Rotten Ride.

RICHARD I guess you haven't seen Barbara on a horse.

LYON (*coming on*) Oh Bebe, that was Harry Cannell, the Chairman of our Company, on the phone. He just arrived from New York and he wants us all to join his family and go on a picnic.

ROBIN Oh boy, I'll be able to dig for ants.

AGGIE You won't have to dig for them. They always know where a picnic is.

BARBARA When's the picnic going to be, Daddy?

LYON Saturday.

BARBARA Oh, no.

RICHARD Pop, you can't do this to us. That's the day we're going riding with Mary and Derek.

LYON I thought that was Sunday.

DANIELS Can't you change it, Barbara?

BARBARA (*dramatically*) Change a date with the boy I love? Mother, put yourself in my shoes.

DANIELS No dear, the last time I did that I broke three toes.

LYON Look kids, it's not often that I ask you to give up anything for me, but this picnic is important. After all, Mr. Cannell is my boss.

RICHARD But why do we have to go?

LYON Because Mr. Cannell wants you to meet his children.

BARBARA	How old are they?
LYON	I didn't ask him, but I imagine the girl and the older boy are around your age and the little boy around Robin's age.
BARBARA	(*shocked*) You mean you don't even know what they look like?
LYON	I don't care what they look like. He's my boss.
RICHARD	We're sorry, Pop, but we can't go.
BARBARA	Yes, we're really sorry to let you down.
LYON	(*martyr*) Oh, you don't have to feel sorry for me. I'm only the person who sweats and slaves to give you every comfort—I don't expect any gratitude. I don't even expect you to stay here and listen to the troubles of a tired father.
RICHARD	(*going off*) Gee, thanks.
LYON	(*shouts*) Richard, you come back here.

'The Clitheroe Kid' originated in Manchester and ran with great success from 1957 until the death of Jimmy Clitheroe in the early 'seventies. Clitheroe was a diminutive comedian with a large following in the north of England. On radio his appeal was universal, and I can remember when Marty Feldman and I were in the throes of 'Round The Horne'—and, to be honest, rather pleased with ourselves—we were brought up abruptly by the Head of Light Programme who suggested we should try to make our programme as popular as 'The Clitheroe Kid'.

The programme was written by James Casey and Frank Roscoe, and produced by James Casey. Casey is the son of the legendary comedian, Jimmy James, and worked in his father's act before joining the BBC as a producer. He invented the Kid for a series called 'Over The Garden Wall' that he was writing for the splendid north-country comedian, Norman Evans, who played 'dame rôles'. But by chance, the first appearance of the character was in a programme called 'The Mayor's Parlour', written by Ronnie Taylor and starring Jimmy James. From there, Jimmy Clitheroe became the chief character in a series called 'Call Boy' about backstage life in a northern music hall, with James Casey playing the stage manager. Eventually, on May 5, 1958, 'The Clitheroe Kid' was born. The series ran for fourteen years in sixteen series and clocked up 279 programmes—only thirty-one fewer than 'ITMA'. The show drew an audience of ten-and-a-half million listeners a week at its peak, and ended in August 1972. Before it could resume, Jimmy Clitheroe had died at the age of fifty-seven.

James Casey's philosophy was simple: his scripts would contain 'anything that could happen and everything that could be said by a bright boy'. Any joke that couldn't pass that stringent test was eliminated. That, I suppose, was what made 'The Clitheroe Kid' a success: audiences can smell authenticity and beam in on it like a homing pigeon. 'The Clitheroe Kid' was firmly domestic, and the episodes revolved around the affairs of a fictitious but believable north-country working-class family. Jimmy Clitheroe was the lynchpin of the whole enterprise and it was his view of life that the show embodied. Wistful and cheeky by turns, Clitheroe presented his audience with an identifiable youngster growing up in urban working-class England in the 'fifties, 'sixties and 'seventies. It was the last of the purely domestic radio comedies and was much missed when it ended.

Here is an extract from 'The Clitheroe Kid', first broadcast on February 2, 1959. The cast included Peter Sinclair, Leonard Williams, Patricia Burke, Diana Day, Peter Goodwright, Fred Fairclough, Karal Gardner, and, of course, Jimmy Clitheroe:

GRAMS *Opening theme*

ANNOUNCER (*Over music*) We present Jimmy Clitheroe as The Clitheroe Kid, with Peter Sinclair as Grandfather, Patricia Burke as Mother, Diana Day as Susan, and Leonard Williams as Theodore Craythorpe, in . . .

CLITHEROE 'A Kid With A Problem.' (*With piano, singing few bars of rock or skiffle tune*)

FX *Door opens*

SUSAN (*coming on quickly*) Jimmy. Jimmy. Stop that.

CLITHEROE (*stops singing and piano stops with him*) Oh, get out. Go—girl—go. (*With piano, starts singing again*)

SUSAN Will you stop that noise!

CLITHEROE (*stops singing and piano stops playing—both suddenly*) Noise? That's skiffle. You're a square.

SUSAN *Me*? A square? Listen, you little Mudlark—*that's* had it. It's all cha-cha now.

CLITHEROE It's *what*?

SUSAN Cha-cha.

CLITHEROE That's a nasty cough you've got there.

SUSAN Oh, aren't you a clever little boy.

CLITHEROE Yes. I'm all there with my cough drops. Shut the door on your way out. (*With piano sings again*)

SUSAN Don't start again.

CLITHEROE (*stops with piano*)

SUSAN I want you out of here. Billy's coming round.

CLITHEROE What, again? Hasn't he got a home of his own?

SUSAN When Billy comes, I want this room looking tidy.

CLITHEROE Well, hide your face under the cushion.

SUSAN I'm not standing for any more of your cheek . . .

FX *Door opens*

SUSAN Get out of here or I'll box your ears, you little horror.

MOTHER (*coming on*) Susan, what's the matter with you?

CLITHEROE Yes. What's the matter, Susan? Has something upset you?

MOTHER All right, Mister Innocent. Look, Susan, I know he annoys you, but there's no need to shout. The neighbours will think you've gone mad.

CLITHEROE Yes. They might send for the vet.

SUSAN You cheeky monkey.

CLITHEROE You monkey's sister.

MOTHER Behave yourselves—both of you. I'm surprised at you, Susan, a girl of your age.

CLITHEROE So am I . . .

MOTHER You keep quiet.

SUSAN I'm sorry, mother, but he just gets my goat.

CLITHEROE Now we're back to Billy again.

MOTHER Jimmy! That's enough.

SUSAN There you are, mother. *Now* will you speak to him?

MOTHER I'm speaking to *both* of you. I'm fed up with hearing you two arguing. It's got to stop.

SUSAN It wouldn't have started if he'd come out of here when I asked him.

MOTHER Look, Susan, Jimmy's as much right in here as you have.

CLITHEROE Yes.

MOTHER *He* lives here as well, you know.

CLITHEROE That's right. *You* tell her, mam.

MOTHER *You* keep quiet.

CLITHEROE I wish you'd make your mind up whose *side* you're on.

MOTHER I'm not on anybody's side.

SUSAN Very well, mother. May I tidy the room up then for Billy?

MOTHER Yes. Jimmy you can play the piano . . .

CLITHEROE Good.

MOTHER After you've done your homework.

CLITHEROE Oh heck.

MOTHER Come on, in the other room . . .

FX	*Door opens*
CLITHEROE	Oh mam, who cares about homework?
FX	*Door shuts*
MOTHER	*We* care. Grandad and I want to see you in the first three at the end of this term.
CLITHEROE	Why? Has grandad backed me each way?

Domestic comedy on radio has a long and honourable history, but it's doubtful whether we'll ever have another Huggett or Lyons or Clitheroe family. They were fun and they served their purpose well, helping people forget their own trials and tribulations for half an hour or so as they listened to episodes in the lives of radio's 'ordinary families'. The reason for the decline and, in fact, the virtual disappearance of domestic comedy on radio is simply a matter of cost. It is much more expensive to buy a script and hire good actors than to mount a quiz like 'Twenty Questions', and with the change in listening patterns that have occurred in the last few years, it just doesn't make economic sense to contemplate a brand new radio domestic comedy series. Nowadays radio buys what it needs from television (for example, 'Dad's Army' and 'Steptoe And Son'), knowing that it's acquiring a ready-made success. Besides, writers and performers tend to prefer television, where their income and audience will be about ten times what they can reasonably expect from radio.*

*That was written in 1975. Today, in 1981, the thinking is somewhat different and original situation comedies are welcomed by BBC radio. One such is 'Never Too Late' starring Thora Hird, and very funny it is, too.

9

Ray & Alan & Tony & Beryl

If domestic comedy was the infantry of radio Light Entertainment, then 'Hancock's Half Hour' was the brigade of guards. Tony Hancock had come to prominence in radio in the post-war years first as a solo comedian, then as one of Archie Andrew's tutors, and then—most impressively—in his own series, 'Hancock's Half Hour'. As Hugh Greene says in *The Passing of The Third Floor Front*: 'By 1960 broadcasting was no longer an occupation for gentlemen'. Hancock—the *fictional* Hancock, that is—was a slob with delusions of grandeur but with feet of clay that stretched up to his hips. The real Hancock was a sensitive genius who found the world so unpleasing that he left it abruptly from a drug overdose in 1968. By then his star had waned, and although it in no way lessens the tragedy of his death, Tony Hancock's career was, to all intents and purposes, over when he died.

A man of passionate aspirations, Hancock wished to excel at everything. At the height of his career he discarded first his supporting players—Bill Kerr, Kenneth Williams and Sid James—and then his writers—Ray Galton and Alan Simpson—and many people felt that he'd developed a Messianic complex and was unwilling to share the spotlight with anyone else. On reflection, I don't think this was so. It is my belief Hancock felt secretly ashamed of not being able to do everything, and wanted to prove to himself even more than to the outside world that he could stand alone and triumph. The film that he wrote with Philip Oakes, *The Punch And Judy Man*, expounds this idea and though it wasn't a success in the cinema, it works remarkably well on television, where it's been shown on more than one occasion. Hancock was a 'small screen' man, the delicacy and detail in his work being best seen and heard in close up. He was Hamlet rather than Henry V. His tragedy was that he wanted to be both, and actually talked at great length of doing Shakespeare in repertory with Richard Burton and Wilfrid Lawson, two actors he admired greatly. His dream was a production of *King Lear* in which he was to play Fool to Burton's Lear, and Lear to Lawson's Fool, then reverse the process and be Fool to Lawson's Lear, and Lear to Burton's Fool—an extraordinary idea which might well have been a triumph but which was never put to the test.

There is no doubt that Hancock's best material was written by Ray Galton and Alan Simpson. The three of them together created some of the most thrilling comedy ever to be heard on radio or seen on television. The early 'Hancock's Half Hours' were a revelation of economy and insight, a mixture of fantasy and the mundane that put the programme right at the top of the heap.

Ray Galton and Alan Simpson first met in a TB sanatorium when they were both in their teens. They wrote sketches for the hospital's own radio station and when they came out, decided to try their hand at selling comedy scripts to the BBC. They sent their first script to Gale Pedrick, then the Variety Department's script editor. He, in turn, put them in touch with Roy Speer who was producing a series called 'Happy Go Lucky', starring Derek Roy, and thus it was that they started selling gags to Derek for five shillings a time. Alan Simpson remembers: 'We used to pick a subject—for instance, fat girls, or thin girls, or "my wife", and write as many jokes as we could think of on the subject. We'd then take Derek about three or four pages of these one-liners and he'd tick them or cross them out and give the resulting sheet to Johnny Vyvyan, his secretary, who'd then count up the ticks and pay us accordingly, five bob a tick.'

Here's a typical Derek Roy routine from 'Happy Go Lucky', transmitted on September 20, 1951. It's conceivable that it includes some Galton and Simpson five-shilling specials, though frankly I doubt it; but at least it gives the flavour of the show to which they were asked to contribute.

ROY What a week I've had! I've been over to the USA to see the big fight. No, not the one you're thinking of. I went to see the signing of the Japanese Peace Treaty. But I did get a seat at the big fight. Only it was so far from the ring that I couldn't even pick it up on television. In fact, that seat was so high in the air,

> I was the only man in my row not holding a harp. And to have a nose bleed before the fight. After the fight I borrowed my friend's car to drive around and look for rooms. That car was so new that instead of seat covers, it had nappies. I think that at some time it must have been loaned to Gypsy Rose Lee—it was stripped of its gears. While driving along the Hudson River I suddenly heard a man shouting, 'Help, I'm drowning!' I shouted, 'What's your name and where do you live?' He shouted back, 'My name's Grady and I live at 6 East 49th Street.' So I rushed over to 6 East 49th Street; I asked his landlady if a Mr. Grady lived there. 'Sure he did,' she said. So I told her he had drowned and could I have his room. She said, 'Sorry honey, but it's let to the guy who pushed him!'

There were several writers on the 'Happy Go Lucky' show. A young Australian named Ralph Peterson wrote a regular feature about a boy scout troop called Eager Beavers, which featured the young Tony Hancock, Peter Butterworth, and Graham Stark. Other material was contributed by John Law and Bill Craig, who received the princely sum of £10 per programme for their efforts. Law and Craig were later to be associated with many successful television shows. Craig, the more serious of the two, wrote episodes of such drama series as 'Callan', and dramatised the novel *Sunset Song*, and Law helped to create Michael Bentine's television success, 'It's A Square World', when script-editor to the Variety Department of BBC Television. However, in the early 'fifties, Law and Craig were working for the *Scottish Daily Express* in Glasgow, and because they often contributed to a feature on local theatres, were frequently backstage at the Glasgow Empire. There they met and wrote for many comedians who were on their way to the glories of 'Variety Bandbox' in London.

Produced by Joy Russell-Smith, 'Variety Bandbox' was the Sunday night Variety show. It consisted of a series of acts linked by BBC compère Philip Slessor, and was designed to present to the public the more avant garde and 'with it' comedians and singers of the day. In contrast there was 'Music Hall' which was broadcast on Saturdays and which had a more traditional flavour, featuring such performers as Elsie and Doris Waters, Vic Oliver, and Robb Wilton. 'Variety Bandbox' was, in Con Mahoney's phrase, 'the show in which the Stars of Tomorrow emerged'. Those stars included Derek Roy, Bill Kerr (whose gloomy predictions about the imminent collapse of the theatre—'I've only got four minutes', and the glorification of his Australian birthplace, Wagga Wagga, made him instantly popular), Peter Sellers and

Miriam Karlin (in a series of sketches, 'Bless 'em Hall', written by Jimmy Grafton), the young Max Bygraves, and Frankie Howerd (who made his debut in 'Variety Bandbox' in the autumn of 1946 and quickly rocketed to fame on the strength of Eric Sykes' scripts, a series of devastating catchphrases such as 'chilly', 'let's get myself comfy', 'what a funny woman', and 'I was amazed', and a comic style which was unlike anything ever heard on the air up to that time).

By 1951 Derek Roy had left 'Variety Bandbox' and been given his own show, 'Happy Go Lucky'. When the producer, Roy Speer, went sick, he was replaced by the young Dennis Main Wilson, who made rapid and sweeping changes, and as a result Ray Galton and Alan Simpson were elevated to being the show's principal writers. After 'Happy Go Lucky', they spent the next months writing single acts for solo comedians—Dick Emery, Peter Butterworth, Bill Kerr and, most importantly for their future career, Tony Hancock. Not long after, the boys found themselves writing 'Forces All Star Bill', yet another act-and-sketch show, which starred Tony Hancock. The following extract is from the show transmitted on January 6, 1953. The cast included Tony Hancock, Joan Heal, Graham Stark, Ted Ray, Josef Locke, Betty Driver, and the trumpet virtuoso, Kenny Baker:

HANCOCK Well, Edward, it's happened. After twenty-eight years of bachelorhood, brisk walks, P.T. and cold showers, Hancock the impervious has had his armour pierced by a member of the opposite mob.

RAY Tony, you don't mean a woman?

HANCOCK Can you think of anything more opposite?

RAY Why, Tony, that's wonderful. Does she reciprocate?

HANCOCK (*shocked*) Ted, please, I've only just met her.

RAY Tony, don't look now but your brain just stuck a white flag out the top of your head. Who is this girl, anyway?

HANCOCK My fiancée, Joan Heal.

RAY Joan Heal! She's a lovely piece of crackling. Your *first* girl friend? Shouldn't you have got something for a *beginner*? Where did you meet her?

HANCOCK Last week, at Broadcasting House. She was waiting for one lift and I was waiting for the other. Then she opened her gates, stepped in and went up, and I opened my gates, stepped in, and . . .

RAY You went up.

HANCOCK No, I went down—the lift wasn't there. And as I was lying there, Ted, my mind began to wander.

RAY You can't blame it, there's a lot of space in there.

HANCOCK (*ignores him*) I started thinking to myself 'Hancock, my boy, this girl is just your type.'

RAY How do you mean?

HANCOCK She was breathing.

RAY With you standing next to her that took a lot of courage. By the way, where is Joan?

HANCOCK Well, I haven't read on, but I believe she's on the next page. You see, she's with us on the programme tonight.

RAY (*excited*) Joan Heal—here on the programme? Oh, that's wonderful, wonderful! Quick, where's the mirror? Just see if I've got my eyelashes on straight. Oh Ray, you brute you . . . (*growls*) How is it you've got so much?

HANCOCK Nobody else wanted it. Anyway, Ray, it's no use sprucing up. It won't do you any good. This bint is Hancock-crazy. She hasn't got eyes for anybody else. She's completely under old Hancock's spell. See how her minces light up as soon as she sees me. Oh—she *loves* me!

FX *Door open*

HEAL (*delightedly*) Why, Teddy—*darling*.

RAY Joan Heal.

(*Applause*)

(*Ted and Joan start necking, ecstatic moans, sighs, kisses etc.*)

HANCOCK (*pause, embarrassed laugh*) Oh—er—Ted, I'd like you to meet my girl friend, Joan Heal.

RAY }
HEAL } (*continue necking*)

HANCOCK (*embarrassed laugh*) I said I'd like you to meet my girl friend . . . I . . . (*embarrassed laugh*)

RAY }
HEAL } (*continue necking*)

HANCOCK (*laugh*) Joan, this is Ted . . . I . . . (*laugh*) Look everyone, Hancock's turning cartwheels! (*Laughs*) Balancing on his little finger, look . . . (*Laughs. Pulls referee's whistle out and gives loud blast on it*)

RAY }
HEAL } (*stop abruptly*)

HANCOCK That's better. Just for that I won't introduce you, so there.

HEAL Oh don't be like that, Chubby Chops. Why, Ted and I don't mean a thing to each other. (*Sexy*) Do we, Teddy darling?

RAY (*sexy*) Why, of course we don't, Joan my sweet.

RAY HEAL	(*necking as before*)
HANCOCK	(*blows another blast on whistle*) Cease! What do you think you're doing, Ray? You're giving me bint a bashing, aren't you?
HEAL	But Tony, darling . . .
HANCOCK	(*hurt*) No, no, don't apologise, the damage has been done. Old Hancock's finished.
RAY	This is no time to start reading your press cuttings.
HEAL	Now look, Tony, my pet . . .
HANCOCK	Nothing you say will alter things. (*Breath*) I release you from your obligation to me. (*Breath*) Everything is over between us.
HEAL	What about the engagement ring?
HANCOCK	Just let me get it off my finger and you can have it back. So farewell, farewell . . . (*going off*) I'm going home to mother.
RAY	(*calls*) Give my regards to the girl in the next cell.
FX	*Door slam*

Out of their collaboration on this Galton, Simpson and Hancock developed the idea of a situation comedy show, 'non-domestic with no jokes and no funny voices, just relying on caricature and situation humour'. As Ray Galton says, 'Jokes are all very well, but you don't really give any of yourself to the writing of them.' Their dream was a show without breaks, guest singers, or catchphrases, something that hadn't been done before. The result was, of course, 'Hancock's Half Hour', which started in 1954, and was produced by Dennis Main Wilson. The cast was Tony Hancock, Moira Lister, Bill Kerr, Sidney James, and Kenneth Williams, of whom Ray Galton says, 'After the first week with Kenneth in the show, bang went our ideas of no funny voices and no catchphrases.' In addition to the regular cast (Andrée Melly subsequently replaced Moira Lister and later still Hattie Jacques joined the team), the writers contributed odd voices.

Alan Simpson enjoyed these moments of performance more than Ray Galton, and created a regular character who always agreed with Tony. He would usually appear as a judge or a man in the pub or the next-door neighbour, and punctuate Tony's long and rambling monologues with placid agreement; for example:

HANCOCK	Of course, this isn't the first time I've been in court, you know.
SIMPSON	I didn't think it was.

HANCOCK Oh, it's you. I haven't seen you for weeks. Where have you been?

SIMPSON On holiday.

HANCOCK You haven't got much of a tan, have you? You should have taken your wig off. Well, as I was saying, I've been here before. I was nicked for collecting betting slips in Hyde Park. Of course, I denied it. I told 'em I was the keeper and I'd lost me stick with the spike on the end. Anyway, they brought me in. There was the judge sitting in the box with the crest on. Like a Command Performance. I was second bookie, on after the drunks. Anyway, the judge started.

SIMPSON Who was he?

HANCOCK You know him. Little bloke. Looks like a cocker spaniel with a wooden hammer.

SIMPSON Oh, him.

HANCOCK Yes, that's right. Easter Humphreys.

SIMPSON Christmas.

HANCOCK Eh?

SIMPSON Christmas.

HANCOCK Oh. Happy New Year.

SIMPSON Thank you.

HANCOCK Good health. Anyway, he was in a bad mood that morning.

SIMPSON Was he?

HANCOCK Can you imagine Gilbert Harding with an ulcer?

SIMPSON Yes.

HANCOCK That was *him*. Well, he heard the evidence and he glowered. I thought, Hello, he's going to make an example of me. He said, 'Were you or were you not'—'cos they talk like that you know—he said, 'Were you or were you not collecting bets for next Saturday's Derby?' I said, 'Yes I was.' Well, that settled it. A mean look came over his face, sort of enjoying it he was, triumphant. He picked up his pen, dipped it in the ink . . . and do you know what he gave me?

SIMPSON What?

HANCOCK Three tanner up-and-down cross doubles any to come one and six on the Lincoln.

SIMPSON Well, well.

HANCOCK That's not the end of it.

SIMPSON No?

HANCOCK No. They all lost.

SIMPSON Really?

HANCOCK Yes. I came out last week.

A very funny interlude in the shows. More vivid and memorable was Kenneth Williams with his 'snide' character and his anguished cry of ''Ere, stop messing about!' Much as Galton and Simpson disliked catchphrases, Kenneth Williams, who had been spotted by Dennis Main Wilson playing the Dauphin in Shaw's play, *St. Joan*, brought a new and vigorous dimension to radio character acting and added a spark of eccentricity to the more phlegmatic Hancock and Co.

Galton and Simpson's greatest contribution to radio comedy was their knack of reproducing mundane conversation and lifting it to the level of high art. Whereas Muir and Norden's skill lay in the elegant contrivances of their parody, Simpson and Galton's trump card was the seemingly spontaneous stream of consciousness decorated by their extraordinary inventiveness. They wrote the character—Hancock interpreted it. It was chamber music of the mind. The excerpt from 'Hancock's Half Hour' which follows was transmitted on February 15, 1955. The cast included Tony Hancock, Moira Lister, Bill Kerr, Sidney James, and Kenneth Williams:

FX *Crowd*

HANCOCK (*On flick. Barker*) Gather round, gather round. My friends, winter is upon us. And with winter come coughs, colds, sneezes and flu. I know, I've had the lot. You couldn't buy this stuff in Harley Street for ten guineas. (*Sidney joins in—slightly off mike*) Now, I'm not asking ten guineas, I'm not asking five guineas, I'm not asking one guinea. I'm not even asking for half a bar. Here you are. One and nine a bottle. This cough mixture I'm offering is unobtainable anywhere else in England. (*Tails off*) Because my friends . . .

JAMES (*by himself*) . . . one of the vital ingredients in this potion is supplied direct to me by an extinct tribe of natives in the South American jungle. And here it is. Doctor Sidney James's Rejuvenator. This isn't just a cough cure, it is an elixir of life.

HANCOCK Hello, somebody's working me act. Oi—you!

JAMES Excuse me, my friends, don't go away. (*On mike*) What do you want, Fatty?

HANCOCK What do I want, Fatty? Clear off! It's bad enough working my pitch, but you've pinched me patter as well. Give you me top hat and you've got the lot.

JAMES Don't be stupid. I've been working the cough mixture game for twenty years—so hoppit.

HANCOCK No. I was here first.

JAMES I've had this pitch for seventeen years. Scarper! As I was saying, my friends—

HANCOCK You can't do this. Police! No, better not. Look, sir, Doctor James—what about me? I can't give up me business stock. I've got four thousand bottles of cough mixture in my suitcases.

JAMES Put some flour in it, flog it as hair cream. (*Barker*) My friends! This is the only genuine cough mixture on the market.

HANCOCK (*Barker*) I challenge that statement.

JAMES Made from a recipe given to me by an old Indian fakir for saving his life.

HANCOCK Passed on to me by a Tibetan Lama on his deathbed.

JAMES Sold to all the crowned heads of Europe.

HANCOCK By appointment to Anna Neagle.

JAMES James's Rejuvenator.

HANCOCK Hancock's Tonic.

JAMES One and nine a bottle.

HANCOCK One and threepence.

JAMES Bob a bottle.

HANCOCK Ninepence.

JAMES Three for one and six.

HANCOCK Just a minute, let's work that out . . . threes into eighteen . . . fivepence ha'penny a bottle.

JAMES Fivepence.

HANCOCK Fourpence.

JAMES Nine for one and fourpence ha'penny.

HANCOCK Hold on. Nine for one and . . . that's . . . see . . . carry . . . minus two . . . that's . . . he's trying to blind you with figures. (*Sotto*) I'll take a chance. Threepence ha'penny.

JAMES Threepence.

HANCOCK Tuppence and fourpence on the bottle!

FX *Crowd gasps. Clamours*

WILLIAMS / GALTON / SIMPSON I'll have one. Three over here. Give us a dozen. Six dozen here. Four gross. Bring the car round, Charlie.

HANCOCK Bighead, now look what you've done—I'm ruined. Tuppence and fourpence on the . . . dozey. . . . (*Kindly*) I'm sorry, ladies and gentlemen. Ha ha. My partner made a slight error. He didn't really mean tuppence and fourpence on the . . .

FX *Ominous crowd*

HANCOCK Well, after all, you can't expect us to give money away, can you. Ha ha ha ha. Cor dear.

WILLIAMS He said fourpence back on the bottle.

FX *Angry crowd*

HANCOCK Friends—*dear* friends—I'd like to but I have to live too, you know.

WILLIAMS You won't if you don't give us the money.

HANCOCK But friends . . . I can't do it . . . no . . . put me bottle down. No—

FX *Angry crowd. Bottles being thrown and smashed*

HANCOCK (*on flick*) Stop throwing me stock about. Ow! Me eye! Friends, please! Help!

FX *Police whistles*

JAMES Scarper—the rozzers!

HANCOCK Up the alley, boys.

OMNES (*general confusion*)

GRAMS '*Hancock rumbled*'

Segue

Slight echo as before

HANCOCK }
KERR } (*laughing*)

KERR Oh dear, it's funny when you look back on it. All your bottles and all Sid's bottles—smashed.

HANCOCK Yes—the street was six inches deep in cough mixture. And then the drains blew up.

LISTER What *caused* that?

HANCOCK 'Hancock's Tonic meets James's Rejuvenator'.

KERR Happy days.

There were one hundred and one episodes of 'Hancock's Half Hour' on radio and fifty-nine television shows, the two overlapping. Here's a moment from one of the later radio show scripts:

JAMES Hello, Hancock. I haven't seen you for days. How's the tortoise I sold you?

HANCOCK It hasn't moved since I put it in the garden.

JAMES Hasn't moved?

HANCOCK Not a step. I haven't even seen it yet. I haven't seen its head or its legs. I picked it up and shook it this morning, there's nothing in there.

JAMES Of course there's something in there.

HANCOCK I don't care about *something* in there, is there a tortoise in there?

JAMES Well, there should be.

HANCOCK Well, I don't think there is. I looked in through the front and I could see right out through his leg holes.

JAMES Well, perhaps he was curled up.

HANCOCK They don't curl up.

JAMES Well, give him a chance, he's only a baby, he's still growing, he hasn't filled the shell up yet.

HANCOCK The shell grows with them. There's nothing in there. I've been poking sticks in through every hole and there's nothing in there.

JAMES Oh well, if you've been doing that, that explains it. He must have got a bit niggly. He probably lifted his shell up and ran for it.

HANCOCK Well, I'm not satisfied, I want my money back.

JAMES No, I'm sorry. I never return money, you ought to know that.

HANCOCK Well, give me another one, then. And no cheating. I want one with a head and four legs poking out.

JAMES You're too late, mate, I'm not in the tortoise trade any more. They live too long. There's no replacement trade worth talking about.

KERR Why don't you sell old ones?

HANCOCK Why don't you sell old ones? What a poltroon this man is. How can you tell how old a tortoise is?

KERR You count the rings on its back.

HANCOCK That's a tree.

KERR Oh. You count its teeth?

HANCOCK That's horses.

KERR Well, you can't be right all the time.

At the end of their relationship, Hancock, seeking new fields to conquer, went to commercial television. Galton and Simpson shrugged and went on writing what they'd always written; comedy of character and observation, most notably, of course, 'Steptoe And Son'. They became actually more successful than in the 'Hancock's Half Hour' days, but sadly Hancock never recaptured his public after he'd shed one by one the people who had helped to make him a star.

Between series of 'Hancock's Half Hour', Simpson and Galton wrote a series for Frankie Howerd called, unsurprisingly, 'The Frankie Howerd Show'. It was a forty-five minute Variety package and the list of guest stars—including Richard Burton, Claire Bloom, Robert Newton, Richard Attenborough, Donald Wolfit and many more—is quite formidable. Frankie Howerd was at the top, and like Morecambe and Wise on television in the 'seventies, he was able to attract the leading straight actors of the day, who enjoyed letting their hair down for once in a while with the country's leading clown.

Galton, Simpson and Howerd had come together when the new script-writer/comedian consortium, Associated London Scripts, was launched. This company was the idea of Spike Milligan and Eric Sykes who, like Ted Kavanagh before them, had wanted to create a writers' collective. Milligan, Sykes, Galton and Simpson set up shop in rooms over a greengrocer's shop in Shepherd's Bush, and engaged a girl called Beryl Vertue as their typist. They wanted to call the company Associated British Scripts but were told by the authorities who govern such things that they weren't big enough, so they compromised with Associated London Scripts. Beryl Vertue, who is today one of Britain's leading film producers and ace seller of British television shows to the USA, remembers the early days and the aspirations of the four writers: 'I don't think any of them had the idea of forming a business to make money, they just wanted to help other writers'. The first one to arrive was Johnny Speight, now world-famous for 'Till Death Us Do Part', but at that time an insurance salesman with no experience of writing. Then came Terry Nation (the man who invented the Daleks) and Dick Barry. Ray Galton remembers them arriving together 'from the Welsh valleys, all hairy tweeds and walking sticks'. Nation and Barry had approached the BBC direct and were recommended to ALS. Beryl Vertue became the agent for all these people, 'not because I was brilliant but because I was the only one in the building who wasn't a writer'. News of the ALS set-up soon went round the business and many more writers joined the group—Eric Merriman and Lew Schwarz ('Great Scott, It's Maynard' and 'The Show Band Show'), Brad Ashton and Dick Vosburgh (who appeared on most writing credits in the 'fifties and 'sixties, writing sketches to order for anyone who wanted them), John Antrobus (author of '*Crete and Sergeant Pepper*' and other plays), and myself.

Soon after it started, Associated London Scripts linked up with Frankie Howerd Scripts Ltd., whose manager, Stanley 'Scruffy' Dale, joined forces with Beryl Vertue to run this unruly empire, and Tony Hancock, who brought in his brother Roger to handle his interests. As a power bloc it took some beating, for if you consider the principals alone, they were writing between them 'The Goon Show', 'Hancock's Half Hour', 'The Frankie Howerd Show', 'Educating Archie', and

Sykes's television shows. They all approached the act of script writing in different ways. Beryl Vertue remembers that 'Spike used to write the first thing that came into his head then he'd rewrite and edit endlessly until it was just as he wanted. Alan and Ray would sit in their office and stare . . . and stare . . . and stare, and then when they had it firmly in their minds they'd write it—and that was it. Scarcely a word had to be changed.' She used to worry about Eric Sykes's deadlines because he seemed to spend all his time on the golf course. 'But then he'd suddenly appear and type like a maniac until the script was complete, and deliver it on time. That's what he'd been doing on the golf course—thinking it all out.' They all used Beryl Vertue as a sounding board—the first audience for their work. 'Spike would read a script aloud, flinging his arms around doing all the voices, Eric would *act* it out, playing the various parts, Alan and Ray would just hand me the script without a word.'

Beryl Vertue has become a very successful agent because, she claims, she is logical. She is certainly cool and unafraid and though today she deals as a matter of course with the biggest show business names in London, New York and Hollywood, she brings the same logic and detachment to bear now as she did when, between making the tea and typing the scripts, she argued with the BBC Contracts Department until they raised a writer's fee by two guineas.

Since the early Shepherd's Bush days things have changed in the ALS set-up. Eric Sykes and Spike Milligan left the group to look after their own affairs, and the agency side of the business has gone, being replaced by personal management of Galton, Simpson, Speight, and Howerd and the fusion of ALS with the powerful Robert Stigwood Group. Today Beryl Vertue spends her time commuting between Britain and America; Frankie Howerd works worldwide; Spike Milligan and Eric Sykes each have their own television series; Johnny Speight, having had 'Till Death Us Do Part' translated into two hit US television shows, 'All In The Family' and 'Maud', has partnered Ray Galton in a couple of TV ventures, 'Spooner's Patch' for ATV and 'Tea Ladies' for the BBC; while Alan Simpson, looking slimmer and fitter than he's ever done is taking life easy.

10

Marty and Me

My long love affair with the wireless began when, as a child, I used to slip out of bed, sit on the stairs, and listen illicitly to 'Band Waggon', my parents' favourite programme. That was in early 1939 and although I was unaware of it at the time, it was then that I must have assimilated the desire to become a broadcaster. My education, interrupted by the war, was in fact, virtually non-existent. By 1943, when I was fifteen, I was consumed by the desire to be a dance band trumpet player, learnt to play, left school—and went to work as an office boy in the music publishers, Peter Maurice. A year there was followed by a brief period at Southern Music Company, then for a time I was a projectionist at a cinema in North London, and in 1946 I was called up for National Service in the RAF.

While at the music publishers, I saw many of the leading broadcasters of the day—Vera Lynn, Bud Flanagan, Peter Brough, Max Miller, and many more—and, delivering music to various BBC studios, I became intrigued by the atmosphere of war-time radio. As a musician in various RAF dance bands (many of my contemporaries are leading players today), I used to tell the lads jokes and finally, on Battle of Britain Day in 1947, told my first joke in public in the gap between band numbers. When the gale of laughter hit me it was like being struck by lightning, and I was sure that my future lay in being a comedian.

On demob, I worked as a stage hand at the now defunct Wood Green Empire, and was able to study the great comedians of the day at close quarters. I left, auditioned for Carroll Levis, and did my first solo broadcast in August 1951. Many people in radio who remember it still insist that it was the best I've ever done—and when you consider I've clocked up something in the region of 900 appearances in front of the mike, that's not quite as complimentary as it at first sounds. It was a case of ignorance being bliss, I suppose, but I had the wit to realise that if I was to continue my comic career I needed fresh material. I was introduced to Eric Merriman, who was then just starting on the rocky road of script-writing, and he wrote my next two or three scripts. His father, Percy Merriman, had been a member of the Roosters Concert Party and one of the very first broadcasters, and Eric was to become a leading writer of solo spots for people like Dickie Henderson in 'Henry Hall's Guest Night', Bill Maynard (a very good comedian who's now become a much sought-after actor), Norman Vaughan (one of the most successful compères of 'Sunday Night At The London Palladium'), Terry Scott and many more. At the time Eric was writing for me, the material was better than my performance, and my radio career languished. I then had the good fortune to meet Len Fincham and Lawrie Wyman, who were part of the Kavanagh Associates Empire, and who were engaged in writing 'Educating Archie'. They told me where I was going wrong, and I was given a chance to prove myself on Ronnie Taylor's series, 'Variety Fanfare', which was broadcast from Manchester. (Ronnie Taylor's career in broadcasting has spanned producing and writing—Al Read's hit show 'Such Is Life' was one of his biggest successes—as well as a spell as Head of Light Entertainment for the commercial television company ABC. Today he is a freelance writer, and guides Cilla Black through the minefield of being funny in public.) My first 'Variety Fanfare' was a big success, my second was frightful, and there never was a third.

A long period in the doldrums followed, and in desperation I started writing my own material, finding to my astonishment that although the jokes were worse they got a better reception; and slowly I began to get more radio work. Eric Merriman and I renewed our acquaintance, and at his suggestion we teamed up to write for other comedians, most importantly for Kenneth Horne who was at that time compèring 'Music Hall'. We found him easy and delightful to write for, and at the suggestion of Jacques Brown (who was producing 'Music Hall'), we devised a thirty-minute show which we called 'Beyond Our Ken'. The pilot programme was fairly successful—particularly Merriman's invention, 'Hornerama', which was a parody of television's 'Panorama'—and the BBC scheduled a series, but before it could start, Kenneth Horne had a stroke which partly paralysed him and it was touch and go whether he would ever work again. However, Horne was a man of granite will-power and fought his way back to health, although he was told by his doctors that he must choose between his business interests and broadcasting, because to continue with both would undoubtedly kill him. Fortunately for listeners, he chose to drop his business interests (he was Chairman of the Chad Valley Toy Company, and on the board of various other companies), and concentrated on radio and television.

'Beyond Our Ken' took to the air in 1958 and was an immediate success. The cast of the first series included Kenneth Horne, Kenneth Williams, Hugh Paddick, Betty Marsden, and Ron Moody, plus singer Pat Lancaster, and the close harmony group, The Fraser Hayes Four. Paddick, Moody, Pat Lancaster and I were appearing at the time in an intimate revue called 'For Amusement Only' at the Apollo Theatre in Shaftesbury Avenue, and we persuaded our theatrical friends to boost the studio audience. For the second series, Ron Moody was replaced by Bill Pertwee. Eric Merriman and I created several long-running characters: Ambrose and Felicity, a pair of doddering idiots played by Williams and Marsden; the frightfully correct Rodney and Charles (Williams and Paddick); and Arthur Fallowfield the farmer (Kenneth Williams), whose response to every question was 'The answer lies in the soil'. There was also one of Kenneth Williams's old men with his catch-phrase 'Thirty-five years', and a script contribution from Kenneth Horne concerning one Cecil Snaith, a BBC commentator (Hugh Paddick) who never completed his commentary, saying whenever disaster struck, as it invariably did: 'And with that, I return you to the studio.'

We wrote forty editions of 'Beyond Our Ken' and then to our great surprise were asked to take over 'Take It From Here' when Frank Muir and Denis Norden quit radio for television. That was our undoing as a writing team. Merriman and I found ourselves constantly disagreeing as to what was good 'Take It From Here' and what wasn't. After much agonising and a lot of brooding silences it was decided that we should split the script and work alone. I found it impossible to write funnily on my own and teamed up with Marty Feldman, a friend of some years' standing. In those days 'Take It From Here' consisted of three comedy spots with two music breaks, one from a girl singer, the other an orchestral number from the Sid Phillips Band. An arrangement was reached whereby Marty and I would write the opening spot—a continuing story of Dick Bentley opening a new theatre on the Thames (an echo of Bernard Miles's Mermaid Theatre, which was much in the news at the time), Eric Merriman would write the main sketch—generally a film parody, and that Marty and I would write the last spot—'The Glums'. The following extract shows what we made of it. It was the last 'Glums' ever, incidentally, and comes from programme No. 325 (the 20th programme in the 13th series), transmitted on March 3, 1960. In this excerpt we find the family about to take ship for Australia:

ANNOUNCER	England is facing an era of new prosperity. The Glums are emigrating to Australia. Surely this is more than a coincidence. Be that as it may, we pick up the saga of our 'ordinary family facing life's problems' on the even of their departure. . . .
ORCHESTRA	*Glums Theme*
WHITFIELD	Oh, Ron. Just think, this afternoon we'll be on the boat to Australia. Nothing can stop us now. Oh, I'm so excited I'm goosey all over. Aren't you excited, Ron?
BENTLEY	No, Eth.
WHITFIELD	But I can see you are. You're trembling with excitement.
BENTLEY	No, I'm not. I'm shivering with the cold. Dad sold my winter underwear. He said I wouldn't need it in Australia. Anyway, it's saved me packing it.
WHITFIELD	Haven't you finished packing yet?
BENLEY	No . . . I can't get this case closed.
WHITFIELD	Let me give you a hand . . . Oh . . . ooh . . . the lid just won't close . . .. What *have* you got in here? Oh, Ron—you can't put a bicycle in a suitcase.
BENTLEY	Perhaps if I let the tyres down?
WHITFIELD	No, Ron. With your case full of bits of bicycle, where are you going to put all your clothes?
BENTLEY	I'm wearing them all, Eth.
WHITFIELD	Yes, I thought you looked a bit lumpy. Oh Ron, you're supposed to wear your rucksack *over* your jacket.
BENTLEY	Well, I don't want anybody to see it, Eth. It's full of my valuables. My yo-yo, a ball of string and a pair of roller skates.
WHITFIELD	Everybody will see that bulge under your jacket.
BENTLEY	I'll say I'm round shouldered.
WHITFIELD	Very well, it's up to you, please yourself.
BENTLEY	(*lecherous*) Right ho—
WHITFIELD	No, Ron, I didn't mean that.
BENTLEY	Go on, Eth—just a kiss.
WHITFIELD	Oh, Ron, you've unfastened my locket.
FX	*Door opens*
EDWARDS	Hello, hello, hello. What's this? It looks like a scene out of *The Hunchback of Notre Dame*. Put her down, Quasimodo.

WHITFIELD	Mr Glum! It's his rucksack.
EDWARDS	Oh, is it? I thought his shoulder pads had slipped. Anyway, I only popped in to get the 'Not Wanted On Voyage' label. I'm sticking it on Mrs Glum.
WHITFIELD	Well, Mr Glum, have you completed your packing?
EDWARDS	Yes, Eth, I have. I've carefully packed all my worldly belongings in my hip pocket.
WHITFIELD	Hip pocket?
EDWARDS	There's my best braces, a change of socks and a bottle opener. That's the trouble, Eth. A man can't go anywhere without the trappings of civilization.

Marty Feldman and I had met on a Variety bill at the old York Empire in the early 'fifties. Marty was part of a three-handed act called Morris, Marty and Mitch, who did a sort of primitive Marx brothers routine using a variety of props and patter which would have seemed inadequate in 'Band Waggon's' 'Chestnut Corner'. What they did have was youth, intelligence, and an off-stage sense of humour that showed promise of flowering in the years to come, but certainly hadn't matured that week in York. I was a more formal comedian. I told some jokes and sang a song. It's debatable which was the worse act, theirs or mine, but we found strength in each other's weakness, I suppose, and by the end of the week, Marty and I were firm friends. We worked two or three weeks later on the same bill at Weston-super-Mare, shared a dressing-room, and spent our off-stage hours together. It was at Weston that Marty changed my professional life with a single sentence: 'You look funnier offstage than you do on.' The reason was that *on* I wore a smartish blue suit and suede shoes—off I wore a tweed sports jacket, a Kangol cap and, as I didn't own an overcoat, carried an umbrella. Marty's suggestion that I should wear this outfit on stage worked. For the first time I started getting big laughs, and under Marty's eagle eye began to improve my patter and my timing.

From there it was only a short step to appearing on the major Variety theatre chain, Moss Empires. Through that I managed to get the job of voice man on a radio programme produced by Dennis Main Wilson, written by Jimmy Grafton, Larry Stephens and Peter Griffiths, and starring Jon Pertwee (still some years away from becoming Dr Who). The show was called 'Pertwee's Progress' and wobbled along for thirteen episodes or so before vanishing for good. My first part was that of an effete whale, an effect created by lisping 'Hello, sailor' through a megaphone onto a suitably tuned bass drum. I was rather less than a riot but slightly more than a flop, and soon after that I nearly replaced

Kenneth Williams in 'Hancock's Half Hour' when he was off making a film. I didn't get the part, but it was encouraging that Dennis Main Wilson should have had faith in me.

Dennis Main Wilson, better known today for his television successes 'Marty', 'The Rag Trade', and 'Till Death Us Do Part', was for many years a radio producer who numbers among the many hits for which he shares responsibility, 'The Goon Show', and 'Hancock's Half Hour'. Dennis is an enthusiast, though sometimes his enthusiasm can be a little overwhelming. I always think of him as the kind of man who, if you asked him the time, would say, 'Ah, it's interesting you should ask me that, because I've just been talking to the man whose grandfather built Big Ben', and then proceed to describe in detail the man, the clock, the history of Parliamentary democracy, and in the process would forget what you'd asked him in the first place. There was a time when it was thought to be a good idea to follow the TV 'News' with a ten minute, fictionalized discussion of the day's events. Dennis booked Johnny Speight and Eric Sykes to appear on the pilot programme. Now, Johnny Speight sports a somewhat aggressive stammer, and Eric Sykes suffers from deafness. Hearing about the show, a wit in the bar at the Television Centre remarked: 'Dennis has done the ultimate, he's got a man who can't speak talking to a man who can't hear.' But Dennis Main Wilson's exuberance is his greatest asset, and in the world of television where cynicism is the norm, his tireless enthusiasm is a tonic indeed.

While Marty and I were working on 'Take It From Here', we were simultaneously doing many other things. Marty was working on 'Educating Archie' with Ronnie Wolfe and Ronald Chesney; together we were writing 'Frankie's Bandbox' for Frankie Howerd; I was making a weekly television appearance as a barman on Rediffusion's 'Late Extra', an early TV chat show in which I did a regular comedy spot. We were also writing the occasional script for the TV programme 'The Army Game' and another radio series, 'We're In Business'. In order to cope with this mass of work, we asked Bill Craig—who by now had moved from Glasgow to London—to help us out with 'We're In Business'. He agreed, and we would rendezvous at his home in Willesden at 10 a.m. and write until the show was completed, possibly at 2 a.m. the next morning. (It wasn't *too* bad—Craig's wife used to serve us wonderful meals!) The essence of 'We're In Business' was that Peter Jones, in the character of Dudley Grosvenor that he'd originally created for 'In All Directions', was living off the naïve Harry Worth. At a low ebb in their fortunes, they were staying in a seedy boarding-house in Paddington, run by a Miss Boot (Irene Handl). The Major

(Dick Emery) was the only other lodger. The following extract was first transmitted on March 11, 1960. Peter Jones, as always, wrote the opening introduction.

DUDLEY How do you do. Well, here I am again, ladies and gentlemen. Another week has passed since I last had the pleasure of addressing you. Seven short days—and what a lot has happened. Seven hundred and sixty-three thousand babies have been born in China; two hundred and ninety-six million cups of tea have been drunk in the Northern Hemisphere alone; and two MP's, a bishop and a rock 'n' roll star have called British bird baths a national disgrace. The coast of Pembrokeshire has moved two millimetres nearer to the Azores; and for the eighty-first consecutive year, oil has been voted the most popular lubricant for sewing machines. This will give you an idea of the kind of week it has been beyond the shadows of Paddington Station. I must admit that *within* the shadows of Paddington Station life has been equally confused and meaningless. Mr Worth and me are still at Miss Boot's repulsive boarding house. As a matter of fact, we did make an attempt to shake the dust of the place off our feet—but alas, owing to . . . well, I'll tell you exactly what happened.

GRAMS *Music link*

FX *Floorboards creaking*

MISS BOOT Time you were having your delicious brekkers. You know my rule about breakfast being from seven to seven-ten. Well—you've two minutes left. You'll find your porridge on the table.

DUDLEY Yes, we'll find it—we've got our magnifying glasses. Come on, Mr Worth.

FX *Door opens*

WORTH What a picture! It looks like a winter landscape. The blackened stumps of the toast silhouetted against the grey of the tablecloth and, here and there, the muffled figure of an egg in its cosy.

DUDLEY Yes, and by the feel of it, Jack Frost has laid his icy hand upon the teapot. Hello, Major, you're too late for breakfast —lucky devil.

MAJOR I'm too excited to eat—I've been waiting for this letter for some time.

DUDLEY If you don't mind my asking, what's the letter about?

MAJOR It's in connection with the regimental dinner. We always have one at this time of year. I wouldn't miss it for the world. Frankly, I'm a lonely man and I like to talk about old times with people who knew them.

DUDLEY Indeed, it is most pleasant to reminisce with one's comrades in uniform.

MAJOR Ah yes, Mafeking, Khartoum, Bombay.

DUDLEY Actually, I was thinking of Dartmoor, Strangeways and Wormwood Scrubs.

WORTH Don't scoff, Mr Grosvenor—those war years forged a bond of friendship that can never be broken. I often wonder what happened to the old mob at Cricklewood Town Hall.

DUDLEY I beg your pardon?

WORTH I only got as far as the medical.

DUDLEY Ah, memories . . .

MAJOR 'Course, a chap's got to keep up a certain style at this sort of function. That's why I've been making all kinds of little economies.

DUDLEY Yes, I noticed you were only taking one spoonful of curry powder in your tea.

Writing for Frankie Howerd was less an exercise in technique than a labour of love. We admired him, we revered him—actually to write for him was more than we'd ever aspired to do. But we had become friends and when asked to do a spot Marty and I leapt to the typewriter and nearly muffed the opportunity completely. As Howerd pointed out, 'You haven't put in the "oohs" and "aahs".' We had assumed that these were his own style, his own contribution to the script, but willingly rewrote, and thus started an association that lasted many years, through dozens of scripts, and is as warm today, now that we're all successful, as it was in the brief but frightening period when Frankie Howerd was in eclipse. The following is typical of the sort of stuff we used to write for him in the early 'sixties:

HOWERD Good evening, ladies and gentlemen. Recently I had the pleasure—yes—quite recently. Last Thursday to be precise. I nearly had the pleasure on Friday an' all but the lady mayoress couldn't oblige. Well, she was our chairlady you see. At this meeting. Yes—I addressed a meeting. Well, you see, what happened was, I was at home making myself a cup of cocoa—and I was trying to get the top off my hot water bottle—yes, I always keep some cocoa in my hot water bottle. Well, after I've got me feet warm there's no pleasure in getting out of bed, so I just have a swig out the hot water bottle. Well, there I was with the bottle—struggling to get me cap off—yes, I always wear me cap in bed—it's somewhere to keep the toast warm—I normally keep a crust jammed under the peak in case of night starvation. Anyway, there I was—in the middle of supper—and the phone rang. So I answered it. I said, 'Hello, who is it?' She said, 'Do you know the Expectant Mothers of Bromley?' I said, 'Well, not by name, but I'd recognise them if I saw them.' She said, 'No. You don't understand—we're in a bit of a spot.' I said, 'Well, I don't see how *I* can help. There's not much I can do at this stage.' She said, 'Would you speak to them?' I said, 'Yes, I'll speak to anybody if they're civil to me. I'm not proud you know.' She said, 'We'd like you to address a meeting on the Common Market.' Well, I had to agree—I mean, you can't refuse an expectant mother when she fancies something. My sister-in-law used to get these mad fancies. Every night she'd wake up mad with desire for whipped cream and faggots. Every night my brother would have to scour the neighbourhood for them. He was out all night sometimes. Well, after about three years he tumbled. Oh, he's no fool! She wasn't pregnant at all—just fat! Well, it's not surprising, all that whipped cream and faggots. Now, what was I talking about before I so rudely interrupted? Oh yes—my lecture. Yes—it was such a success that I've been asked to repeat it tonight on the BBC. So now here's Part One of the Howerd Common Market Lectures—this week—France!

ORCHESTRA *Four bars Can Can music*

HOWERD Yes. The French National Anthem. What pictures does that stirring music conjure up? La Belle France! Population fifty million—main industry—increasing the population to a hundred million. The language that is spoken is, for the most part, disgusting foreign rubbish—consisting of such phrases as 'Ooo La La'—'Où est la plume de ma tante', and 'Would you like to buy some naughty pictures, Johnny?' Mind you, my experience is limited to one street in Paris. The currency is grubby and smells of garlic. And however much you have in your pocket is always just the right amount to pay the cab fare. The men all wear berets, striped pullies and are very hostile. The women all wear tight skirts split up the side and are very friendly—very hospitable, in fact. They think nothing of inviting you home with them although you may be a stranger. Once again I must stress that my experience is limited to one street in Paris. This, then, is the country we are asked to join. And why do they want us to join? They're after our false teeth. See, we've got the NHS. Yes. They don't want us for ourselves—no, they just want us for our teeth. Gummy lot they are—poor devils. Stands to reason they need our teeth. You can't have a good gnaw on a frog's leg if you haven't got good choppers. See, they ruin theirselves crunching them snails. It's not the chewy centre so much as the crusty bits. Anyway—there they were—fifty million hungry mouths to feed and no hampsteads. You have to pity them. They're in a right old potage. Those French loaves—useless—you can't put 'em in a toaster. And it's not only our teeth they want to get their hands on—they've got their eye on our pudding an' all. They haven't got Yorkshire Pud over there—or Black Pudding—there's not a slice of Spotted Dick between Boulogne and Monte Carlo. No—they're Spotted Dickless—and Roly Poly Pudding-less as well. That's why they want us—they want to get their false teeth into our Roly Polys. So people of Britain—I implore you—stand firm on your false teeth . . .

GRAMS *Creep in 'There'll Always Be An England'. Bring up under following speech to crescendo*

HOWERD The battle still has to be fought, but remember we have fought before, and so I would like to finish by quoting the speech from Henry the Fifth—script by William Shakespeare—from the book of the same name.

GRAM *Music up louder here*

HOWERD Once more unto the breach or not to be. And when the blasted war rings in our sinews and ring out the old, that nation shall speak peace unto we happy few—that gentlemen of England now abed—on the beaches and in the streets of this—our Septic Isle—cry Havoc for King Harry and a kingdom for his horse—shall not perish from the earth—and the best of luck!

When Marty Feldman and I were asked to write the show that was subsequently called 'Round The Horne', we were involved in a speculative piece of radio writing for Clive Dunn. Marty had written a 'one-off' for him called 'Wilkie' which had worked well, and there was interest in a series. We were about half way through the script when we received a call from John Simmonds, who had taken over the production of 'Beyond Our Ken' from Jacques Brown sometime before, and he asked us if we'd like to meet him, Roy Rich (the Head of Light Entertainment), Edward Taylor (the script editor), and Kenneth Horne, to discuss it. Actually it was Taylor's idea that we should be asked, his feeling being that as I had been one of the original writers of 'Beyond Our Ken', I'd know more about it. We duly met up, and were asked to take over the Horne show as Merriman was no longer interested in writing it. When he and I had split after our disagreements on 'Take It From Here', Merriman had written 'Beyond Our Ken' solo and had created a number of new characters, and Marty and I were very dubious about taking on what could well turn out to be a hot potato. 'Beyond Our Ken' was a success and we doubted if we could do better, in spite of the fact that the show was to have a new title, format and characters. We naturally admired the cast enormously, and in the forty-odd 'Beyond Our Ken' shows that I had written with Merriman, I'd learned a good deal about their strengths and weaknesses. But—we felt 'Hasn't it all been done already?' What could we do that would be sufficiently different to justify taking it on? And supposing it flopped? If we weren't careful we would wind up, as Kenneth Williams might say, with 'omelette sur le visage'.

We agreed to go home and think about it, went home, thought about it and spent the next day or two restlessly discussing the problem. Supposing we *did* do it? Well, we could do a modern day Mayhew's London, we could write a feature on wives of famous men, we could echo the Kings Road/Carnaby Street swinging England image that was erupting at the time. We could. . . . In short, we talked ourselves into it, wrote a pilot which was called 'It's Ken Again', changed it to 'Round The Horne' and the show went on the air in 1964. It took us about six episodes to really get on top of it, by which time we'd invented the camp characters Julian and Sandy (they actually started as two old actor laddies down on their luck and were changed at the insistence of John Simmonds); Rambling Syd Rumpo, the folk singer; the ham actors, Fiona and Charles; and the rest of the oddities with which we peopled the shows. It became a solid success, with learned articles written about it in the posh dailies, and was sold worldwide. In fact it can *still* be heard on local radio stations in Canada and the USA, and I'm told it's a big hit in Fiji today!

Marty Feldman and Barry Took, 1968 (Topix)

'Round The Horne': l. to r., Hugh Paddick, Kenneth Williams, Kenneth Horne, Betty Marsden and announcer Douglas Smith, 1968

(BBC)

'The Navy Lark': l. to r. (front row): Heather Chasen, Judy Cornwell; (centre row): Stephen Murray, Richard Caldicot, Leslie Phillips; (back row): Ronnie Barker, Jon Pertwee, Michael Bates, Tenniel Evans

(BBC)

'I'm Sorry, I'll Read That Again': l. to r., Bill Oddie, John Cleese, Tim Brooke-Taylor, Jo Kendall, Graeme Garden and David Hatch (producer), 1968

(BBC)

It was the happiest of shows, there were no disagreements, and I think that for the first time since 'Much Binding In The Marsh', Kenneth Horne really bubbled. The work of Kenneth Williams, Hugh Paddick, Betty Marsden and Bill Pertwee was superlative, developing even further than 'Beyond Our Ken'. Recordings were like a West End first night and John Simmonds's iron-fist-in-a-velvet-glove approach to the production gave it a polish that many radio series have equalled but few have surpassed. Marty and I wrote fifty episodes in all, and when he decided to go back to performing, I carried on with other writers—Donald Webster, now better known as an actor, and Johnnie Mortimer and Brian Cooke, who later created the television shows 'Father, Dear Father', and 'Man About The House'. Though Marty wasn't officially writing, he and I would still get together occasionally and write the odd sketch. 'Round The Horne' was a powerful stimulant.

When Kenneth Horne died (on stage of a heart attack at the SFTA Awards Ball), the BBC went on with a revamped series called 'Stop Messing About', but such was my emotional attachment to Kenneth Horne that I felt unable to work on it. The memory of his presence was too strong and I felt his absence too acutely. To me he was like a father, encouraging, thoughtful, understanding and generous. He was an enchanting man. In December 1970, I wrote this tribute to him in *The Listener*:

> 'When Marty Feldman and I started work on "Round The Horne" it was the extraordinary personality of Kenneth Horne that enthralled us. He was an unselfish performer, but it was still always *his* show. You just knew it. A Martian would have known it. His warmth tempered the sharpness of the writing. Our attacks on people and institutions were often, I regret to admit, cruel and unfair. We snapped at almost every radio and TV personality of the period. Such hallowed figures as Malcolm Muggeridge, Lord Willis, Albert Schweitzer, Archbishop Makarios, Ken Dodd, Canon Collins, Jimmy Clitheroe and Sir Cyril Black were invoked. Rereading the scripts, I wonder how we managed to stay out of prison let alone on the air. We attacked everybody—ourselves included. We described the show as "star-studded rubbish", "catchpenny horseplay", "whimsical muck" and "thirty minutes of trivial, sick-making hoo haa". But we really let our hair down when it came to naming our characters. Rambling Syd Rumpo, J. Peasmold Gruntfuttock, Dame Celia Molestrangler and Binkie Huckaback, Beatrice Clissold—"the pure brass of the music halls"—and her butler Spasm, Otto von Kuckpowder (the German air ace), Milo Nostradamus (an Armenian pastry cook of no fixed abode),

Troilus Lackwind (a man so simple he used to set fire to the living-room curtains to get a ride on the fire engine), Brown-Horrocks, MI5, Dr. Gaylord Haemoglobin, Yeti Rosencrantz, Old Widow McGanderpoke—the mind boggles.

The comic announcer is common to almost all radio shows. Our announcer was Douglas ("I dreamt I went to the opera dressed only in my Dobbitex Equine cummerbund") Smith. We made jokes about an LP called "The Chipmunks Sing Handel's Messiah", of a film called "Where No Hippos Fly", and gave the fashion hint "Bosoms are on their way back", which was greeted by Horne's "I'll keep a light burning in the window: come home, bosoms, all is forgiven"—such sallies were all right in their way, but only the fact that we wrote thousands and thousands of them is in any sense remarkable. . . . When we couldn't find the right words we invented new ones. When there were complaints we attacked those who complained. When we couldn't think of anything we said so in the scripts.

Central to the action, making it all happen, was Kenneth Horne. To say that everyone loved him sounds like every obituary ever written—nonetheless it's true. In the last years of his life we met frequently and corresponded even more. Hardly a day would go by without a scribbled note from Kenneth. Here is one of the last things he wrote apropos "Round The Horne": "My dear Barry, a tremendous series—easily the best, and what's more without a word of discord." '

Horne was one of the few great men I have met, and his generosity of spirit and gesture have, in my experience, never been surpassed. I mourn him still.

Here are some extracts culled at random from 'Round The Horne'. The first is from the transmission of June 4, 1967:

SMITH And now a show that we humbly dedicate to Lady Dartmouth, with whom we'd like to couple The Flying Scot—'Round The Horne'.

ORCHESTRA *'Round The Horne' signature tune*

HORNE Hello again. Well, today marks the start of Baste an Archdeacon In Syrup Of Figs For Fun And Profit Week, and there will be many events to celebrate it. On Tuesday there'll be a display of Old Tyme Frog Bottling in the round at the Wimpole Street Porridge Bar. There's international free-style gnome fingering at the five-minute

Hippo Wash, Brompton Oratory, and chip fumbling in the great vat of St. Pauls. On Thursday the Over Eighties' Nudist Basket Ball Team are playing an exhibition match against the Harlem Globe Trotters. This will be followed by the presentation of a medal to the nudist voted most likely. I shall be interested not so much in who gets the medal as where it's pinned.

PADDICK And now, in association with the Lew and Leslie Grade Clerical Sportswear Boutique, Lambeth Cut, we present—

SMITH Part Two of 'The Admirable Loombucket'. [This actually comes from the 2/4/67 transmission].

HORNE My name is Lord Tantamount Horseposture. Whilst on a world cruise with my young, incredibly beautiful daughter, Wisteria, played incredibly by Betty Marsden, and her fiancé, the Reverend Isambard Mousepractice—played by tiny, agile Hugh Paddick—we were shipwrecked. Only timely intervention by my butler, Loombucket, exquisitely portrayed by Bolivian Sex Goddess Kenneth Williams, saved us from disaster. Bill Pertwee was in it, too, but I can't remember what he did. We landed on an uninhabited desert island—our only provisions six gramophone records and an inexhaustible supply of Roy Plomley. What was to become of us?

ORCHESTRA *Music*

FX *Distant waves lapping, seagulls, etc.*

MARSDEN Safe at last. Where are we Loombucket?

WILLIAMS The lost island of Gonga, your ladyship.

PADDICK But how do you know?

WILLIAMS I recognise the signs.

HORNE What signs?

WILLIAMS There, look—that one says, 'The Lost Island of Gonga welcomes careful castaways.'

HORNE And see there—dominating the island, the sacred volcano of Gonga—played by Douglas Smith with a hole in his head and steam coming out of his ears.

PADDICK What an awesome sight—snow mantling his mighty summit and lava oozing down his sides.

SMITH That's porridge, actually. I had a hurried breakfast this morning.

HORNE Shut up, Smith, you're a volcano. You just loom over us and rumble ominously.

SMITH Yes, I told you. I had a hurried breakfast.

HORNE Shut up, Smith.

SMITH Rumble rumble.

HORNE That's better.

PERTWEE I have heard it said that when the god of the volcano gets angry he can only be placated by having a young maiden thrown to him.

HORNE I think that's a rumour put about by Smith on the off chance that some gullible twit will believe him.

MARSDEN But how are we to live here in this desolate spot? It may be years before we're rescued.

HORNE Loombucket—build us a rude hut.

WILLIAMS Yes, my lord. Right away. I shall need a rude hammer, some rude nails and a rude saw.

PADDICK What about 'Confucious he say man who lose soap in bath find . . .'

HORNE All right, Mousepractice—you're not at the Ecumenical Council now. Right, Loombucket—get started.

WILLIAMS Yes, my lord.

FX *Hammering, sawing, etc, very fast*

WILLIAMS There you are, my lord—it's finished.

HORNE Good heavens, wasn't that quick—a life-size replica of Windsor Castle. Oh well, it'll have to do.

MARSDEN Oh, Loombucket, you're so masterful. I'd follow you anywhere.

PADDICK Well, Wisteria, you're obviously infatuated with him. There's no point in my staying here. I shall go back to camp with Lord Horseposture.

WILLIAMS Chacun à son goût.

MARSDEN Loombucket, we're alone. Come, sit here beside me on the sand. I love you, Loombucket, and you, Loombucket, love me.

WILLIAMS Perhaps so, my lady, but it can never be. I know my place and you know my place, don't you, my lady?

MARSDEN Yes, Loombucket.

WILLIAMS Right. See you at my place in ten minutes. If I'm late, start without me.

ORCHESTRA *Music link*

HORNE The weeks dragged into months and the months into years and as our clothes became more tattered and torn so Loombucket revealed his qualities of leadership—among other things. Each Sunday he'd swim three hundred miles to the mainland to fetch the Sunday papers—sometimes

	not returning till the following July. He prepared us succulent dishes made with native fruits.
WILLIAMS	More paw paw, my lady?
MARSDEN	Not first thing in the morning. Keep your paw paws to yourself.
WILLIAMS	But all the time the sacred Douglas Smith brooded over us.
SMITH	Rumble—rumble—puff—puff—
HORNE	And then one day—
SMITH	Rumble shudder—quiver quiver—pow kersplot.
HORNE	Kersplot?
SMITH	I think I've erupted.
PERTWEE	The volcano is angry. I warned you, on page three, but you wouldn't heed me.
MARSDEN	What are we going to do?
WILLIAMS	We must propitiate it with a sacrifice.
HORNE	Which of us is it to be?
PERTWEE	It has to be a young maiden.
HORNE	Oh well—that rules me out.
PADDICK	And me.
PERTWEE	And me.
MARSDEN	And me.
	(*Pause*)
WILLIAMS	What are you all staring at me for? All right, I'll do it. I'll black up and go in drag. It's an old trick but it might just work.
HORNE	And without further ado the Admirable Loombucket scaled the volcano, paused—touched his forelock for the last time and plunged into the awful bubbling maw of the sacred Douglas Smith.
WILLIAMS	(*screams*)
SMITH	(*gulps, swallows, smacks his lips*) Thank you. You've made an old volcano very happy.
FX	*A vast electronic burp*
ORCHESTRA	*Playoff*
HORNE	So ends our saga of the Admirable Loombucket. It might not have been as good as the original but you must admit we managed to drag it out for two weeks. And so to our roving reporter—Sunday night TV personality, Seamus Android.
PERTWEE	Hello—all right and welcome yet again to the first of what I can only hope will be the last of many—which have given me great pleasure—in the past—as I know you have. So

before I introduce my first guest who has travelled nearly two hundred yards to be with us tonight, personally, in person herself, I'd like to tell you some of the things that have been said about her, but I've never heard any of them and so without further ado I can think of nothing more apt to say by way of introduction than—good night.

HORNE Thank you, Seamus Android—a man of many parts, most of which he forgets. Women play an important part in medical research—if only behind the scenes, and many films have been made which depict love blossoming among the test tubes and specimen jars. One such film was *The Wayward Streptococcus*, starring Dame Celia Molestrangler and ageing juvenile, Binkie Huckaback.

GRAMS '*Isn't It Romantic*'

MARSDEN Oh Charles, are you still experimenting?

PADDICK Yes, Fiona. I must carry on. I think I've stumbled on something big—very big indeed.

MARSDEN You must rest, Charles. You can't keep driving yourself like this.

PADDICK I can't give up now. It's all I live for. I think I've hit on something. Look through this microscope.

MARSDEN In here, Charles?

PADDICK Yes, at these slides.

MARSDEN Good heavens, Charles. It's me on a donkey at Margate.

PADDICK And here, look—see, hundreds of them.

MARSDEN They're terribly small, Charles.

PADDICK You can't see them with the naked eye—but for years I've known they were there.

MARSDEN Bacteria, Charles?

PADDICK No, thanks, not while I'm working. There, see—just an ordinary piece of Gruyère cheese.

MARSDEN But I don't understand. What are you doing with it?

PADDICK It's an experiment, Fiona. Watch—I do this—and this and that.

MARSDEN Don't do that, Charles.

PADDICK Oh I'm sorry, not that. I'll do this, then.

MARSDEN That's better.

PADDICK Then I take it so and hold it over the Bunsen burner. Now do you see what I've been up to all these years?

MARSDEN Oh Charles, you've done it at last. One day millions of people will recognise your achievement.

PADDICK Yes, Fiona. I shall be known as the man who discovered— Welsh Rarebit.

The following 'Julian & Sandy' sketch was first transmitted in March 1967. I think it's fairly typical.

HORNE Now, many people complain that they are misrepresented by the Press—and the reporters don't respect their privacy. This certainly hasn't been my experience—until last Tuesday when two representatives of the Fourth Estate came to interview me.

FX *Doorbell. Door open*

PADDICK Good morning. I'm Julian and this is my friend, Sandy.

WILLIAMS We're from the *Daily Palare*. He's the man you follow around and I'm the one you can't gag.

PADDICK Can we have five minutes of your time?

HORNE It depends what you want to do with them.

WILLIAMS Well, our editor said, Why don't you troll off to Mr. Horne's lattie . . .

HORNE Flat or house—translator's note.

WILLIAMS And have a palare with him.

PADDICK We'd like something hot and personal.

HORNE How about this mustard plaster?

PADDICK No thanks, we've just had breakfast.

HORNE How did you two become newshounds?

PADDICK We was Aunt Ada.

WILLIAMS You know—advice to the lovelorn—palones with pimples in love with older men—that sort of thing.

HORNE And you advised them?

PADDICK Well, we did what we could, but we run into a few snags. For instance, Indignant of Chatham—remember him, Sand?

WILLIAMS Do I? He's etched on my memory he is—etched he is—deeply—Indignant of Chatham.

HORNE He took your advice?

PADDICK Yes, he's still indignant.

WILLIAMS But he's had to move from Chatham. Then there was Curly of Wimbledon.

PADDICK He had a personal problem and we told him what to do in a plain envelope.

HORNE I tried to and it was absolutely useless.

WILLIAMS 'Ere, are you Curly of Wimbledon?

HORNE Not any more I'm not, thanks to your advice.

PADDICK	Still, it's cured the blushing.
HORNE	Now, what did you come to see me about?
PADDICK	Well, we heard you'd done something absolutely staggering with a marrow at the Church Hall.
HORNE	The vicar's wife was astounded.
WILLIAMS	We can't go back to our editor with a story about how you won a prize for a marrow.
PADDICK	Where's the titillation in that?
WILLIAMS	We've got to tart up the story somehow. Whip out your reporter's companion and take this down. Now, Mr. Horne—let me see—ah—is that a picture of you on the wall?
HORNE	Yes. It was taken when I was eighteen months—on a bearskin rug.
PADDICK	It's a good likeness.
WILLIAMS	Right, get this down, Jule. Kenneth Horne, former nude photographic model—
PADDICK	. . . graphic model.
WILLIAMS	Now, let's see. You won the competition. Did the vicar charge an entrance fee?
HORNE	Yes, there was a small charge.
WILLIAMS	Right—yes—Jule, I've got it. I've got our headline—'Kenneth Horne nude photographic model admits vicar's charge'.
ORCHESTRA	*Playoff chord*

This chapter would not be complete without mention of two producers: Jacques Brown, the producer of 'Beyond Our Ken', and John Simmonds, who produced 'Round The Horne'. Listening to 'Danger—Men At Work!' I grew up with the sound of Jacques Brown's voice in my ears. I first met him in 1952 when I was broadcasting in the 'Midday Music Hall' series. I was pretty raw and very nervous. Just before I went on, he turned to me and said, 'You're not nervous are you, Barry?' I told him I was petrified. He said, 'You mustn't let those stupid so and so's worry you. Go out there and enjoy yourself.' And oddly enough I did, and was never really frightened by the microphone or a studio audience again. He booked me fairly frequently from then on, keeping a fatherly eye on me, and when I started writing with Marty Feldman, he became a great ally, singing our praises to all who would listen. He was a very puzzling man, at times light-hearted and flippant, at others sombre and suspicious. He produced many shows and almost invariably came to hate them. Con Mahoney, who knew him much better than I, explains that 'Jacques was one of the kindliest of men. He would devote an enormous amount of time to people whom he thought were genuinely interested in what he had to offer, but within the BBC Jacques was a loner. He always felt that he was unwanted by the management. Somehow I always thought that this had something to do with his being a Jew, and I believe he felt that he was at a disadvantage within a working society that was overwhelmingly non-Jewish.' Jacques died tragically in a road accident in Hampshire; he will not be forgotten by those of us fortunate enough to have experienced the sunny side of his odd dual personality.

John Simmonds joined the BBC in 1935 as an effects boy at thirty shillings a week. Today, now retired, he looks back at a career spangled with hit shows. His admiration for and understanding of writers is boundless. One of the first to impress him was Vernon Harris, who wrote much of the pre-war 'Fol de Rols' and 'Band Waggon' series, before going on to a distinguished career in serious drama and becoming a top-flight film writer. Simmonds's approach to production could only be described as impeccable, a far cry from his experiences as studio manager for 'Danger—Men At Work!', where the casual approach of producer Max Kester must have been sheer mental torture to a man of Simmonds's meticulous scrupulosity. For example, Simmonds produced 'Henry Hall's Guest Night' for many years and on one occasion Rex Harrison and his then wife, Lilli Palmer, were guests. In his introduction Henry Hall called her Lillian, a slip of the tongue that distressed him intensely. The show was recorded and when editing it, Simmonds was able to out the 'an' from Lillian so that it sounded like Lilli. 'Henry listened to the programme that night in anguish, waiting for his terrible gaffe—and then to his great relief realised there wasn't one.' To John Simmonds this was all in a day's work, but I think it was illustrative of his entire approach. He knew and understood radio and cared for it deeply. He didn't claim to be a perfectionist but sought always to put the very best on the air, in the best way possible.

11

Larking About

By the end of 1975, 'The Navy Lark' had become the longest-running situation comedy ever, its life span of seventeen years surpassing even such shows as 'Take It From Here', 'Educating Archie', 'ITMA', and 'The Clitheroe Kid'. Admittedly, there haven't been as many episodes, but in terms of years it has outstripped all its rivals in the comedy field.

The programme began in 1959, when Lawrie Wyman approached producer Alistair Scott-Johnston and said he'd like to write a show for Jon Pertwee. At that time Pertwee had just completed 'Pertwee's Progress', which had not been a great success, and Scott-Johnston told Wyman he saw Pertwee 'not as a comedian but as an actor, a comic actor admittedly, but an actor. I felt it would be good to do a show with a services background and as I'd been in the army and Lawrie had been in the RAF, I suggested the navy on the grounds that that way we wouldn't argue about detail.' Once that was agreed they had two elements for a show—a star, Jon Pertwee, and a setting, the fictitious HMS Troutbridge, an accident-prone frigate in the Royal Navy. Scott-Johnston recalls, 'Jon's on-stage personality was brash, and to counterpoint this we needed someone who was smooth, and we hit on Denis Price. Then I felt we needed an idiot, and there was no-one better at playing idiots than Leslie Phillips, so we got him.' The supporting cast were gathered together and a trial recording made. It was good, and the show duly went on the air. As Scott-Johnston says, 'It was one of those shows that worked from the start. Well, to be honest, we never got the first three pages of the first script right, but thereafter it was spot on. It always worked.'

In its seventeen years there have been surprisingly few changes. Denis Price left after the first series to work in America, and was replaced by Stephen Murray. Ronnie Barker left when his television commitments clashed with the 'Navy Lark's' Sunday recordings. Judy Cornwell appeared only in one series, but Heather Chasen has never missed an episode, and Jon Pertwee was only missing once, even though at one time he suffered agonies with lumbago, and was literally tied to a studio chair in order to avoid any unnecessary movement, from which odd position he broadcast brilliantly.

Alistair Scott-Johnston's career as a BBC producer is fairly typical. He joined the Corporation in 1939 as an effects boy in the Drama department, and remembers vividly the occasion when, during a major production about the events leading up to the start of the First World War, one of his gramophone turntables caught fire. 'It happened just as I'd shot the Archduke Ferdinand and I was desperately trying to carry on with my remaining five turntables and at the same time prevent myself asphyxiating. The Effects Studio was in the bowels of Broadcasting House several floors away from the main studio. The producer kept coming through on the talk-back, asking what the hell was going on—and I couldn't tell him.' Luckily a passer by saw his predicament and grabbed a fire extinguisher. The programme finished with Scott-Johnston engulfed in thick black smoke in a foam-filled sound effects room.

When the war started, he enlisted in the Grenadier Guards and was in due course commissioned, serving in the armoured division all over the world. After the war he returned to the BBC as a junior producer doing 'a bit of everything—light music, Outside Broadcasts, comedy,' and eventually took over the highly successful 'Henry Hall's Guest Night'. 'Henry taught me showbusiness, particularly the need for planning. He taught me that if you haven't got a show before you go into the studio—go sick!' Though this advice was not always possible: once when he was producing 'The Frankie Howerd Show', Denis Price, that week's guest star, phoned to say he might be a little late. Scott-Johnston asked why. Denis Price said, 'Well you see, I'm phoning from Zurich.' Eventually, thanks to Swiss Air and a police escort from Heathrow, Price arrived in time, but only just. The programme was already on the air. On another occasion during that same series, Richard Burton was the guest star and really didn't have enough to do. The writers quickly added a sequence based on the idea of an actor's audition piece, in which Burton had two pages of histrionics running the gamut from 'Oh darling, I love you' to

'Look out, he's got a gun!', and other such clichés. Every line had a change of mood, and it was a tour de force. Unfortunately, they'd forgotten to tell Frankie Howerd of this addition to the script and when Richard Burton launched into his tirade, Howerd started searching furiously through his script to try and discover what was going on. Eventually Burton reached a ringing climax, and the audience stood and cheered for two minutes. Howerd shambled up to the mike and in one of the epic 'toppers' of all time said, 'Show me *that* in the script.'

'The Navy Lark' was one of Scott-Johnston's biggest successes and one of which he is justly proud. Lawrie Wyman now writes the show with George Evans, and there seems no earthly reason why 'The Navy Lark' shouldn't survive as long as the British Navy which it so genially mocks. Here is a typical sequence. The accident-prone duffers of HMS Troutbridge are on a Hovercraft familiarization course.

RATING	Excuse me, Commander Ward, sir.
WARD	What is it, Stonehouse?
RATING	The two officers and the CPO from Troutbridge are ready to make their first solo trip in the Mark Five Hovercraft, sir.
WARD	I always knew that one dark day they'd send us somebody from Troutbridge for instruction. Are the rescue and fire services standing by?
RATING	Yes, sir.
WARD	All shipping in the area been warned?
RATING	Yes, sir.
WARD	Everyone on the station been warned to take cover?
RATING	Yes, sir.
WARD	Oh well, that's all we can do. I may as well go out to the apron and send them off. It's at times like these one realises that they should never have let the Home Guard stand down.
RATING	Good luck, sir.
WARD	Don't be ridiculous, Stonehouse. We all know what my luck is today. It wouldn't be quite so panic making if that blond one didn't keep saying, 'Honestly, sir, it's just like driving a car.'
RATING	Well, in a way I suppose it is, sir.
WARD	Possibly, Stonehouse, but blondie can't drive a car *either*. Come on—let's get them launched. Six to four they buzz off backwards at forty miles an hour.
GRAMS	*Music link*
FX	*Hovercraft running*
PHILLIPS	Honestly, sir, it's just like driving a car.

MURRAY Is it really? I suppose that's why you backed us out of the garage at forty miles an hour.

PERTWEE Here—that Commander Ward is pretty nippy, isn't he, sir? *I've* never seen anyone clear an eight foot fence from a standing jump before.

MURRAY It was the way he was still able to run like fun afterwards that fascinated me.

PHILLIPS I think he was trying to catch up with Able Seaman Stonehouse, actually.

PERTWEE Catch him? In twenty yards he'd overtaken him.

MURRAY Odd the way some people panic, isn't it? Anything on the radar screen, Chief?

PERTWEE No, sir. I've been wondering about that. Either the radar isn't working or somebody must have warned all the shipping in the area that we're out for a spin.

MURRAY Well, that would make sense. Jolly disappointing, though.

PERTWEE Disappointing, sir?

MURRAY Yes. It would have been fun to wave at some of the chaps from this thing.

PHILLIPS Then why don't we buzz into the dockyard, sir? A quick slither round Troutbridge so that Commander Bell and all the others can have a butchers at us.

PERTWEE Oh no, sir—please.

MURRAY Certainly not. I absolutely forbid it.

PHILLIPS Perhaps you're right, sir.

MURRAY It's out of the question.

PERTWEE Completely, sir.

MURRAY Ye-es. (*Pause*) It would have been fun though.

PHILLIPS It would have shaken them rigid.

PERTWEE (*pause*) Did Commander Ward actually *say* we weren't to go into the dockyard, sir?

MURRAY Well, no, but obviously . . .

PHILLIPS Oh, *obviously*, sir, yes.

PERTWEE Quite so. It *would* have been fun though.

MURRAY Oh, enormous. Pity.

PHILLIPS Shame.

MURRAY Oh, absolutely. (*Pause*) Pom-pom-pommerty pom—diddle diddle pom—pommerty pom. Of course, he didn't actually *say* . . .

PERTWEE Not a word, sir. Not a word.

MURRAY Even so . . .

PHILLIPS Oh, go on, sir—*let's*.

MURRAY Oh, all right then. Push the stick forward, Mr. Phillips and head for the dockyard. And for pity's sake don't rip your skirt on a mooring buoy.
PHILLIPS Pardon? Boys don't wear skirts . . .
PERTWEE The rubber skirt round the hovercraft, sir!
PHILLIPS Lumme—that's a relief.
MURRAY Increase speed up to forty knots and head for the dockyard, Mr. Phillips.
PHILLIPS Aye aye, sir. Now, which way would that be?
PERTWEE Oh, toss for it like you usually do, sir. Heads it's that way—tails it's behind us—and if it lands on its edge, we're there.
MURRAY So *that's* how he navigates—I've often wondered.
PERTWEE Well, now you know, sir. Now you know.

Edward Taylor has in his time produced two of radio's longest-running shows, 'The Men From The Ministry' and 'Does The Team Think?', a compendium of all known jokes, devised by Jimmy Edwards. Taylor is proud of his connection with 'Does The Team Think?' which he inherited from Jacques Brown in 1959 and which ran for over three hundred editions.

'Does The Team Think?' starred Jimmy Edwards, too, and featured any three out of Ted Ray, Tommy Trinder, Arthur Askey and Cyril Fletcher, depending on who was in town at the time. Taylor said of it, 'It doesn't suffer from the passage of time, and it's no strain on anybody because Jimmy and company have trained themselves to be funny on tap.'

He was much more concerned with 'The Men From The Ministry', however, which he invented in 1962, and which was entirely his own idea. He wanted to write for Richard Murdoch, to whom he is devoted, and he wanted to team Murdoch with Wilfred Hyde White, which he did. Placing these two against a Civil Service background, he came up with 'The Men From The Ministry'. Although from time to time he had co-writers (Johnnie Mortimer and Brian Cooke, now at the top of the television writing tree, started on the show), 'The Men From The Ministry' is very much Edward Taylor's brain-child. Curiously, its biggest audience was overseas where the BBC's World Service disseminated it to anyone who happened to be listening—and there were a lot of such listeners. Taylor once had a letter from Turkey saying, 'I like your show because our government service here is just like yours over there.' 'The Men From The Ministry' was also a big hit in Sweden, where they bought the scripts, translated them into Swedish and used local actors, but kept the locale in London, presumably because they thought British bureaucracy was funnier.

Here's a typical sample from the programme, starring Richard Murdoch, Deryck Guyler, Ronald Baddiley and Norma Ronald.

FX *Door opens*

BADDILEY Aha! I want a word with you two!

GUYLER Do come in, Sir Gregory, and have a seat.

MURDOCH A cup of tea, sir? And may we press you to a jam doughnut?

BADDILEY You may not, Lamb.

MURDOCH Thank you, sir. Well, I've checked our books as you asked, and you'll be delighted to hear that our Entertainment and Expenses account shows a substantial surplus.

GUYLER No less than seventy-five pence, sir.

MURDOCH (*aside to Mildred*) There—I knew Sir Gregory would be delighted. Look, he's smiling.

RONALD (*aside to Murdoch*) Oo-er. He's not smiling—he's baring his teeth.

BADDILEY The 'E and E' account has a *surplus* you say?

GUYLER That's right, we have it here, sir—in the Petty Cash box.

FX *Rattle of coins in box*

BADDILEY (*quiet menace*) *Seventy-five pence* surplus, eh?

MURDOCH You're not delighted, sir? Not even a teeny weeny bit?

BADDILEY (*shouts*) Of *course* I'm not blasted well delighted! You know the government's policy! If a department doesn't spend its full allocation in any financial year, next year they receive less!

GUYLER Oh dear.

BADDILEY 'Oh dear' is right, Lennox-Brown. If that seventy-five pence isn't spent, and spent quickly, this department's expense account will be cut.

MURDOCH You mean—less medicinal brandy in the first aid cupboard!

BADDILEY Exactly! I could find myself going on fact finding tours of the Midlands instead of the South of France!

GUYLER We're very sorry, sir.

BADDILEY It's no use being sorry, Lennox-Brown! Just see that you lose seventy-five pence, and be quick about it! (*Going off*) Or heads will roll—even square heads like yours.

FX *Door shuts*

MURDOCH Well, I suppose we could have fish *and* chips for lunch today.

GUYLER Don't be silly, Two—we can't spend that money on *ourselves*! You know the Civil Service rule—you can waste as much public money as you like, as long as no one benefits! If you benefit, it's corruption!

Almost the last star in the galaxy of big time radio comedy was 'I'm Sorry, I'll Read That Again'. It was full of up and comers—that is to say, they *were* up and coming when the series started—and the cast included John Cleese, Graeme Garden, Tim Brooke-Taylor, Bill Oddie, Jo Kendall and David Hatch, who co-produced. The other co-producer was Peter Titheridge, who had been a BBC script editor for some years and whose knowledge of and interest in the younger generation of funny people helped keep BBC radio in business in the late 'sixties.

'I'm Sorry, I'll Read That Again' was a young people's 'Round The Horne', a kaleidoscope of funny voices, catchphrases and innuendo revolving at breakneck speed and with a complete disregard for logic. It had sprung indirectly from a visit that Peter Titheridge and Edward Taylor had paid to Cambridge in 1963 to see that year's Cambridge Footlights revue. They made the pilgrimage rather in the way that before the war Harry S. Pepper and Ronnie Waldman had toured the concert parties looking for talent. The outcome of their visit was that they offered gainful employment in radio to Humphrey Barclay, Bill Oddie, and John Cleese. Humphrey Barclay had produced the Footlights show and its undoubted stars were Cleese and Oddie. Bill Oddie was more interested in pop music and had written what John Cleese describes as three superb send-ups of pop songs which were the big successes of that year's 'Footlights'. Oddie declined the BBC's offer but Barclay and Cleese each accepted a contract as writer/producer. In the event, Barclay didn't do any writing and Cleese didn't produce.

John Cleese's first BBC writing assignment was a Christmas show starring Brian Rix and Terry Scott called 'Yule Be Surprised'. According to Cleese, he was told that there were too many jokes in it, and he had to remove them. He then went on to write for Dick Emery and Deryck Guyler, doing cross-talk routines for them as two characters at a bus stop. Cleese recalls, 'Trevor Nunn had once paralysed me telling me about a Peter Cook sketch about a man who sat down next to somebody and told him interesting facts but got them confused. For instance, he'd say "A great six-foot Arab can live on a grain of rice for a year, isn't that interesting? You wouldn't think that a great big strapping six–foot Arab could live on a grain of rice." And he'd go on and on and then he'd say, "No, wait a moment, it's a mosquito. A mosquito can live on a grain of rice. I get them confused because in my dictionary mosquito comes next to mosque." ' Cleese wrote pages of such inconsequentialities for Emery and Guyler.

The following excerpt from 'I'm Sorry, I'll Read That Again' was first transmitted on April 6, 1969.

HATCH This is the final programme of our series and tonight's survey is, appropriately enough, the last one. 'I'm Sorry, I'll Read That Again' examines love . . .

BAND *Bright chord*

HATCH Sex . . .

BAND *Brighter chord*

HATCH And marriage.

BAND *Dismal chord*

HATCH So let's begin with sex . . . (*pause*) Ah, that was nice—and now let's get onto love. Without it, what would we all be?

ODDIE Frustrated.

HATCH What is that certain something that first attracts a boy to a girl? No one can say.

ODDIE I can.

HATCH Not on radio. I suppose really the special allure of a woman was probably best summed up by an eminent psychoanalyst when he said:

CLEESE Chooooor!

HATCH The French, they tell us, often die for it.

TAYLOR Oh, I'm dying for it.

HATCH But . . . to different people love is many different things. To some it is dancing cheek to cheek on a moonlit balcony with a lissome blonde, to others it is a warm cuddle and a cup of tea by the fireside with the wife. To me, it's a quick snog in the one and nine's with Cynthia Prune of 17 Chepstow Villas —oh Cynthia! Are you listening? I love you, Cynthia. . . . And where better to start a study of the ways of love than Cynthia Prune.

OMNES NO!

HATCH Or than a spring day in the country. . . .

GRAMS *Spring music*

HATCH As the dewdrops hang on the cobwebs like so many dewdrops hanging on cobwebs, the female spider, having laid her eggs, enacts the last rite of her ritual breeding cycle by tenderly eating the male—

KENDALL That's what I call bed and breakfast.

HATCH A cheeky little chaffinch beckons to his mate.
GARDEN Oi—mate!
HATCH And a dainty turtle dove calls his loved one.
ODDIE (*like phone*) Coo coo coo coo coo coo coo coo
KENDALL (*distort*) Sorry, there's no reply.
HATCH Down in the orchard the mayflies merrily play at piggyback, and even the lowly maggots munch away in pairs, and apples and plums . . . and in the meadow even the humble cow knows the promise of romance.
TAYLOR Fear not, Buttercup—you shall go to the bull.
HATCH Love—love is everywhere; birds do it, bees do it—
ODDIE Even educated Cleese do it—
HATCH Ah, how wondrous it all is, how pure, how good—and see, see—here comes a country lad with his lady fair, tripping hand in hand.
GARDEN My love is like a red red rose
All newly sprung in June,
My love is like a melody,
HATCH And her name is Cynthia Prune . . . Cynthia . . . come back, Cynthia.
TAYLOR David! Don't humiliate yourself any more. Can't you see, she's no good for you.
HATCH Cynthia!
TAYLOR Let her go—you're worth something better than Cynthia—she's no good. She's never been any good. She's deceitful.
HATCH Deceitful . . .
TAYLOR She's a wanton hussy . . .
HATCH Wanton . . .
TAYLOR She's corrupt, promiscuous, wicked and evil—and besides, she's coming out with me tonight.
GARDEN But if love remains strangely abstract—sexual impulses are infinitely more definable. How well most of us recognise those desires first awakened so long ago when Eve offered Adam the apple . . .
KENDALL Here, have a bit.
ODDIE *Crunch* (*real apple*)
KENDALL And another . . .
ODDIE *Crunch munch munch mm, etc. Sigh*
KENDALL Now?
ODDIE Oh, I can't eat another one.
HATCH Courtship is always a tricky problem—it is up to the man to make some indication of his wishes and the woman to under-

stand and decipher his needs. Sometimes lovers use the language of the eyes.

GARDEN Aye aye.

Shortly after, an enterprising impresario took the Cambridge Footlights revue to New Zealand and the United States. The cast included John Cleese, Bill Oddie, Tim Brooke-Taylor, Graham Chapman, Jonathan Lynn, David Hatch, Humphrey Barclay, and Jo Kendall. At the end of the tour the others returned to England, but Cleese remained in the States working first as a journalist on *Newsweek*, and then in a touring version of *The Establishment Show*. By the time he returned to England, 'I'm Sorry, I'll Read That Again' had already been on the air for a season. Instigated by Edward Taylor, the show had been produced by Barclay (with Peter Titheridge overseeing), and Graeme Garden was now in the cast. Garden had joined Cambridge Footlights at the same time as the rest of those who were to become the 'I'm Sorry, I'll Read That Again' gang. He joined the radio team in 1966 while still a medical student, although he had to drop out for a while when he was 'delivering babies in Plymouth', replacing Graham Chapman when Chapman, also a medical student, had to take time out to qualify. Garden finally gave up medicine to become a full-time performer in a television series called 'Twice A Fortnight' with Oddie and Jonathan Lynn, before graduating from that to 'Broaden Your Mind' with Tim Brooke-Taylor, and eventually to 'The Goodies'.

David Hatch joined the BBC in 1965 as a producer/writer on a similar contract to the one that Barclay and Cleese had, and after a stint on such shows as 'Roundabout', an early evening magazine programme, joined 'I'm Sorry', as writer/producer/performer. As he was crucially involved in performing, Peter Titheridge shared the production. As his career developed, Hatch produced many programmes, including panel games like 'Tennis Elbow Foot Game' and 'Just A Minute', adaptations of Richard Gordon's 'Doctor In The House', and television-to-radio transfers such as 'Brothers In Law', and 'All Gas And Gaiters'. He then started the late-night Friday satire on the week's news, 'Week Ending', with Nigel Rees, Bill Wallis, and David Jason, and was the first producer of 'Hello Cheeky'. But of David Hatch, more in the next chapter—it is sufficient for now to say that he has gone up the promotion ladder of the BBC with the speed of the proverbial scalded cat.

Humphrey Barclay moved from radio to television and today is Head of Comedy with London Weekend Television. John Cleese spends his time between Monty Python films and his own television series, 'Fawlty Towers', and Jo Kendall is a frequent broadcaster on radio and television. They formed a sprightly and talented group, and 'I'm Sorry, I'll Read That Again' was a classic of inconsequential knockabout nonsense, as epic in its way as 'Danger—Men At Work!', and 'The Goon Show'. It certainly attracted an audience of enthusiasts. As John Cleese says, 'Performing to that studio audience was like playing in front of a Cup Final crowd. They were fiercely partisan and *cheered* the jokes.'

One recent comedy series to create any noticeable stir of enthusiasm is the confection called 'Hello Cheeky', which has done away with plot, shape and style and has gone back to the fundamentals of comedy—jokes. It's written by and stars Tim Brooke-Taylor, Barry Cryer and John Junkin, all of them by now old hands at the scriptwriting and performing game. It's about as subtle as a poke in the eye with a sharp stick, and has already become not only a radio show but a TV series as well. I don't suppose its creators will claim that it's the greatest radio show ever, but by reducing everything to the bare essentials they've managed an elegant conjuring trick. Here's a typical routine from a show first broadcast in 1975, produced by Bob Oliver Rogers:

TAYLOR We apologise for the fact that our programmes are running a little late but this is due to a technical fault in Terry Wogan. It will therefore be necessary for our next three programmes to be broadcast simultaneously. So here are 'Z Cars', 'Gardeners' Question Time' and 'A Book At Bedtime'.

GRAMS *Romantic music*

JUNKIN *To Drink At The Fountain* by Denise Holloway, Episode 8.

GRAMS *Music fades*

TAYLOR Spring came early to Broadmead that year. To Harvey, walking down the lane, suitcase in hand, memories came flooding back of . . .

JUNKIN (*scouse*) Two ponces in the public bar, and that one-eyed tart from the docks.

TAYLOR (*scouse*) If he starts on me, he'll get a mouthful of . . .

JUNKIN Leaf mould and compost in equal parts. Spread this on the . . .

TAYLOR Dining-room table with little cucumber sandwiches. It was just as Harvey remembered it. Mother, still like a Dresden shepherdess, fragile and sweet, gave an impish smile and murmured . . .

CRYER (*woman*) Get stuffed, you big git, nobody's pushing me into . . .

TAYLOR A bone china tea pot. 'Just look at these'—it was Dorothy, from the French windows, as he'd always pictured her, with an armful of . . .

JUNKIN Window boxes and small greenhouses. On the other hand, you may prefer to bed down early with . . .

CRYER Sergeant Lynch . . . if he's not there, get hold of . . .

TAYLOR Dorothy's bosom, heaving with emotion . . .

JUNKIN I can assure you, they look lovely side by side . . . particularly if you have a red one and a blue one. Don't forget, this is also a good time of year for . . .

CRYER Robbery with violence, indecent exposure and grievous bodily harm.

TAYLOR 'Yes please,' said Dorothy, and she clapped her . . .

JUNKIN Tulip bulbs, but they do tend to wilt in an early frost.

CRYER Look, son, there's a dead body been found in the car park, and I want to ask you a few questions, for a start, like . . .

TAYLOR 'Will you marry me?' Dorothy blushed like a . . .

JUNKIN Dead ferret that I found once, behind the potting shed. I think he must have got there . . .

CRYER (*scouse*) By cycling from Runcorn.

TAYLOR (*scouse*) But he can't—I know for a fact that he was in the Red Lion that night, playing the piano . . .

JUNKIN Which is a habit ferrets have that not many people know about. Another question that gardeners often ask me, is: 'How can I treat a vegetable marrow that has . . .'

TAYLOR Been in love with Dorothy since she was a schoolgirl. 'I can see you now,' smiled Harvey, 'in your little summer frock with the . . .'

CRYER Handcuffs, truncheon and a couple of tear gas bombs just in case.

JUNKIN (*scouse*) Why, Sarge, are you expecting trouble in . . .

TAYLOR The back pocket of Harvey's trousers. Pulling it out, he said: 'I know this is only a photograph, but it'll give some idea of what it looks like.' 'Good heavens,' said Dorothy, 'it's . . .

JUNKIN The biggest stick of rhubarb in East Anglia.

TAYLOR Harvey said nothing. He simply . . .

CRYER Smashed her over the head with a water jug, stole her holiday money and got out of town disguised as a . . .

JUNKIN Turnip and a bag of King Edwards.

TAYLOR 'Oh Harvey,' said Mrs. Heatherington, 'how sweet of you to get Dorothy . . .'

CRYER In the club with two drag artists and a dodgy soprano.

TAYLOR (*scouse*) There's only one way to stop him, Sarge . . .

JUNKIN Cut off the end with a pair of secateurs . . .

TAYLOR 'It'll never be the same again,' said Harvey, smiling bravely.

JUNKIN This could have been due to too much weed killer or . . .

CRYER Doing it out in the open where everyone can see—that's your job. What's the good of a uniformed copper creeping round corners . . .

TAYLOR Kissing Harvey on the tip of his nose.

JUNKIN And using a dibber where it's needed most. But the short answer at this time of year is . . .

CRYER Grab the villain by the scruff of his neck, sling him into one of the charge rooms and . . .

TAYLOR Be the mother of his child.

12

Up To Date

One of the most intriguing elements of radio comedy is that it grows and develops almost unnoticed and suddenly you find a new mood in the comedy—a change of direction, new voices, different jokes. And that has happened in BBC radio during the time I have been writing this book. It has been generated by the energies and enthusiasms of a group of people who have found in the 'seventies and 'eighties a fascination with the medium that older practitioners found in the 'forties, 'fifties and 'sixties. But these bright men and women don't spring, as it were, fully formed from the brow of Zeus. They emerge gradually into the light.

The new mood of radio comedy can be directly attributed to a quartet of alert, shrewd, young practitioners—John Lloyd, Simon Brett, Humphrey Barclay and David Hatch. I've mentioned Hatch earlier in connection with 'I'm Sorry I'll Read That Again', but when he was promoted to Head of Light Entertainment (Radio) in February 1978, he took a successful but rather static, traditional department, shook it warmly by the throat and out popped some excellent new programmes and, more to the point, a new generation of writers, producers and performers. His former secretary, Sandra Pronger, has seen a great deal of the development of contemporary radio. She thinks Hatch's great strengths were that he wasn't put off by opposition and that he was always brimming with new ideas.

'He tried a lot of things which didn't work, but it was innovation all the time. He's something of a catalyst and starts little whirlwinds everywhere he goes but he leaves a lot of new thinking behind him.'

Among the things David Hatch inherited when he took over the Light

Entertainment Department was the tradition of panel games. Quizzes, parlour games and the like are deeply imbedded in the history of radio. In the 'thirties the fashion was for spelling contests known as 'Spelling Bees', and during the war the general knowledge quiz was a constant and popular element of many variety shows. One of the most popular programmes ever was 'The Brains Trust' in which, during the 'forties and 'fifties, the top minds of the day (Julian Huxley, C. E. M. Joad and Commander Campbell, among others) tackled various important topics with varying degrees of erudition and plain horse-sense.

At the other end of the scale was 'Ignorance Is Bliss' which, as its title suggests, was the antithesis of erudition and in the hands of Harold Berens, Michael Moore and Gladys Hay—and the seemingly out-of-control chairman, the Canadian sports commentator turned show host, Stewart McPherson—became a mêlée of inconsequential but hilarious foolishness.

Between these two poles numerous shows of a more or less whimsical nature flourished, most of them based loosely on Victorian parlour games. There was 'Twenty Questions', a variation of the old 'Animal, Vegetable Or Mineral', which is still going strong under the latter title on BBC World Service. Then there was 'My Word', now in its twenty-sixth year and which is, in the main, a test of what *Reader's Digest* would describe as 'word power' plus a sequence in which Frank Muir and Denis Norden play havoc with a well-known phrase or saying as I have described at some length earlier in this book. Another game to have found a more or less permanent niche in the radio calendar, is 'Just A Minute' where a mixed quartet of actors, writers and politicians are invited to speak without hesitation, repetition or deviation for one minute, their efforts being thwarted by the other panellists who can, and do, challenge the slightest deviation from the strict letter of the contest. This game is chaired by the urbane Nicholas Parsons and is the brainchild of Ian Messiter, whom we have to thank for many successful radio quizzes.

I have appeared as a panellists on many game shows, including 'Call My Bluff' when it was on radio, 'The Tennis Elbow Foot Game', a dizzying game based on word association but which is no longer on the air, 'My Word' and 'My Music', where I deputise for both Frank Muir and Denis Norden when either is unavoidably absent, 'Funny You Should Ask', a show-business quiz, 'Pros And Cons', where panellists have to decide whether a dramatised sketch involves a confidence trick and if so what the trick or 'con' *is*, and 'Just A Minute'. To be honest I prefer the role of chairman or quiz master. It's infinitely more soothing to ask questions than to have to answer them.

My first venture in this line was a series called 'Sounds Familiar' where a panel of show-business celebrities had to answer questions based on recorded extracts from the archives. When I left the BBC briefly to work for commercial television, my place was taken by the talented and versatile Jack Watson, who vacated the hot seat on my return with an audible sigh of relief. Jack Watson's career in radio has been long and honourable. He started as a stooge to his father, Nosmo King, in the double-act Nosmo King and Hubert (Jack being Hubert). From there he graduated to compering war-time variety shows billed as Petty Officer Jack Watson, did a solo act as an impressionist, and has since become one of our finest film and television character actors. 'Sounds Familiar' ran for several years and was produced by many excellent men, including John Simmonds, John Cassels, Bobby Jaye and, for most of its life, the impeccable John Dyas.

My next 'chair' was of the stimulating, if raucous series, 'The Impressionists', devised and produced by the sprightly Richard Willcox. It started in 1974 and I revelled in the refreshing atmosphere created by the splendid young impersonators—Roger Kitter, Peter Goodwright, Dave Evans, Ray Fell, Aiden J. Harvey, Janet Brown, Faith Brown, Johnnie More, David Jason and the rest—who brought zest and mischief to what could have been a fairly ordinary show. In fact, audiences love it and it's become a welcome fixture in the Radio 2 schedule, now chaired by the brilliant ventriloquist and compere, Ray Alan.

In 1979 I took over Radio 4's 'News Quiz' from Barry Norman when, owing to television commitments, he was unable to continue in the chair. Unfortunately, I lack Norman's control and fluency—so much so that what Richard Ingrams regularly describes as 'the chairman's speech impediment' has become a running gag and is greeted by studio audiences as an old and much-loved friend. However, I've tried to make up for my shortcomings by turning the show into a sort of free for all: so while the main object of the programme—answering questions about the week's news—is adhered to a great deal of inconsequential nonsense gets aired, too. Produced in alternate series, by Danny Greenstone and Alan Nixon, the 'News Quiz' has gone from strength to strength and almost every leading British journalist has now appeared on the panel, many making their radio début.

There is a cachet in being involved in a successful show and the advantage of panel games like 'News Quiz' is that, for the participants at least, they aren't time consuming. A brief check for voice levels at the microphone, ten minutes in the hospitality room for a glass of wine—dubbed by Alan Coren, the editor of *Punch* and a permanent member of the 'News Quiz' team, 'Chateau Trethowan'—and, after a suitable introduction to the studio audience, the personality can let rip to the listening millions.

The joy of the 'News Quiz' is that while the questions are not especially difficult for the working journalists on the team to answer, their *reaction* to the question and their way of answering it reflects in many ways their own individual journalistic style. Simon Hoggart, the political columnist, for instance, is quirky, succinct and ironic; while Valerie Grove, the literary editor of the *New Standard*, tends to be amusing but more detailed in her replies, as if she were herself rewriting the news item on which the question was based. All the panellists are idiosyncratic but none more so than the regulars, Alan Coren, Richard Ingrams, the editor of the satirical magazine, *Private Eye*, and John Wells, a man equally at home in the world of radio, television, theatre and journalism and who includes among his activities producing opera and appearing in beer commercials.

Here is a transcript of some moments from the totally unscripted answers or exchanges that emerged during our recordings in 1980. First, Alan Coren replying to a question about the SAS assault on the Iranian Embassy in London. The question was: Explain how the few who dared—won?

COREN: Is it the people selling balaclavas to the Iranians?

TOOK: I suppose that's one way of looking at it.

COREN: A number of balaclava'd salesmen in the pay of the government were attempting to peddle their wares to a group of cold foreigners who'd come to these shores to blow things up and set fire to things. They were sitting huddled in their room in Knightsbridge and these balaclava salesmen sprang through the windows and forced their attentions on them. They trade under the name of SAS—it's a mail order company. 'Get bombed in your own home . . .'

When Richard Ingrams was partnered by John Wells, the following jollity ensued. The question was about Eton School's abandoning 'fagging' and, after a lot of prompting, Richard duly came up with the answer, and added the information, 'John Wells used to teach at Eton.' John Wells interjected, 'I'm prepared to draw a veil over Richard Ingrams's career at Shrewsbury if he'll just belt up.' And Alan Coren added laconically, 'I didn't know he wore a veil at Shrewsbury. I thought that came later.'

Equally successful is 'Quote, Unquote', devised and chaired by Nigel Rees and produced by Alan Nixon. It's a programme where a knowledge of who said what is indispensible but, as with 'News Quiz', it's the embellishments that the panellists add to their answers that make the show so amusing and interesting.

The third of the current crop of excellent game shows—one which appears to have few, if any, rules—and those it does have seem to be made up on the spot—is 'I'm Sorry I Haven't A Clue', an illogical extension of 'I'm Sorry I'll Read That Again'. Chaired by Humphrey Lyttelton and produced by Geoffrey Perkins, those mainly involved are Barry Cryer, Willie Rushton, Tim Brooke-Taylor and Graeme Garden.

The three scripted comedies that seem to me to be the pick of the crop of recent radio light entertainment are 'The Burkiss Way', 'News Huddlines' and 'Week Ending'.

At its birth in 1970, 'Week Ending', the brainchild of Hatch and Brett, was an innovation in that it was topical, political and dispensed with a studio audience. It was not universally popular either with the listeners or within the BBC but, thanks to the backing of the Controller of Radio 4, then Tony Whitby, the show was nurtured and it flourished. Sandra Pronger was, at this time, secretary to the then Head of Light Entertainment Radio, Con Mahoney, and tried her hand at verses and lyrics for the new programme. Her first contributions were greeted by Peter Spence, the head writer of the show, with the comment, 'The mad poetess strikes again!'—but together with the brilliant Roger Woddis she became a valued contributor of verses and lyrics to the series in its early years. She was one of the few women to figure regularly in the credits and is a good example of the many part-time writers who find 'Week Ending' a rewarding outlet.

In the summer of 1980 while writing an article on radio comedy for *Radio Times*, I sat in on the weekly script conference of 'Week Ending' and, hard as I found it to keep my trap shut—I felt like an old war horse who hears the distant bugles sound the charge—I was delighted to be there. Nine writers were present, and the producer, Jimmy Mulville, apologised for the sparseness of the meeting, explaining that many of the team were on holiday and that 'Week Ending's' principal writer, Guy Jenkin, had already delivered his material for that week's programme. They looked as, in my experience, all writers *en masse* look, like the crowd outside Marylebone Magistrate's Court waiting for the proceedings to start. The meeting was held in a smoke-filled room and the writers sat round a table littered with newspapers—*The Times* and the *Guardian* predominating.

The conversation was peppered with 'Week Ending's' own private jargon—'Let's make it an A and B runner'. 'This should be very one liney', 'What'd be the punch line then?' and more obscurely, 'Put crumhorns from your mind, Brian.' On the date of that particular meeting the Moscow Olympics were at their height or, depending on your point of view, depth, and several comic 'olympic' ideas were floated. The marathon taking months to run because of security checks, and so on. Someone mentioned that Ian Wooldridge had written something in the *Daily Mail* to the effect that from where he was sitting he could have 'shot Brezhnev'. Someone else commented drily, 'No, he couldn't. He's a lousy shot.' Jim

Mulville rattled through a list of subjects culled from the week's papers—Zimbabwe, Afghanistan, worst July weather for three hundred years, the setting up of a joint audience research board for BBC and ITV, the actors' strike in Los Angeles featuring Liza Minelli ('I'm striking with a K not striking with a C,' warbled someone), the continuing saga of the Carter family and many more. Different writers claimed the subjects they fancied, Mulville made a note and pressed on, often making the best jokes himself, and was convulsed by a report in one of the tabloids of a punch up in Red Square with the headline GBH FROM KGB.

Time passed, the room became smokier, inspiration flagged, the menu for the week's show was getting full. 'OK, only good ideas from now on, lads,' said Mulville, and at 12.15 the meeting ended. The deadline for delivery of the promised material was 3.30 the following day. By the recording, the day after, the script had been collated, edited, typed, last-minute topicals added and the cast—David Jason, Bill Wallis, Sheila Steafel and David Tate—had received their scripts, rehearsed and recorded them. Just another edition of a show that has run, with few interruptions, for over ten years. Here's a typical sketch from 'Week Ending', the week ending in question being Saturday, 17 January 1981. The writer is John Langdon.

FX: *Airport atmosphere*

FX: *Ding dong*

STEAFEL: (*As British Airways announcer—very upmarket*) This is the final call for flight BA 104 to Bahrain. Would the passenger please make his way to gate 14? Thank you.

FX: *Ding dong*

STEAFEL: British Airways announce the departure of flight BA 105, non-stop to Boston, boarding at gate 10: standby seats are now on sale at £98. Thank you.

FX: *Ding dong*

STEAFEL: British Airways flight BA 105 to Boston . . . Boston via New York . . . ? Via New York *and* Miama, then. Now boarding at gate 10 . . . Make that gate 5—no gate 4 *and* we'll lend you a trolley. Standby seats are still available, at only £78 . . . Call it £70 and you can keep the trolley. Thank you.

FX: *Ding dong*

STEAFEL: (*as an afterthought*) Which does, of course, include free ear-phone, free movie . . . two if you like, drinks, in-flight catering, souvenir biro and key-ring. Thank you.

FX: *Ding dong*

STEAFEL: (*beginning to sound desperate*) This is the final call for flight BA

105 to Boston via Paris and Dar es Salaam. Boarding when you're ready—no, I tell you what, stay where you are, and the crew will come and pick you up. Thank you.

FX: *Ding dong*

In the beginning, April 1970 to be precise, 'Week Ending' was presented by Michael Barratt with a spot from such expert writers as Basil Boothroyd and Andrew Alexander, and a cast of actors drawn from the BBC Repertory Company. It was written originally entirely by Peter Spence, but as the years went by he was joined by many others, including Andrew Marshall, David Renwick and Colin Bostock-Smith. It is today, as my experience of the script conference showed, a proving ground for a great many writers.

How can the BBC, particularly radio, afford all those writers? The answer comes in three parts—no individual writer gets much for his work, the average being about £10 a minute for material used; many of them are involved in other shows and 'Week Ending' represents only a part of their working week; and the radio moguls have realised that if you don't invest in writers, comedy dries up. However gifted or popular the actor, he's soon stranded without good material. David Hatch, now risen to the dizzy heights of Controller of Radio 2, is responsible, together with BBC Television's Head of Light Entertainment, James Gilbert, for a writers' scheme whereby radio and television each puts £5,000 a year into a kitty to employ three young writers on a one-year contract. The only proviso is that there is no contract for a second year, and the writers must then fend for themselves. The value of this scheme is obvious, and that it's fruitful is apparent: already Guy Jenkin, Rory McGrath, Rob Grant and Doug Naylor, and Jimmy Mulville have benefited from it.

Radio is a great training ground for would-be comedy writers, such as Muir and Norden, Galton and Simpson, Esmonde and Larby, Mortimer and Cook, Peter Spence (his creation, 'To The Manor Born', was written for radio but in fact became a television hit), Chris Miller, David Renwick and Andrew Marshall, Andy Hamilton, and many, many more, including, I need hardly add, Marty Feldman and Barry Took.

The advantages to television are obvious, too, as witness 'Not The Nine O'Clock News' where John Lloyd, Griff Rhys Jones, and Rowan Atkinson, who all started in radio, played a major part in the show's success. Rhys Jones was also a radio producer, but after much heart-searching gave up the security of radio production and became a freelance actor. He was discovered by John Lloyd in an ex-Cambridge Footlights group revue, 'An Evening Without'. The fact that Lloyd is scarcely older than Rhys Jones is neither here nor there. The radio crowd—Geoffrey Perkins, Jimmy

Mulville, Danny Greenstone, Alan Nixon, Jonathan James-Moore (who produces the successful 'News Huddlines'), Richard Edis and the rest—are constantly forming new combinations of writer/performer/producer to invent new shows in many different fields.

'News Huddlines' ('forty writers no waiting') is among today's most successful radio shows. The team led by the ebullient Roy Hudd, backed by the gifted Janet Brown and Chris Emmett, sprays its mixture of music hall gags (' 'Ere missus, 'ere's one') and sharp political satire to most exhilarating effect. Here is part of a broadcast on 20 November 1980. This particular sketch was written by Terry Ravenscroft. Those taking part are Roy Hudd, Chris Emmett and Norma Ronald.

HUDD: I see that one of Harold Wilson's houses is up for sale. About seventy years old . . . rambling and detached—and the house isn't bad either. I wonder if he's found a client yet?

BAND: *'English Country Garden' link*

FX: *Country atmosphere. Ring of doorbell. Door opens.*

MAN (HUDD): Sir Harold Wilson?

WILSON (EMMETT): If it's about Lord Kagan I don't even wear denims.

WOMAN (RONALD): No, we've come about the house.

WILSON: Oh, I see. Well you'd better come in then. Wipe your feet on the doormat.

MAN: There isn't a doormat.

WILSON: Sorry I was forgetting, she's out giving one of her poetry readings. Well, come in then, this is the hall.

WOMAN: Hmm, it needs decorating.

WILSON: No trouble—any preference, the OBE, CBE, Knight of the Garter . . . ?

MAN: My wife means that the wallpaper is hanging off and all the paintwork is scratched.

WILSON: Yes, when Wedgie-Benn was round here last week he had one of his turns. I had to lock him up in the Keith Joseph padded broom cupboard until he'd calmed down.

WOMAN: The Keith Joseph padded broom cupboard?

WILSON: Yes, you see I've named all the rooms in the house after politicians. There's the Harold Macmillan room, the Jim Callaghan room, the Ted Heath room, the Anthony Eden room and the Winston Churchill room.

FX: *W.C. flushing*

WILSON: Oh yes, and the Margaret Thatcher room. Well, I

	suppose you'd like to look round.
WOMAN:	Please.
WILSON:	Well, this room here is the Ted Heath room.
FX:	*Door opens*
WILSON:	As you can see I've chosen the furnishing to reflect his personality.
MAN:	But it's completely empty.
WILSON:	Quite.

In 'News Huddlines' as with 'Week Ending', the emphasis is on topicality and jokes of the moment, an area that, curiously enough, television appears to ignore. There's no reason why radio should be more topical than television but the tradition of 'instant radio' is a long and well-established one. As I have mentioned earlier in this book, Tommy Handley, the star of 'ITMA'—the nearest thing we've ever had to a show with universal appeal—used to listen to the six o'clock news and incorporate what references he could into his 8.30 show, and today 'News Huddlines' and the rest follow the same tradition. It's said that too much topicality can be dangerous—a joke about, say, the Shah of Persia made an hour before he died, or worse an hour *after* he died would have seemed in dreadful taste but, frankly, I've never seen the job of the comedian or the comedy writer to be 'safe' or 'reliable'.

Freedom itself is a dangerous business and whilst we still live in a free society, a little licence—indeed a great deal of licence—is no bad thing in broadcasting, comic or otherwise. Which brings me, at a bound, to 'The Burkiss Way', an irreverent, surreal romp through the conscious and unconscious mind of the 'seventies and 'eighties. It's written as if Sigmund Freud and A. J. P. Taylor had joined forces with John Cleese and the result, while not to everyone's taste—indeed 'The Burkiss Way' can be outrageous—is, to my mind, very exciting.

The history of the show is briefly this: Simon Brett, who was to radio in the early 'seventies what Irving Thalberg was to Hollywood in the 'thirties, and who has since left radio to concentrate on writing detective novels, concocted a comedy for Radio 3 called 'The Half Open University', with writers, David Renwick, Andrew Marshall and John Mason. The idea was reasonably simple—a correspondence column of the air which featured a Professor Burkiss. After a lapse of time while Radio 3 digested this oddity, it was reshaped by Renwick and Marshall, and guided by Brett became 'The Burkiss Way To Dynamic Living'. Subsequently, the show was produced by John Lloyd and David Hatch, and the cast, Nigel Rees, Jo Kendall, Fred Harris and the physicist-turned-impersonator-turned-writer, Chris Emmett (also a Brett discovery), have carried the ball since then. Emmett's character, Eric Pode of Croydon, rates in my mind with the best of Kenneth Williams's 'monsters' and I can think of no higher praise.

Here are three brief extracts from a recent series. To get the full flavour of 'The Burkiss Way' you really need a full half-hour to absorb the constant shifts of attitude and changes of direction, but I hope that these extracts give the authentic tang of the show.

GRAMS: '*The arrival of the Queen of Sheba*'

KENDALL: (*over*) England, 1739, and King George the Second the First makes a state visit to one of his favourite composers . . .

GRAMS: *Quite long but not that long, fanfare. Then:*

FX: *Modern doorbell. Door opens.*

WOMAN: (*gruff*) Yes?

KING: I am His Britannic Majesty King George the Second the First.

WOMAN: Oh. I'll have two yoghourts then, please.

KING: And I have come to speak to . . . what?

WOMAN: Two yoghourts. One sour flavour, one very sour, and one screwed-up-face-and-thumping-your-fist-in-the-table flavour.

KING: What are you talking about? I am the King!

WOMAN: I thought you said milkman.

KING: Don't be absurd! How could you possibly mistake the phrase 'His Britannic Majesty King George the Second the First' for milkman?

WOMAN: I'll have a pair of tights, please, as well if you've got them. I snagged the last ones on a sailor with a wooden leg.

KING: Look, for the last time, I am *not* . . . Oh, bloody Nora! Coachman—pass me that handcrate. Here's two homogenised, one sterilised, two yoghourts and a packet of twelve-deniers.

FX: *Tap on door*

REES: Come.

FX: *Door opens. Strange squishing noises and sound of something pouring into a chair.*

REES: Ah, good morning. Jobes, isn't it?

EMMETT: Jobes is my name, sir. My name is Jobes. And in truth I am none other than he which aspires to that cognomen of which you speak. (*A strange French accent comes into play.*) Je suis Monsieur Jobes. I am Meeeeesterr Jobes. C'est moi, eet ees me, Je am il, Jobes ergo sum. I who art Jobes hath in no wise that nomenclature which is nor of the seed of they that Jobe the Jobes, wheretofore Jobes of that ilk being that by which I am known, be it testament to ever having been Jobes, that it *is* Jobes, and evermore *shall* be Jobes.

pause

REES: Fine, well I think that's thrashed that one out, Jobes. Now, by my calculations, you've been employed here at the Department of Civil Service Staff Recruitment and Fisheries now for just on two and a half years.

EMMETT: (*sings very feebly*) Working in a coal mine, going down, down, down . . .

REES: Shut up.

EMMETT: Sorry, sir.

REES: And I think, to save ourselves time, Jobes, we may as well be blunt with each other on this one. You are . . . an amoeba.

EMMETT: Yes, sir.

REES: Now, employed as you are, as a token protozoan under the Employment Protection (Unicellular Beasts) Act of 1978, one is obviously prepared to make certain allowances for your somewhat microbial status. What concerns me most, however, is your behaviour in the office canteen.

EMMETT: Working in a coal mine . . .

REES: Shut *up*. It has been brought to my attention, Jobes, that you have been reproducing asexually by mitosis during firm's time.

EMMETT:
HARRIS: (*in unison*) I'm very sorry, sir.

(This came from the conclusion of an episode based on Edgar Allen Poe's *The Masque Of The Red Death* . . .)

PROSPERO: Oh God, no! . . . I . . . I feel all hot and feverish. My skin is growing red and blochy . . . what manner of evil horror have I caught?

PODE: Eric Pode of Croydon.

PROSPERO: Good Lord! What are you doing in this little room all by yourself?

PODE: What do you think?

PROSPERO: Oh, I beg your pardon.

PODE: I'm washing my smalls.

PROSPERO: Yes, I noticed you were in the bath. But, er . . . I see you haven't got any water in it.

PODE: Eh?

PROSPERO: You haven't got any *water* in it.

pause

PODE: You know, I wondered why the duck kept sinking.

PROSPERO: Ha ha ha ha, isn't he a panic?
PODE: 'Ere, I'm going to climb out now. Would you like to turn round and look the other way?
PROSPERO: No, I think I'll stay with my back to you, thanks.
PODE: All right—the offer was there.
PROSPERO: I don't think I've seen you round here before, Mr Croydon. What job do you do?
PODE: I'm the castle's chief rat-catcher.
PROSPERO: What made you pick that?
PODE: I can't find my handkerchief.
PROSPERO: No, the job.
PODE: Oh, sorry. Well I enjoy the work.
PROSPERO: And what about hobbies?
PODE: I've only got one main hobby.
PROSPERO: And do you get much time for that?
PODE: About six months usually. Haaaa . . . 'Ere, I nicked that one out of Bernard Manning's dustbin.
PROSPERO: That sounds a bit risky.
PODE: It was, he was still wearing it. Haaaa . . .

Simon Brett's many other production credits include 'Week Ending', 'Lord Peter Whimsey', and 'Frank Muir Goes Into . . .', and the first episode of Douglas Adams's 'The Hitch Hiker's Guide To The Galaxy', *the* cult comedy of the 'seventies.

Douglas Adams wrote 'Hitch Hiker' when he was penniless and struggling. He says, 'In those days I used to type a note to myself at the end of a day's work: "If you ever get offered a proper job—take it." ' So when he *was* offered a proper job as a radio producer, he took it. It only lasted six months as he was then offered and accepted the post of Script Editor to the TV science fiction series, 'Dr. Who'. During this time, 'Hitch Hiker' was slowly working its way through the system and Adams was eventually commissioned to write 'Dr. Who' for television and 'The Hitch Hiker's Guide To The Galaxy' for radio, on the same day.

Geoffrey Perkins replaced Simon Brett as producer and was responsible for the next eleven episodes. Amazingly there have only been twelve in all but, as Perkins remembers—'It really took off after the fourth episode'—and became required listening for millions. Since then it has become a best-selling book, an LP, and has been staged three times: once at the ICA in London, on tour in Wales with the Theatre Clwyd, and with only moderate success at the north London venue that specialises in rock concerts, the Rainbow Theatre. It failed in this vast auditorium for the simple reason that Adams has written a precise, intimate script full of nuance and subtlety, and the cavernous Rainbow is no place in which to be subtle.

Subsequently, it has been translated with great success to television where it acquired a whole new group of *aficionados*. Those twelve episodes, on two of which Douglas Adams had the collaboration of John Lloyd, undoubtedly made more impact than possibly any other series in the history of radio. Why did it work? Adams says, 'In most comedy shows the emphasis is on parody, on a distortion of what is already known. With "Hitch Hiker", the supposition is that this is what is actually going on.' And audiences are fascinated and excited by the concept that the ideas expressed in the programme could really be true.

It's a brilliant *tour de force* helped not a little by the cool *savoir-faire* of Peter Jones as the narrator. Douglas Adams: 'I had in mind a sort of Peter Jonesy type of voice—and it eventually occurred to me to ask Peter Jones.' Apart from Peter Jones's contribution it's a noisy show and, indeed, on its débût a distinguished critic described it as 'noisy and confused'. Since those days the only confusion exists among the show's detractors who can't for the life of them understand why 'The Hitch Hiker's Guide To The Galaxy' is such a colossal success.

The latest incumbent of the Head of Light Entertainment (Radio) post is Bobby Jaye. Jaye has had a long and honourable career in radio which began in 1941 when, as a sixteen-year-old, he left the leafy charms of the Isle of Wight where he was born, to become a sound effects operator at the BBC in London.

As a member of the engineering staff he was in a reserved occupation until the age of twenty-three, but it is typical of the irrepressible Jaye that at seventeen-and-a-half he joined up, whizzed through Sandhurst, was commissioned into a cavalry regiment, and spent the rest of the war in the Far East. When the war ended, the now Captain Jaye returned to broadcasting. He remembers, 'During the first show I did on my return to the BBC, I stood there poised, with this enormous pile of cans in front of me, holding a very big hammer ready to knock the whole contraption to the ground on the cue from Jimmy Jewel and Ben Warriss, and I remember thinking, I wonder if knocking over a pile of cans in "Up The Pole" is a progression for a captain in the cavalry.' But Bobby Jaye loved the exciting life of post-war radio, and graduated to becoming a studio manager where he worked happily with the Goons and Bernard Braden among others, and learned from and became friends with the great producers of those days, in particular George Inns and Pat Dixon.

Bobby claims, and with justification, that he's always had a pretty outrageous sense of humour (I can remember one warm summer night after a broadcast Bobby waltzing my wife down Northumberland Avenue for no other reason than that he felt full of *joie de vivre*), and his joyful, irreverent attitude to life made him an ideal working companion to Spike Milligan, and later Ken Dodd. Bobby Jaye admits that when he was asked to produce the Ken Dodd shows he was 'terribly excited because I felt that Ken Dodd was a genius'. Genius though Dodd doubtless is, he is inclined to be erratic; and recording a Ken Dodd show could take hours with Dodd suggesting to the cast *during* the recording, 'try this as a Welshman', or 'try this as a Scotsman', when in fact the poor actor had rehearsed the part in quite another accent, a situation liable to cause embarrassment. On one occasion the script was eighty-four pages long—the norm is thirty—and 'a lot of it,' says Jaye, 'was pretty horrendous.'

But Bobby Jaye, recognising the great talent of the man, laughs as he remembers and says, 'All right, you haven't got the genius that this man has—appreciate it, be careful with it, deal with it gently.' And that, I suppose, is Bobby Jaye's attitude towards talent.

A man with a different type of genius is Basil Boothroyd and, after Ken Dodd, it must have been refreshing for Jaye to work with this punctilious master of language. Boothroyd's radio series, 'The Small Intricate Life Of Gerald C. Potter', starring Ian Carmichael, won a well deserved BAFTA award, and is one of the shows of which Bobby Jaye is most proud, saying of Basil Boothroyd, 'He has taught me more about the art of script writing than anyone.'

Today Bobby Jaye is the boss of one of radio's indeed the BBC's, most lively departments. Aided by Edward Taylor (his deputy) and Martin Fisher (Script Editor) he has the flair and the experience to make it even more successful, and Jaye feels very optimistic about the future of radio. 'In the past couple of years I've noticed that people are listening more, particularly the youngsters, and I feel we're on the crest of a wave. If we can ride that wave, we in radio comedy are going to be desperately important. Let's face it, life at present is pretty awful, but as long as we can laugh at the awfulness of life then I think that there's hope for us all.'

Radio is like a busy railway station, new shows and people arrive, old ones depart. It's always changing and yet always much the same. My thirty years in the business of making people laugh have left me with a profound respect for the engineers and producers, writers, actors, comedians and musicians who fight the eternal battle to amuse, enlighten and entertain. I salute them.